PROOF:
EVERYONE'S UNDER A SPELL

How to Break Spells and Curses

SHANE WALL

Godly Writes
PUBLISHING

Godly Writes Publishing, LLC
Orangeburg, SC

Copyright © 2025 by Shane Wall

All rights reserved. No part of this publication may be reproduced, stored in a retrieval system, or transmitted in any form or by any means, electronic, mechanical, recording or otherwise, without the prior, written permission of the publisher.

Published by:
Godly Writes Publishing
P. O. Box 2005
Orangeburg SC 29116-2005

Unless otherwise noted, Scripture quotations taken from the Amplified® Bible (AMPC),

Copyright © 1954, 1958, 1962, 1964, 1965, 1987 by The Lockman Foundation

Used by permission. lockman.org

Scripture quotations marked KJV are taken from the King James Version of the Bible.

Public Domain.

Proof: Everyone's Under a Spell — How to Break Spells and Curses

ISBN: 978-0-9967997-9-9

Disclaimers:

This book is a work of nonfiction. The stories and testimonies shared are true to the best of the author's knowledge and are presented to bring biblical insight and understanding. The content of this book is not intended to replace professional advice for spiritual, emotional, or psychological issues.

The name satan and related terms are intentionally not capitalized in this book, except when appearing in direct Scripture quotations or beginning a sentence. This decision reflects our choice to deny him the dignity of recognition, even at the expense of conventional grammar.

Cover and Interior design by Greg Jackson, ThinkPen Design

10 9 8 7 6 5 4 3 2 1

For Worldwide Distribution, Printed in the U.S.A.

WWW.SHANEWALL.COM

DEDICATION

This book is lovingly dedicated to the legacy of my father, Hoover Wall.

His quiet yet unwavering support of my life and ministry was unmatched. For the final 16 years of his life, he honored me by trusting me to be his pastor. He shared my writings, sermons, and quotes with full confidence and pride.

The day after I preached his eulogy, the Holy Spirit gave me a perspective I'll never forget. He said:

"Good doctors do everything in their power to make sure their patients go back home. Good attorneys do everything in their power to make sure their incarcerated clients go back home. And good pastors do everything in their power to make sure their congregants go back home."

I'm deeply grateful—and profoundly moved—that my daddy is back home in Heaven, with our Lord and Savior, Jesus Christ.

TABLE OF CONTENTS

Chapter 1: **Characterizing Spells and the Gospel** 7
Chapter 2: **Characterizing Curses** 33
Chapter 3: **The Power of the Gospel** 69
Chapter 4: **How to Believe** 103
Chapter 5: **Practical Steps to Overcoming Bondage** 129
Chapter 6: **Walking in Freedom** 141
Chapter 7: **Overcoming Fear and Anxiety Spells** 157
Altar Call and Prayer for Salvation 185
Daily Prayer for Daily Power 187
Blessings that Break Curses 191
Spell and Curse-Breaking Prayers 199
Spell and Curse-Breaking Declarations 213
Spell and Curse-Breaking Affirmations 227
About the Author 241
Contact 242

CHAPTER 1:
CHARACTERIZING SPELLS AND THE GOSPEL

What is a Spell?

You might find it surprising that after over 40 years of preaching and over 20 years of pastoring, I don't subscribe to "practicing what I preach." Instead, I believe in preaching what I'm already practicing. This approach allows me to connect with congregations more deeply, sharing the lessons I've learned and the pitfalls and challenges congregants will likely face as I did. Through this lens of experiential wisdom, I aim to guide by giving practical insight, helping everyone navigate and overcome life's difficulties with outstanding success.

I've encountered spells and curses of varying types, personally, and I know how God's power has freed me from some challenging forces. As a result, I trust you can experience the same freedom as I have.

This approach brings us to a significant biblical truth concerning practices. In Deuteronomy 18:9-22, God warned the Israelites about avoiding the practices of the pagan nations surrounding them. Verse 11 is the first explicit mention of a *spell* in the Bible, introducing the Hebrew word *chabar*, which means "to charm" or "to bind." The concept of *chabar* involves the acts of manipulating, controlling, or binding individuals through incantations or enchantments, and it's strongly associated with spell-casting. This mention marks the first time the Bible explicitly addresses the idea of spells, revealing God's clear stance against such practices.

> 9 When thou art come into the land which the Lord thy God giveth thee, thou shalt not learn to do after the abominations of those nations.

> *10 There shall not be found among you any one that maketh his son or his daughter to pass through the fire, or that useth divination, or an observer of times, or an enchanter, or a witch.*
> *11 Or a charmer, or a consulter with familiar spirits, or a wizard, or a necromancer.*
> *12 For all that do these things are an abomination unto the Lord: and because of these abominations the Lord thy God doth drive them out from before thee.*
>
> Deuteronomy 18:9-12 (KJV)

In this passage, God listed a series of occult practices, including divination, sorcery, and necromancy. Verse 11 specifically mentions the *charmer*, someone who uses spells to bind or enchant others. These practices, deeply rooted in the pagan cultures surrounding Israel, were condemned by God as abominations—actions that are detestable and contrary to His nature. According to research, the definition of *abomination* is something that God never wanted to be created—emphasizing His absolute hate for those practices.

God's abhorrence for these occultic practices stemmed from their deceptive nature, drawing people away from His truth and into the darkness of demonic influences. Instead of relying on occult practitioners and their spells, God desired His people to trust in Him alone. His hatred for these methods is why He made clear that such practices were forbidden and the very reason He would drive out the nations that practiced them.

God provided an alternative for His people, promising to raise up a prophet they could listen to instead of turning to those who dealt with the occult. Deuteronomy 18:15 KJV says, "The LORD thy God will raise up unto thee a Prophet from the midst of thee, of thy brethren, like unto me; unto him ye shall hearken;" This prophetic promise pointed to the coming of Jesus Christ, the ultimate Prophet, who would lead His people into truth, contrasting with the lies and deceptions of the occult.

Verses 19-22 highlight the seriousness with which God regards His words spoken through this Prophet:

> 19 And it shall come to pass, that whosoever will not hearken unto my words which he shall speak in my name, I will require it of him.
> 20 But the prophet, which shall presume to speak a word in my name, which I have not commanded him to speak, or that shall speak in the name of other gods, even that prophet shall die.
> 21 And if thou say in thine heart, How shall we know the word which the Lord hath not spoken?
> 22 When a prophet speaketh in the name of the Lord, if the thing follow not, nor come to pass, that is the thing which the Lord hath not spoken, but the prophet hath spoken it presumptuously: thou shalt not be afraid of him.
>
> Deuteronomy 18:19-22 KJV

These verses stress that anyone claiming to speak on God's behalf has to be accurate and faithful to His message. If a prophecy did not come to pass, the lack of accuracy was proof that the prophet had spoken presumptuously. This divine standard distinguished the true Prophet, whom God promised to raise from the false prophets and occult practitioners who sought to deceive God's people with spells and lies.

The Mystery of Spells Solved!

In the quiet corridors of language, a hidden power lies dormant, waiting to be discovered. The seemingly innocent word *spell* carries a profound secret that has echoed under the radar for centuries. Beyond its ordinary definition, it unravels a tale of enchantment, manipulation, and the unseen forces that have shaped each life. You are about to discover that all of us have unknowingly allowed influential spells to rule and govern the ultimate decisions we've made.

In 1250, when knights roamed and castles stood tall, the term *spell* debuted in Middle English. But this wasn't just a linguistic evolution; it marked the convergence of meaning and mysticism. At its core, *spell* meant more than mere words; it meant talking, conversing, and announcing. Let's rewind to the year 900, when we encounter the term *spell* in Middle English, defined as *a story, a tale, a narrative*. Gothic (extinct East Germanic language) defines *spell* as a *fable or story*. These earlier meanings become personal and somewhat alarming as they awaken us to realize that every story that causes us to believe, every narrative our hearts embrace, and every tale we privately or openly endorse becomes a spell cast upon our lives.

A spell is designed to lead a person to believe and act on a particular story until those actions develop into a controlling habit or lifestyle.

Each of us navigates a world shadowed by the mystery of spells, yet not all are entangled in the grip of curses. As we embark on this journey to unravel the puzzling existence of spells and curses, our primary focus will be on the subtle yet powerful influence of spells. Our emphasis on spells is necessary because many individuals, even after freedom from curses, are trapped by spells—embedded belief systems that took root in their hearts during their time under a curse. What exactly are spells and curses? How do they weave their way into our lives, and why do they seem to cling to us persistently? This book aims to demystify spells and curses, as people often fear what they do not understand.

How to Know You're Under a Spell

Herein lies the revelation: spells aren't just mystical incantations in dusty sorcery books; they are the stories we hear, accept, maintain, and live out. Whether it's the story of our diets, relationships, or even our identity, spells influence the narratives, tales, and stories we've chosen to believe and cling to.

Psychology 101 teaches that the desire to gain pleasure or avoid pain drives human behavior. Those who cast successful spells, often called *spellers*, exploit this fundamental behavior to subtly convince their victims that the new influence is simply an extension of their current lifestyle. This manipulation makes the victims believe they can introduce these new actions into their lives to their advantage. In reality, they're unaware that the decision and control were inconspicuously yet deliberately implanted by the speller for the victim's strong consideration and eventual adoption. (I will delve further into when spells are cast upon unaware victims later in this chapter.)

Victims susceptible to spells sent by someone are often unaware that spellers control them remotely, thinking their actions are self-directed. Once the initiator casts a successful spell, the ideas become ingrained in the victims' psychological makeup, seamlessly integrating into their lives as an evilly influenced and operated coping mechanism for various situations and circumstances. This insidious influence replaces the guidance and protection offered by God's loving and caring nature, leading the individual away from His divine direction.

Spells and curses often leverage fear to convince victims that new behaviors are essential for self-defense and protection from perceived threats. This fear-driven manipulation creates a sense of urgency, making the victim believe that adopting these behaviors is crucial for their survival. In truth, these individuals often guard themselves against *imagined* dangers, which may be the harmless and hopeful reality God has prepared for them. The cunning nature of these spells lies in their ability to obscure the victim's own discernment, making them feel that they must rely on these false safeguards.

Spellers foster a climate of fear through falsified stories that paint a gloomy outlook. They distort their victims' perception of reality, steering them away from the genuine peace and security that God offers. Recognizing this tactic is crucial for breaking free from the psychological hold of spells and reclaiming the divine assurance and tranquility that God has intended for us.

Let's embark on a journey to unravel the spells woven by the stories we tell ourselves or believe from others. What stories have we embraced? What narratives hold us back? What spells are we living out now? We're about to uncover the unseen forces that could hold us back for days, weeks, months, or years.

The Unseen Weaving of Stories

In the rich fabric of language, the Old High German and Old Norse tales, we find our lives interwoven with the definition of *spjall*, "saying, tale." The Gothic (extinct East Germanic language) *spill* (from which *spell* derives) is a *story* or *fable* that reveals a spoken word's underlying power. Here, we confirm the startling truth that the stories we subscribe to continuously govern our actions, shape our emotions, and dictate our chosen paths.

Understanding these spells begins in something other than occult books or secret societies, but in language and history. Stories weave their silent spells into the fabric of our lives, revealing a profound understanding that can reshape our destiny. We are standing at the threshold of this revelation, peering into the ancient past to uncover the ever-present power of narratives—forces that shape our actions and very being.

Think of what many call the "spell of love," not as a whimsical enchantment but as a deeply held narrative that guides our hearts and choices. Many say, "I can't help who I love," or "I can't control how I feel." They don't realize these sentiments are the essence of a spell—a story believed and acted upon. Yet, the teachings of Jesus offer a counter-narrative: "Let not your heart be troubled…" (John 14:1a KJV), reminding us that we are not mere puppets to our emotions, but master controllers and protectors of our hearts and, ultimately, our destinies.

> Keep and guard your heart with all vigilance and above all that you guard, for out of it flow the springs of life.
>
> Proverbs 4:23 AMPC

The Origin of *Gospel*

The word *gospel* has an interesting origin. The first element of the Old English word had initially been a long-o (ō). Still, it shifted under mistaken association with *God*, as if *God-story* (i.e., the history of Christ) to *good-story*, which is the correct translation. It comes from the Old English word *gōdspell*, which means "good news"—the good news story about Jesus Christ. *Gospel* was formed by combining parts of the words *good* and *spell*. Therefore, the transition from *God-story* to *good-story* is intentional for clarification.

Indeed, the gospel is the good spell that can annihilate every evil spell. Now, as we consider these verses from the Bible and replace *gospel* with *good spell*, what was once a mystery now becomes evident—the power of the gospel is a good spell (story) that we believe. The good story produces an impenetrable force against any evil spell (story) it encounters:

> For I am not ashamed of the Gospel (good news) of Christ, for it is God's power working unto salvation [for deliverance from eternal

death] to everyone who believes with a personal trust and a confident surrender and firm reliance, to the Jew first and also to the Greek,

Romans 1:16 AMPC

Interestingly, the Greek origin of the word *salvation* extends far beyond the prayer we offer to receive Jesus into our hearts and lives. Too often, we, as Christians, have limited salvation to when we first surrendered to Jesus in prayer, as if the gospel's power stopped working after we said, "Amen." If salvation was limited to that single moment of prayer, the gospel's effect would be short-lived. However, the original Greek meaning of *salvation* encompasses, *the full sum of benefits and blessings that Christians, redeemed from all earthly ills, will enjoy after Christ's visible return from heaven in the consummated and eternal kingdom of God.* The power of the gospel spans beyond the moment of salvation—lasting until Jesus Christ returns to receive us as His own. Oh, what a glorious day that will be!

The gospel's power doesn't just save us; it keeps us from future oppositions determined to carry us back to a life of sin against God and a lack of close relationship with Him.

Think of it this way: If the gospel was only strong enough to rescue us from hell but powerless to deliver us from the spells, curses, and strongholds that still try to dictate our lives, then what kind of power is that? No, God never intended us to treat salvation like a one-time transaction. The good spell of the gospel is the only spell that continues working every day, breaking the false narratives, the generational curses, and the destructive beliefs that try to rewrite our story.

The enemy wants people to think salvation is a mere door we walk through once. But the gospel is not a moment; it's a movement. It is not just a past event; it is present power. And it is not just an escape from hell; it is total victory over the forces of darkness every single day. That's why the gospel is the only spell that can break every other spell.

For in the Gospel a righteousness which God ascribes is revealed, both springing from faith and leading to faith [disclosed through the way of faith that arouses to more faith]. As it is written, The man who through faith is just and upright shall live and shall live by faith.

Romans 1:17 AMPC

The gospel of Jesus Christ is a good spell in its purest, unadulterated form—a glorious narrative of redemption, love, and hope. When we choose to live by the gospel, we align ourselves with a good spell—the only proven spell that promises and delivers freedom from all demonic binding and crippling spells. We possess tremendous power to resist evil spells when we live according to the life-giving power of the good spell—the gospel. Many believe the gospel's purpose is complete once they offer the prayer for salvation. Did you know that the power of the gospel continues to work in and through our lives long after we first pray to receive Jesus Christ for the salvation of our souls? I'll share more about the gospel's long-standing effect in the next section of this chapter.

Do not let yourself be overcome by evil, but overcome (master) evil with good.

Romans 12:21 AMPC

The Gospel (Good Spell): Beyond Salvation

A widely accepted notion is that the gospel of Jesus Christ has reached its capacity when it offers salvation to those not previously in a relationship with Jesus. Yet, the reality is that after salvation, the gospel's effectual work in our lives continues to complete us unto God's glory. In the New Testament of the Bible, *gospel* is used in several phrases: the Gospel of the Kingdom (Matthew 4:23, Matthew 9:35, Matthew 24:14, and Mark 1:14), *Gospel of Jesus Christ* (Mark 1:1), *Gospel of Christ* (Romans 1:16, Romans 15:19, Romans 15:29, 1 Corinthians 9:12, 1 Corinthians 9:18, 2 Corinthians 4:4, 2 Corinthians 9:13, 2 Corinthians 10:14, Galatians 1:7, Philippians 1:27, 1 Thessalonians 3:2), *Gospel of God* (Romans 1:1, Romans 15:16, 2 Corinthians 11:7, 1 Thessalonians 2:2, 1 Thessalonians 2:8, 1 Thessalonians 2:9, 1 Peter 4:17), and several other phrases, including the *Gospel of peace*.

The term *gospel* first appeared in the New Testament when Jesus began preaching. Since His crucifixion, burial, and resurrection had not yet taken place, the gospel had a broader impact than just the moment of the salvation altar-call prayer—and indeed, it did.

> *And Jesus went about all Galilee, teaching in their synagogues, and preaching the gospel of the kingdom, and healing all manner of sickness and all manner of disease among the people.*
>
> Matthew 4:23 KJV

The gospel of the Kingdom of God that Jesus preached includes profound lessons on how God, our King, operates on Earth. Jesus taught us to seek God's Kingdom first (Matthew 6:31-33), promising that God would add necessities to our lives. The Kingdom of God represents how God governs life in Heaven and on Earth, emphasizing our obedience to His laws as revealed by Jesus. Jesus referred to His teachings as *the gospel*, which remains a vital part of the good news that can liberate us from all evil influences, whether sent to us or self-inflicted.

The New Testament books of Matthew, Mark, Luke, and John are *the Gospels* because the entire story of Jesus Christ comprises the good spell that still empowers us thousands of years after Jesus ascended. Bible scholars have noted for centuries that the gospel expands from Christ's birth to His return to Earth.

> *...The reason the Son of God was made manifest (visible) was to undo (destroy, loosen, and dissolve) the works the devil [has done].*
>
> 1 John 3:8b AMPC

Again, the gospel is not merely a means to salvation that loses its power once God performs that miracle. The good spell of the gospel remains with the one who continues to build his or her relationship with Jesus, continuing His purpose on the Earth by annihilating the works of the devil. Every spell woven and every curse cast comes under the authority of Jesus Christ. As scripture commands us to overcome evil with good (Romans 12:21), let's continue to discover how the gospel of Jesus Christ, the good spell, can eradicate every spell and curse causing us or someone we know to suffer.

A Coworker Casts a Spell

Spells hide in plain sight, even in my hometown, Orangeburg, SC. Like wicked sorcerers, some weave words of harm, crafting curses masquerading as fate. Yet, the greater power of the gospel of Jesus Christ exists, which can shatter all dark enchantments. Not just in shadowy rituals do people cast spells. Family members' taunts, a stranger's cruel whisper, and even the pronouncements of community leaders can bind us with the unseen cords of spells. Tales of fear, judgment, and superstition circulate in our lives, casting dark shadows on the oblivious. But remember, chanted incantations aren't controlling us; instead, the stories and narratives we choose to believe are what shape our destiny.

As a college dropout in the late 1980s, I worked in a drafty warehouse that reeked of dated cardboard. Each shelf I stocked fed into the low self-esteem I silently suffered from. Former classmates casually paraded through as customers, fresh from graduation with new beginnings, cars, and houses. I didn't need a devil to torment me because my own thoughts were weaving spells of failure, leading me to believe that I'd be trapped here, stocking shelves forever.

I was living with my parents and attending church services faithfully, though none of this seemed to matter. An unseen script played in my mind, a story convincing me that worthlessness was my destiny. One day, a coworker glared at me, irritated by my conversations about Jesus. His fingers pointed at me and danced in a strange, taunting gesture. He then made an ominous prediction: "You're going to have a car accident on your way home today, and you're going to be killed." Each word felt like a fresh knot in the spell. But as I met his gaze with a smile, something in me shifted. I replied, "I'll see you tomorrow." With every syllable I uttered, I felt each thread of that intended and failed dark spell unravel.

The key to breaking spells, or wannabe spells, like this food warehouse story, lies not in perplexing rituals but in embracing a glorious, more authentic narrative. God's true, uplifting revelation replaces the stories of fear and limitation with the story of the gospel, which is the narrative of the good news of Jesus Christ. Living according to the gospel is genuine spiritual warfare, not a battle of chants and incantations. Spiritual warfare is an intentional effort to claim or reclaim God's original intent for our lives.

Jerry's Spell Story

At midmorning on this occasion, I stood in line with one of my spiritual sons, DeJaun, in a local Starbucks. As I turned around, I noticed a man I didn't know standing behind me. Instantly, the Holy Spirit revealed aspects of his heart and spirit to me. I exclaimed, "Mighty man of God! What's up, son?" His jaw dropped, eyes widened, and he covered his mouth with his hand and started laughing. Then he said, "I was just in the car listening to Dr. Myles Munroe, and he mentioned that we need godly people around us so that we can excel." While he continued sharing how my words confirmed what he had just heard moments before entering the restaurant, DeJaun and I listened intently.

We ordered and sat together as Jerry, the man I had addressed, began openly sharing his life story and how he had belittled himself. Not wanting to create an embarrassing moment, I refrained from mentioning his apparent nervous condition, evidenced by his trembling hands. As he spoke about the spells and possible curse that had affected his life, he eventually acknowledged the trembling and admitted he couldn't control it.

Jerry continued to say that he had just prayed the day before, asking God to give him a mentor and a church to attend. After he spoke more concerning his life, DeJaun and I prayed for him and invited him to attend the next Sunday morning service at The Feast of the Lord, the church I pastor. Jerry attended and became a member almost immediately. He shared his testimony with me and wanted me to mention it in encouraging others to know what God can do in their lives.

I have prayed that your faith and courage will increase as you read Jerry's story:

> *My name is Jerry,* and I dealt with severe anxiety and fear throughout my entire life. Growing up, I was bullied and accused of acts I didn't commit, which caused me to hate myself. I also blamed myself for

actions other people engaged in that I had nothing to do with. I isolated myself from these issues by playing video games or hanging out with bad influencers. At around 11 or 12 years old, I began to have thoughts of suicide, thinking that my family would be better off without me. I soon went into indulging in drugs and bad relationships—deep-rooted in problems I had no idea how to fix. I didn't smile in any of my photos. I hated myself. Yet, I kept pushing through life, despite how certain family members treated me.

I knew about God and went to church, but was never really able to find what I needed. Sometimes I think back and realize that most churches I was familiar with wanted children to play and have fun to ensure they would continue attending, but that amusement only lasted a couple of hours. Then, we young churchgoers returned to horrible situations where all the fun and games were absent.

I needed something from the church that would help me overcome the hatred I had for myself because of the trials I faced. I needed something or someone to help me win against the terrifying life I encountered at home and on the streets.

Apostle Shane Wall was the main speaker during a ministry service I attended one evening. Toward the end of the service, he invited those dealing with anxiety and spiritual problems to come to the front of the stage for prayer. Desperate for freedom from the evident spells and curses I was under, I went up, knowing I could receive my healing because I'd witnessed times before how Jesus used Apostle Wall to help people recover from many ills.

Before this evening, I suffered almost daily with extreme anxiety. I was constantly overthinking, my hands and stomach would shake uncontrollably, and fearful thoughts haunted me throughout many days. Cold chills plagued me day and night. I can't even count the multiple times I went to the emergency room only to be told my vitals were fine, even while I was in the throes of a spiritual attack. The spells and curses I endured were mental and physical burdens for so many years, and I'm only 26 years old, married, and with a beautiful little daughter.

At the service this day, I saw people delivered as the power of God was evidently freeing them. When Apostle Wall reached me, he laid his hands on me, and God's power surged through me as he spoke to the evil spirits tormenting my mind and body. I can only describe what I felt afterward as a release, as though whatever gripped my entire being let go and left me.

I had only known Apostle Wall for a few weeks and respected him as a great Bible teacher. This day, while praying for me, he taught me through this deliverance. He said, "Now, you can't worry anymore because you'll bring back the activity of evil spirits to taunt you again." I learned that I had to do my part to stay free by not yielding to future temptations of worry, fear, and anxiety.

Ever since that moment, which was almost two years ago, I no longer have cold chills. My hands and stomach don't shake. I have a clearer and stronger mind and can control my thoughts better than ever. I love how I respond to situations now by being calm instead of nervous and irrational. I'm grateful for how God used Apostle Shane Wall, and he always gives God all the glory whenever I mention how God used him to bless my life.

After Jerry renewed his commitment to Jesus Christ, his life underwent a profound transformation. He attended church services regularly, prayed more fervently, and lived for God with greater sincerity. The gospel of Jesus Christ is indeed the power of God unto salvation, and this good spell continues its power throughout the rest of our lives, as Jerry experienced firsthand.

Today, Jerry is an ordained minister who has brought many people to a deep and rewarding relationship with the Lord, just as he has come to know Him. Only God knows how many spells and curses He dismissed from people's lives after Jerry experienced the gospel's transformative power for himself and lovingly shared his testimony with others.

Jerry has hosted several small groups to help people with anxiety and fear. He's a trailblazing soul-winner who goes to a local gym to play basketball with other young people, witnesses to them regarding Jesus, and invites or brings them to church. No matter where Jerry goes, telling strangers about the love and power of Jesus Christ is his joy and passion. He uses the gospel (good spell) to break spells on lives he encounters daily. To God be all the glory for the story of the gospel that can destroy spells and curses anywhere in the world!

The Ancient Echoes of Narrative Power

Think about how the Bible shows the world-shaping power of story. From the start of Genesis, God literally speaks everything into being! Later, Jesus uses parables, everyday stories, to reveal deep spiritual truths. These aren't dusty old tales but living, spiritual words that still change lives today.

The gospel's story has fueled some of humanity's most extraordinary transformations in recent history. For example, the gospel enlightened Dr. Martin Luther King Jr.'s belief in equality and nonviolence. Dr. King channeled this narrative into words and actions that ignited the civil rights movement, bending unfair laws and opening hearts to righteousness and truth.

Mother Teresa, who lived out the gospel message to care for "the least of these," showed the world love that shattered the idea that wealth equals worth. Her service to the less fortunate transformed the lives she humbly served and altered our thoughts today about human dignity.

Even fiction can spark powerful change! C.S. Lewis's *Narnia* books also showed children as well as adults qualities of sacrifice, redemption, and hope in a fantastical setting. He proved that stories can bridge old truths with new ways of understanding, drawing people closer to the heart of the gospel.

These stories remind us that we aren't just passive listeners. We're permitted to choose narratives that spread truth and love. What is your own gospel story? Have you seen its power change your life? Through how we speak, act, and even what we create, we help write the ongoing story of God at work in the world—an account that has the power to change everything.

Negative Narratives: Unraveling the Spells of Our Lives

Breaking free from negative tales starts with noticing them. Think about those spells ingrained in us as to what brings happiness—like the need to wear the latest fashions. How others value fashion struck me in 7th grade. In the '80s, you could buy three pairs of knock-off sneakers for ten bucks—and that's what I had. One of my classmates called attention to my shoes while the teacher was out of the classroom. He said, "I saw those shoes in the sales paper. I bet your mom got you all three pairs!" Everyone cracked up with jeering laughter, and I writhed with a sense of shame, feeling like I could melt into the floor and disappear from that embarrassing moment. Instead of owning up to his claim of my mom's choice to purchase all pairs, I lied and said she hadn't. I even lied to my mom when I came home that day. I told her the shoes hurt, prompting her reluctant acceptance of my lie.

I'd bought into the suggestion that my worth came from my clothes. We must help children navigate these situations to avoid their making the same sort of mistake. We want them to look at how these little moments shape us and remind them their value doesn't come from outside opinions. Let's teach them that real happiness isn't in owning things but in who they are and the good they bring into the world.

The direct critique from my classmate took me by surprise. Decades have passed, and now, with the benefit of hindsight, I envision a reply that might have turned my classmate's jest into a moment of empathy. I could have retorted, "Well, my parents probably don't make as much money as your parents, but they love me and try to give me the best they can. I'm glad your parents have the money to buy you more expensive shoes so nobody will tease you." Whether this would have evoked sympathy from my classmate remains unknown, but one thing is clear: such a response would have steered me from succumbing to a narrative that eventually led to deceiving my mother. This reflection opens up the conversation about various tactics to counteract and dismantle the harmful delusions and spells we might encounter.

> *But you shall [earnestly] remember the Lord your God, for it is He Who gives you power to get wealth, that He may establish His covenant which He swore to your fathers, as it is this day.*
>
> Deuteronomy 8:18 AMPC

I don't advocate for what's often referred to as the "prosperity gospel." However, I hold true to the scripture that states God doesn't directly bestow wealth upon us; instead, He grants us the ability to acquire wealth.

A cherished memory came to mind recently of the late Dr. Audrey Brunson, a pastor who graced my home church as a guest minister on several occasions. One of her impactful messages included a comment she famously and comically stated, "I'm not waiting for a pie in the sky when I die. I want some steak on my plate and some ham where I am." She firmly rejected the notion that a commitment to Christ necessitated a life of poverty, refusing to let it cast a spell over her life.

Weary not yourself to be rich; cease from your own [human] wisdom.

Proverbs 23:4 AMPC

We sometimes also inadvertently place a spell on our lives by tirelessly striving to accumulate wealth. How can we discern whether we live in unnecessary poverty or overburden ourselves in the chase for riches? When we seek God's guidance through prayer to understand and embrace His financial blueprint for our lives, He assures us that we're no longer under a spell that keeps us from living up to our God-given potential.

Spells Cast upon Unaware Victims

People often believe that spells purportedly cast without the victim's knowledge work on a subconscious level. In some belief systems, the thought is that these spells can influence a person's ideas, emotions, or behaviors without their conscious awareness. Such spells may effectively tap into the subconscious mind, planting suggestions or manipulating perceptions without the individual's recognition.

This theory aligns with concepts from psychology, such as subconscious influence, suggestion, and priming. Even if an individual is unaware that someone cast a spell on them, they may still be susceptible to its effects if their subconscious mind is receptive to the suggestions or influences within the spell.

An example of this method of spell casting and manipulation occurred when Samson fell victim to Delilah's deceit. In Judges 16, Samson, known for his extraordinary strength, was unaware of Delilah's true intentions as she persistently sought to discover the secret of his power. Delilah's manipulation worked on a level that Samson didn't fully perceive. She used her influence over him to gradually wear down his resistance and extract his secret. When Samson finally disclosed that his strength lay in his uncut hair, Delilah acted on this information, leading to his capture by the Philistines.

This real-life tale highlights how subtle influence and deceit can operate similarly, affecting someone's actions and decisions without the victim's conscious awareness. Delilah's manipulation and charm allowed her to infiltrate Samson's subconscious, leading him to trust her and believe the story that she would never betray him.

The account of Samson's experience emphasizes the importance of vigilance and discernment in contextualizing the breaking of spells and curses. Just as Samson's downfall came from underestimating the influence of those around him, individuals today must be aware of the potential for subconscious manipulation. Recognizing these influences and seeking divine guidance can provide protection and clarity. By staying attuned to God's wisdom and surrounding oneself with trustworthy and faithful individuals, one can guard against the subtle deceptions that may lead to spiritual or personal harm.

I Was Under a Gluttonous Spell

As a heartfelt disclaimer, I realize that breaking spells that have fostered unhealthy habits requires deliberate effort and careful planning. This effort is worthwhile because the alternative can lead to dire consequences. While this section focuses on steps to overcome overeating, the same principles apply to any spell-induced behavior that threatens to bring destruction to areas of our lives. We must approach these changes seriously, recognizing the need for thoughtful strategies and consistent work. Additionally, I recommend using available resources to explore natural (material and ordinary) ways to reverse harmful practices, ensuring a comprehensive and balanced approach to breaking free from injurious habits.

While I'm not a health or mental health professional, I am someone who has personally experienced the challenges of overeating and understands the spiritual battle behind it. My insights come from years of walking this path, seeking God's guidance, and learning from successes and setbacks.

I once had a terrible habit of eating until I was overly full. The Holy Spirit would rebuke me often, and I would repent, only to fail again at the next meal and many meals after that. The spell or false narrative I accepted about myself was: "Eating doesn't satisfy me unless I'm overly full." As simple and harmless as this thought may seem, it is far from it. This belief can lead to sickness, disease, and even death for many who share this misguided story. I've watched episodes of *My 600-Lb Life* and have seen people explain how they can't stop eating until they've just stuffed themselves with food and beverages.

My stomach often felt uncomfortably tight and strained, a sensation I detested every time I encountered it. Despite this, I found myself overeating repeatedly. The spell's grip on my mind was so firm that I would forget the discomfort of previous overeating episodes because my enjoyment in constant food intake overpowered any memory of former misery. My focus was solely on the pleasurable flavors and textures of the food and beverages I consumed right then.

What was the solution that freed me from that spell? I will take my time to explain and pour out my heart because I want you to understand how to break free from spells, especially when it seems as though you have inadequate strength to defeat the spell. But we can have hope during our struggles. The tools I will share are spiritual as well as natural, proven concepts. Please read this entire section to understand all the solutions I discovered.

> *But I say, walk and live [habitually] in the [Holy] Spirit [responsive to and controlled and guided by the Spirit]; then you will certainly not gratify the cravings and desires of the flesh (of human nature without God).*
> Galatians 5:16 AMPC

We must resist the lure of physical pleasures and align our lives with God's will by surrendering to the Holy Spirit. I'll share more of my struggle to stop overeating now to help you fully grasp the solution I discovered.

Repetitive sin, especially when we know it's wrong yet consciously repeat it, is what Paul faced when he wrote:

> *For I fail to practice the good deeds I desire to do, but the evil deeds that I do not desire to do are what I am [ever] doing.*
>
> Romans 7:19 AMPC

I loved munching the entire time I watched TV. So, I tried refraining from watching television while eating, thinking that being entertained was the root of my problem. Yet, even without the television, I would still sit, eat, talk, snack, and overindulge. Again, I would repent for disobeying the Holy Spirit's instructions. The spell of overindulgence also had me bound in the grips of repetitive sin.

Is gluttony sinful? Since, in the Bible, God commanded us to avoid anything that leads away from His will, then yes, gluttony is indeed sinful. Overeating, like other forms of excess, can become a form of idolatry, where we place our desires for physical satisfaction above our obedience to God. The more we give in to these desires, the more we allow this spell to take hold, keeping us in a cycle of sin that is difficult to break. I now realize that true freedom can only come from surrendering to the Holy Spirit and aligning our actions with God's Word.

> *20 Do not associate with winebibbers; be not among them nor among gluttonous eaters of meat,*
> *21 For the drunkard and the glutton shall come to poverty, and drowsiness shall clothe a man with rags.*
>
> Proverbs 23:20-21 AMPC

These verses strongly urge us to avoid associating with those who overindulge. Engaging in gluttony is much easier when surrounded by others who do the same. The second verse highlights that gluttony leads to drowsiness, which can eventually cause laziness, neglect of our responsibilities, and poverty.

> *They are doomed and their fate is eternal misery (perdition); their god is their stomach (their appetites, their sensuality) and they glory in their shame, siding with earthly things and being of their party.*
>
> Philippians 3:19 AMPC

This verse addresses gluttony more seriously, stating that gluttons effectively make their bellies their god. In this context, the term *belly* signifies more than physical fullness; it symbolizes surrendering to the pleasures of the palate, indulging in gluttony.

The true root of any gluttonous behavior isn't merely the desire to be overly satisfied but rather the drive to satisfy our palates—finding something pleasing to our desired tastes. Reflecting on my struggles, I realize my goal was never just to overstuff my stomach but to please my senses. This insight into Philippians 3:19 helps me understand that gluttony stems from pursuing sensory pleasure, not overconsumption.

Whatever story a spell causes us to believe and live by can be broken similarly by seeking God's Word for insights, as well as understanding that we should discover and take charge over the pleasure point associated with the spell that challenges us.

Overcoming any overindulgence involves integrating spiritual insights and practical, natural applications. From the scriptural perspective, immersing oneself in God's Word and embracing the guidance of the Holy Spirit provides the foundational shift to grasping the harmful impact of excess and the need for repentance and renewal.

Practically, the first step is to develop wisdom about natural (material) and learned habits. For those who are overindulgent in food, this means paying close attention to what, when, and how much we eat. Keeping a food journal can help track eating patterns, making identifying triggers for overeating easier. Before taking any action that could lead to spell-controlled behavior, such as eating a meal, pausing a moment to pray, and sincerely thanking God for the food (in this case), can also help shift the focus from mere consumption to appreciation and purposeful eating. This practice aligns with the guidance of Psalm 119:105, where God's Word becomes a guiding light, helping us make better choices.

Thy word is a lamp unto my feet, and a light unto my path.

Psalm 119:105 KJV

Incorporating activities based in good behavior can also play a significant role in curbing overindulgence. Physical exercise promotes a healthy lifestyle and is a practical deterrent to gluttonous eating—exchanging an unhealthy habit for a healthy one. Replacing negative actions with positive ones engages both natural and spiritual dimensions. To act effectively, one must harmonize the heart, mind, spirit, soul, and body, ensuring a holistic approach to transformation.

We must openly declare that our corrective actions replace harmful past behavior. This practice reinforces our determination and encourages others to become unofficial accountability partners with us. Further, hearing ourselves declare the words of determination aloud builds encouragement and endurance.

Additionally, establishing a supportive environment is crucial. Surrounding ourselves with individuals who encourage and engage in healthy habits themselves while providing support can significantly impact our ability to overcome overindulgence or other unfavorable habits. Sharing struggles and victories with a trusted friend or a small group can foster a sense of community and shared purpose, as emphasized in Proverbs 27:17 AMPC: "Iron sharpens iron; so a man sharpens the countenance of his friend [to show rage or worthy purpose]."

Setting realistic and achievable goals is also vital. Breaking down the journey into manageable steps, such as reducing portion sizes, choosing healthier food options, and scheduling regular meals, for instance, can help maintain progress without our feeling overwhelmed. Celebrating small victories along the way reinforces positive behavior and motivates continued effort. Since spells influence our lifestyle, these suggestions help us build and maintain healthy, long-term routines after breaking the spell.

These practical strategies, combined with the spiritual strength derived from God's Word and the Holy Spirit's guidance, make the possibility of breaking free from the spell of overindulgence and other spells a foreseeable reality. We want to focus on release from engaging in excessive or otherwise sinful pleasures, possibly causing irreversible harm to ourselves. This practical and spiritual holistic approach nurtures and balances life's physical and spiritual aspects. This leads to a healthier, more fulfilling existence that aligns with God's will for our bodies, minds, and souls. (3 John 1:2)

The Secret Weakness Spells Wait For

We often overindulge because we're trying to relieve a feeling. But what we're sensing is not just an emotion; it's a spiritual presence. Excessiveness manifests because we're attempting to replace something spiritual with something material. However, the spiritual will always overpower the material unless we exercise God's wisdom. For example, when experiencing a spirit of frustration, we might turn to food or other calming substances to try to numb that sensation. Yet, no matter how much we indulge, our material choices cannot alleviate our spiritual discomfort.

Trying to force a natural solution to deaden spiritual misery can lead to increased consumption of desired things. Too often, this consumption becomes excessive, and tragically, many have lost their very lives trying to overpower a spiritual battle using harmful, ordinary substances. The key to breaking this cycle is recognizing that only spiritual solutions, such as prayer, worship, and seeking God's guidance, can bring relief and healing from feelings such as fatigue, frustration, anxiety, and so on.

Fatigue is one of the greatest enemies of our mental, physical, and spiritual well-being. Whether extreme or moderate, it can weaken our resistance to temptation and leave us vulnerable to the persistence of a spell. When we're tired on any level, our bodies and minds crave relief, and in seeking to escape exhaustion, we may turn to harmful activities such as sexual immorality, alcohol, drug abuse, overeating, or other destructive habits. However, the relief our bodies crave and require is found in restful sleep, which restores and rejuvenates us.

The illusion that harmful pleasures can provide lasting fulfillment from feelings of tiredness is a deceptive spell that can never satisfy the underlying requirement for restorative sleep. Recognizing and definitively addressing our genuine need to relax or even nap are keys to breaking free from this destructive cycle of providing unsuitable solutions for sensible rest. Let's look to Holy Spirit-led activities that weaken a spell's hold on our lives until we're entirely free from its grip.

Spells of Pleasure

What is your point of pleasure? It varies for everyone. Those who engage in premarital or extramarital sexual activities—despite the Bible's clear teachings against them—aren't just passing the time. They are indulging in a specific pleasure point, which often goes beyond the act itself. For me, overeating led to the physical sensation of a full stomach. But the intensified moment of pleasure was satisfying my appetite. For someone else, that person's weakness might be cake, but cake holds no appeal for others. The point of pleasure is personal and unique to each individual. The key to understanding it is discovering the story we've embraced that convinces us this pleasure will bring fulfillment.

Consider someone caught in a cycle of sexual immorality. This individual's pleasure point might stem from the belief, "Nobody cares about me enough to give me their undivided attention." Once they accept that narrative, they believe it so deeply that it becomes their truth, causing them to disregard the true intentions of others. They overlook potential harm and become entangled in the trap of seeking immediate satisfaction through acceptance. Their need for attention and approval blinds them to the consequences—finding themselves driven by pleasure, validation, or engagement—even at their own expense.

For yet another person entangled in illicit affairs, the point of pleasure might be as simple as an innocent touch on the shoulder or back, signaling the affection they crave. The story behind this might be, "People avoid me as if I'm contagious. I feel like I'm invisible in every crowd." If this resonates with you, know that you are not poison. God has a plan for your life. Instead of seeing yourself as avoided by people, recognize that God protects you for a higher purpose than you may realize.

We must be vigilant, guarding ourselves against the vulnerability that comes with desiring pleasure so intensely that we allow spells to infiltrate our lives. The story we believe about ourselves or how others treat us, combined with the trigger of someone satisfying the pleasure point created by the spell we're under, can lead to sin that spirals into a destructive lifestyle with unpleasant, even deadly, consequences.

Since these spells have pleasure points, we naturally seek the pleasure they promise. However, we can permanently cancel the story we've believed by embracing the truth found in the gospel's good spell. The gospel isn't just about Jesus coming to Earth to die; it includes His birth, teachings, miracles, and everything He did as part of His divine mission before fulfilling the prophecies of His death and resurrection.

Jesus also promised never to leave or forsake us, which means the power of the gospel is still at work today. The books of Matthew, Mark, and Luke in the Bible are *synoptic Gospels* because they tell similar accounts of Jesus' life. We must not omit any part of Jesus' life or legacy from the gospel—the good spell and good news that encompasses all He did and continues to do in, for, and through us.

Prepare to Go Deeper

In the coming chapters, we will explore the stories that have trapped us and the narratives that have dictated our choices and emotions. We will uncover the spells and curses we've lived under and, more importantly, learn how to break away from them through the power of the gospel. Applying the solutions in this book is not just an academic exercise; it is a journey toward freedom, a battle to reclaim the narrative of our lives from the spells that have bound us.

Our task is straightforward: identify the spells and curses that have controlled us, sever their hold, and embrace the truth that sets us free—the message of Jesus Christ. This good spell liberates us from the negative narratives that bind us.

Understanding the power of narrative and belief to shape our lives sets the stage for exploring what being under a spell or curse means. This understanding brings us to a crucial point: the gospel's transformative power, the good spell that can shatter the chains of negative narratives.

But what does living under a good spell indicate? It is not merely about attending church or reading the Bible, although those are excellent life-event choices; it is about a profound, personal transformation that reshapes our understanding of reality. Embracing the truth involves recognizing whether the stories we've believed are rooted in reality or deception and discerning the powerful truth of the Gospel of Jesus Christ, which sets us free.

Jesus included specific manners and customs of His earthly life in Israel to help His audiences better familiarize themselves with the points of His Kingdom teachings. As we delve into the material history and psychology behind the spirituality of spells and curses, we will explore how ancient cultures understood these concepts and how modern understanding of human thought provides insights into the power of belief and narrative. This journey will take us from the dusty streets of ancient Jerusalem to cutting-edge cognitive psychological studies.

Furthermore, we will discuss real-life stories of individuals who found themselves under damaging spells—stories of shame, despair, and hopelessness—and how the gospel's transformative power broke those spells, leading them to a life of freedom, purpose, and joy.

In dissecting these stories, we'll uncover the common threads—the lies believed, the truths ignored, and the moments of revelation that led to freedom. These narratives will prove the power of the good spell and guide readers in identifying and breaking spells and curses in their own lives. The remaining chapters will be more than instructional; they will be a call to action—a challenge to step into a new story, the story of freedom and truth found in Jesus Christ.

Before we move on to the next chapter on Curses, I sense the Holy Spirit prompting me to lead you to ask our Father, "Lord, are any stories or narratives I believe in right now causing me to live under spells? Please reveal them to me and guide me in removing them from my life. In Jesus' name, I pray. Amen."

CHAPTER 2:

CHARACTERIZING CURSES

Understanding the Roots of Curses in Our Lives

In the 1960s, A. A. Allen, a renowned healing evangelist, encountered a woman possessed by a demonic spirit at one of his revival meetings. Although the companion who brought the demon-possessed lady referred to her condition as a "spell," what this dear lady suffered through was undeniably a curse that was evilly placed on her life. As Rev. Allen prayed for her, the demon verbally manifested, declaring, "I am lucifer!"

The companion who brought the woman to the meeting recounted how the demon had tormented the victim, explaining on a 1964 Miracle Revival Recordings vinyl, "When she was a young girl, there was a lad that wanted to marry her, and she wouldn't marry him, and he cast a spell upon her, and then her parents took her to a witchcraft doctor because of the pain in her chest [caused by the demonic possession resulting from that spell]. They wanted her to be healed, and they didn't know any other place to go. She was Roman Catholic, and every year, they say they'd keep that spell cast upon her…."

The companion continued, "When we go down to her home, [we'd] drive down to her home to get her for a prayer meeting; you could see the evil powers around the home. You could feel in the house…the force of the devil there. The devil tries to kill her, tries to kill her child, and hates her husband, and whenever we talk to her about her husband and child, she couldn't talk. When this spell comes on her, it just keeps her speechless."

Rev. Allen cast the devil out of the woman in that revival meeting. God freed that precious lady from demonic oppression and possession through the power of prayer, command, and faith in Jesus Christ. The following biblical proclamation remains true today: When we surrender to Christ, the power of the gospel can liberate us from all depths of spiritual captivity.

The gospel of Jesus Christ is powerful enough to break even the strongest of spells and curses, such as the demon-possessed woman suffered from in this true story. In the following verse, Jesus declared:

> *The Spirit of the Lord [is] upon Me, because He has anointed Me [the Anointed One, the Messiah] to preach the good news (the Gospel) to the poor; He has sent Me to announce release to the captives and recovery of sight to the blind, to send forth as delivered those who are oppressed [who are downtrodden, bruised, crushed, and broken down by calamity],*
>
> Luke 4:18 AMPC

Jesus also demonstrated His authority over demonic forces when He commanded an unclean spirit to leave a man:

> *25 And Jesus rebuked him, saying, Hush up (be muzzled, gagged), and come out of him!*
> *26 And the unclean spirit, throwing the man into convulsions and screeching with a loud voice, came out of him.*
>
> Mark 1:25-26 AMPC

Believers have been given this authority through Christ and can overcome any spell or curse by way of the power of the gospel through the Holy Spirit. Words alone do not expel demons. We cast them out only by the authority of Jesus Christ because His gospel empowers us through faith in Jesus, belief in His Word, and obedience to His command to cast out demons.

What is a Curse?

From human to human, a curse is an act of imprecating or invoking evil upon someone, a prayer to an evil entity that a curse or calamity may befall someone. Delving into curses' origins is crucial to break free from them effectively. Curses can arise from various sources, each with its unique impact on our lives. Understanding these roots is not about assigning blame but seeking clarity and direction for our journey toward freedom from curses.

Although biblical references firmly establish that curses are genuine and effective, in contemporary secular society, the concept or belief in curses is often more symbolic than literal. Also, the methods used to *produce* curses vary widely, depending on cultural and personal beliefs. Some of the ways people might believe they can produce curses include:

Words and Intentions: The power of spoken words is profound and undeniable in the complicated experiences of human interaction. A belief among many is that words infused with intense negative emotions or intentions can manifest as a curse—a verbal incantation wishing harm or misfortune upon another. This notion is rooted in the understanding that our tongues wield the dual power of life and death.

> *Death and life are in the power of the tongue, and they who indulge in it shall eat the fruit of it [for death or life].*
>
> Proverbs 18:21 AMPC

The same bodily instrument that can inflict pain and sorrow can also harness the power to breathe life, hope, and healing into existence. This duality reminds us of the weight our words carry and the responsibility we are expected to uphold. By consciously choosing to speak words of life, we can counteract and overpower the destructive force of negative intentions, transforming a cursed life into a blessed one, from darkness to light. In this dance of words, the intentionality of our tongues becomes a powerful tool for change, shaping our reality and the world around us with each utterance.

A dear friend of mine is a pastor who testified that he went to his medical appointment only to discover that the doctor had urgent news for him. The doctor told him that he had diabetes. Without a second thought, he responded, "No, I don't." The doctor repeated that the diagnosis was a fact, that my friend had diabetes. Again, he replied, "No, I don't." After quite a few weeks had passed, he revisited his doctor for a checkup following the determination of diabetes. To the doctor's surprise, he could no longer confirm the pastor's previous diagnosis. By faith, my friend believed in his heart and confessed his faith in God with his mouth!

Symbolic Actions: A mystique that transcends the ordinary

Oppositely, some believe that specific rituals possess the power to invoke a curse. The act of burning an effigy or writing a name on paper only to destroy it carries an intention to inflict harm, weaving negative energy into the fabric of reality. These actions are thought to channel and project the caster's will, transforming mundane objects into conduits of a hostile force. In this realm of symbolism, the physical act becomes a manifestation of intent, believed to have the power to alter destinies and shape the unseen forces that govern the victims' lives.

> *But no weapon that is formed against you shall prosper, and every tongue that shall rise against you in judgment you shall show to be in the wrong. This [peace, righteousness, security, triumph over opposition] is the heritage of the servants of the Lord [those in whom the ideal Servant of the Lord is reproduced]; this is the righteousness or the vindication which they obtain from Me [this is that which I impart to them as their justification], says the Lord.*
>
> Isaiah 54:17 AMPC

When I stepped out of the front door of my home, heading to work, I encountered an unsettling sight—a dead cat in my front yard. Living on a dirt road in the rural parts of Orangeburg, SC, I was no stranger to stray cats, but finding one deceased on my property was a first. As I neared the cat, I noticed its body was positioned unnaturally, and the surrounding ground bore the marks of a circular pattern. It was clear to me that this was an attempt to cast a curse on me or my family.

I dismissed the feeble attempt with a laugh: "You devils, is this all you've got? I apply the blood of Jesus over this ground and nullify your schemes because they will not prevail!"

Upon returning home from work, I found the area pristine, as if nothing had ever happened. The cat and the eerie ground drawing had vanished. This experience, though bizarre, didn't frighten me; it merely appeared to be a failed attempt at witchcraft aimed at my family or me. I saw it as a tangible representation of a weapon formed against me, and just as surely as it was formed, it was thwarted by God's divine protection and authority granted through my faith in Him. Knowing that the continued work of the gospel of Jesus Christ empowers our lives, we can defeat whatever spell or curse any caster envisions.

Technological Means: In the digital age, the landscape of curses has evolved, with some believing that the virtual world offers a new avenue for hatred. Some view the act of sending threatening or harmful messages through social media or other electronic means as a contemporary form of cursing. This modern twist on an ancient practice leverages technology as a vehicle for delivering ill intentions, allowing words and images to traverse the Internet to cause distress. In this context, the screen becomes a medium for delivering supernatural injury, transforming keystrokes into a tool for wielding influence and harm from afar.

On several occasions, biblical content I've shared on my social media pages has drawn criticism. While simply deleting negative comments is tempting, I prefer to seize distinct moments as educational opportunities. Often, those who comment critically are under the spell of long-held beliefs that need the light of wisdom or further understanding for them to break free. With the help of the Holy Spirit, it's key that we discern whether someone is genuinely attacking or merely seeking enlightenment, whether they're aware that they're seeking help or not. By responding with sound wisdom and understanding grounded in God's Word, we wield the power to break spells and curses by guiding others to the truth.

Psychological Influence: As with spells, the power of belief can be a double-edged sword, especially regarding the realm of curses. The psychological impact of believing oneself to be cursed can be profound, leading to a spiral of self-fulfilling prophecies or psychosomatic symptoms. In this mental maze of convincing thoughts, the line between reality and perception blurs, and the mere conviction of being cursed can manifest in tangible ways, shaping one's experiences and health. This phenomenon underscores the intricate connection between mind and body, highlighting how deeply our thoughts and beliefs influence physical and emotional well-being. With belief and reality, the mind becomes both the battlefield and the weapon, capable of conjuring its own curses from the shadows of doubt and fear.

> *Why are you cast down, O my inner self? And why should you moan over me and be disquieted within me? Hope in God and wait expectantly for Him, for I shall yet praise Him, Who is the help of my countenance, and my God.*
>
> Psalm 42:11 AMPC

This verse is particularly moving, capturing a profound conversation between the human spirit and its soul. It reflects on the moment God formed Adam from the dust of the ground, breathed a living spirit into him, and transformed him into a living soul. Adam's creation highlights the divine origin and complex connection between our spiritual and physical natures.

Psalm 42:11 is a verse I often turn to as a justification for talking to myself. Throughout my life, I've struggled with expressing my emotions. When I grew up in the 70s and 80s, men were frequently told to keep their feelings to themselves because such restraint was considered manly. However, in recent years, a shift has come about, encouraging men to express their emotions more openly. I find myself caught between these two perspectives. The actuality isn't that I don't want to share how I feel, but I often struggle to identify and articulate my emotions. Yet, through prayerful reflection and conversations with others, I've become more in touch with my feelings than ever before.

This newfound understanding began when I realized my spirit could communicate with my soul. In Psalm 42, the psalmist portrays a moment where his spirit questions the downcast state of his soul. Understanding that my spirit can discern the condition of my soul and strengthen it has freed me to express my feelings more openly because I now grasp what's happening within me spiritually. Communication from my spirit to my soul has become vital when I'm not feeling my best in the spiritual parts of my being, such as my mind, heart, and spirit.

This is not New Age teaching. We do not believe that the human spirit or soul is divine in and of itself. We follow the clear teachings of the Holy Spirit as echoed throughout the Old and New Testaments. Every truth shared in this book is grounded in Scripture and aligned with sound biblical doctrine. The verses provided are not twisted or removed from their intended context; rather, they reinforce that this revelation is rooted in God's Word and not in mystical or man-made ideologies. My aim is not to introduce a strange or new theology, but to illuminate how the Bible already speaks to these spiritual realities in ways that bring clarity, healing, and deliverance.

Recognizing the role of my human spirit makes me aware of the continual nourishment my spirit requires—through prayer (in both English and tongues), fasting, Bible study, and more. Romans 8:16 tells us that the Holy Spirit bears witness with our human spirit that we are children of God. Therefore, I must keep my spirit sensitive to the Holy Spirit by feeding it with God's Word and whatever else He deems necessary for my growth and well-being.

Then the Lord God formed man from the dust of the ground and breathed into his nostrils the breath or spirit of life, and man became a living being.

Genesis 2:7 AMPC

The human spirit is an innate part of us, designed to seek, search, and explore beyond the surface of our existence, constantly longing for deeper understanding and connection. The sensory input we receive from our environment—what we see, hear, and experience—enters our spirits, influencing our hearts and souls, shaping how we think, speak, and act. Given this profound connection, we must be vigilant about what we expose ourselves to. What we absorb affects the human spirit, which God created with the purpose of seeking His truth. Therefore, guarding our eyes and ears is critical to nurturing a spirit that remains aligned with God's design.

> *I call to remembrance my song in the night; with my heart I meditate and my spirit searches diligently:*
>
> Psalm 77:6 AMPC

> *My soul yearns for You [O Lord] in the night, yes, my spirit within me seeks You earnestly; for [only] when Your judgments are in the earth will the inhabitants of the world learn righteousness (uprightness and right standing with God).*
>
> Isaiah 26:9 AMPC

However, we must guard ourselves against absorbing evil sights and sounds; God desires us to profoundly understand the good that emanates from Him while remaining uninformed about the world's evil. This refusal of wickedness enables God's power to manifest through us as He overcomes the devil's schemes and weapons aimed at us.

> *19 For while your loyalty and obedience is known to all, so that I rejoice over you, I would have you well versed and wise as to what is good and innocent and guileless as to what is evil.*
> *20 And the God of peace will soon crush Satan under your feet. The grace of our Lord Jesus Christ (the Messiah) be with you.*
>
> Romans 16:19-20 AMPC

After God formed Adam from the dust of the ground and breathed a spirit into him that gave him life, Adam became a living soul (Genesis 2:7 KJV). This soul encompasses a person's will, intellect, and emotions, serving as the essence of human experience and identity.

> *I will greatly rejoice in the Lord, my soul will exult in my God; for He has clothed me with the garments of salvation, He has covered me with the robe of righteousness, as a bridegroom decks himself with a garland, and as a bride adorns herself with her jewels.*
>
> Isaiah 61:10 AMPC

10 When wisdom entereth into thine heart, and knowledge is pleasant unto thy soul;
11 Discretion shall preserve thee, understanding shall keep thee:

Proverbs 2:10-11 KJV

And He said to them, My soul is exceedingly sad (overwhelmed with grief) so that it almost kills Me! Remain here and keep awake and be watching.

Mark 14:34 AMPC

Another integral part of our being is the heart, which is the territory where belief is birthed and cultivated. Our deepest convictions and faith are held in this region of our existence, influencing our decisions and guiding our actions.

For with the heart a person believes (adheres to, trusts in, and relies on Christ) and so is justified (declared righteous, acceptable to God), and with the mouth he confesses (declares openly and speaks out freely his faith) and confirms [his] salvation.

Romans 10:10 AMPC

The spirit, soul, and heart collectively steer our existence, making it pivotal that our souls do not merely surrender to what the spirit seeks, finds, and delivers for the heart to believe. When the soul ponders, decides, and acts upon these inputs, it shapes our reality. Such dynamics can lead to psychological influence, causing individuals to live in a perpetual state of terror, convinced they are under a curse or spell.

Singing and listening to songs that direct our worship toward God or Jesus, praying at every opportune moment, reading the Bible to deepen our understanding of Jesus and His teachings—all these practices ensure that our spirit has only godly and righteous resources to draw from. Dedication to these disciplines as a lifestyle helps guarantee that our spirit, soul, and heart remain consecrated to God's pleasure and usage, ensuring we are protected against the intent of spells and curses formulated by other human beings.

In the realm of curses, practitioners often adhere to the principle that faith is proven by works, believing that specific words and actions, executed with precision, can bring about a desired outcome. This belief in the power of ritual and incantation is rooted in a deep conviction in the effectiveness of their practices. By contrast, God calls Christians to a higher standard of faith, one anchored in His promises and teachings.

If those who conjure curses operate with such conviction in their rituals, how much more should Christians, who have the truth of God's Word, exercise our faith to produce works of strict obedience? This dutifulness, born out of genuine faith in God, has the potential to unleash God's desired outcomes in our lives, transcending the limitations of human effort and tapping into the divine power that transforms destinies.

> *Do not let yourself be overcome by evil, but overcome (master) evil with good.*
>
> Romans 12:21

The Prophetic Role of Curses

Prophets in the Old Testament sometimes pronounced curses as part of their divine mandate. These curses were declarations of God's judgment against unfaithfulness, idolatry, and injustice. For instance, the prophet Jeremiah cursed those who trusted in mere mortals instead of the Lord.

> *Thus says the Lord: Cursed [with great evil] is the strong man who trusts in and relies on frail man, making weak [human] flesh his arm, and whose mind and heart turn aside from the Lord.*
>
> Jeremiah 17:5 AMPC

However, it's essential to note that the purpose of these prophetic curses was not to bring harm for harm's sake but to call the people back to repentance and faithfulness to God. The ultimate aim was restoration and reconciliation, not destruction.

Curses in the Bible often carry a prophetic dimension. Prophets were God's messengers, tasked with conveying His warnings and judgments. When they pronounced curses, such an action was a call to repentance and an emphatic reminder of the consequences of continued disobedience. This prophetic dimension means curses weren't just random threats or punishments; they were specific declarations from God regarding future consequences if people continued disobeying His Word. Scripture clearly shows this prophetic aspect, highlighting that God always revealed His intentions through His prophets before bringing judgment. Scripture confirms this role of prophets clearly:

> *Surely the Lord God will do nothing without revealing His secret to His servants the prophets.*
>
> Amos 3:7 AMPC

Thus, when prophets like Moses or Isaiah pronounced a curse, they weren't speaking merely from personal conviction. Instead, they spoke under divine authority, declaring events that would occur if people refused to obey God's commands. The prophetic role of curses was not merely punitive but redemptive. The ultimate goal was to turn the people's hearts back to God, prevent the fulfillment of the curse, and restore those who had wandered from a righteous path to a place of blessing. This purpose highlights the dynamic nature of curses in the biblical narrative, where even the harshest warnings were infused with the hope of redemption.

Reflecting on the prophetic role of curses reminds us of the importance of heeding God's warnings in our own lives. Here, censure encourages us to listen to the voice of the Holy Spirit, be attentive to areas where we may be straying from God's path, and respond with humility and obedience.

When God Curses

When God bestows a curse upon an individual or a group in the divine realm, the consequences are far more profound than any earthly exchange of curses between humans.

> *8 Will a man rob or defraud God? Yet you rob and defraud Me. But you say, In what way do we rob or defraud You? [You have withheld your] tithes and offerings.*
>
> *9 You are cursed with the curse, for you are robbing Me, even this whole nation.*
>
> *10 Bring all the tithes (the whole tenth of your income) into the storehouse, that there may be food in My house, and prove Me now by it, says the Lord of hosts, if I will not open the windows of heaven for you and pour you out a blessing, that there shall not be room enough to receive it.*
>
> *11 And I will rebuke the devourer [insects and plagues] for your sakes and he shall not destroy the fruits of your ground, neither shall your vine drop its fruit before the time in the field, says the Lord of hosts.*
>
> *12 And all nations shall call you happy and blessed, for you shall be a land of delight, says the Lord of hosts.*
>
> Malachi 3:8-12 AMPC

The passage in Malachi challenges us to consider the weight of our actions, particularly regarding tithes and offerings. It reminds us that our relationship with God is not just about what we receive but also about what we give. The act of giving is not merely a transaction; it's a testament to our trust in God's provision and our commitment to His Kingdom.

When God withholds His blessings, a curse most assuredly ensues. In the profound words of Malachi, we find a divine principle that speaks directly to the heart of every believer. When God withholds His blessings of protection, provision, etc., it is not merely a passive act but a deliberate withholding that is a stark reminder of a richer spiritual truth. The withholding manifests the underlying meaning of such a curse: the absence of God's blessings. This absence is a divine response to the actions or inactions of an individual. Simply put, God does not actively unleash curses upon people; He curses people by refusing to bless them.

When we fail to honor God with our tithes and offerings, we position ourselves outside the realm of His blessings, as if we're standing in the shadow, just outside the warm glow of His favor. The curse, therefore, is not a random punishment but a natural consequence of our disconnect from the Source of all blessings.

This scriptural text also invites us to introspect and realign our priorities with God's Law (His will), ensuring that our giving reflects our gratitude and trust in God's unwavering faithfulness. It's a call to step back into the light, to bask in the abundance of God's blessings, and to experience the joy of being in harmony with His divine will. Without God's goodness in our lives, we will experience many seemingly random yet automatically occurring curses.

In Jeremiah 17:5-8, God draws a clear distinction between those who place their trust in human strength and those who trust in Him. He declares a curse on those who rely on people:

> 5 *Thus says the Lord: Cursed [with great evil] is the strong man who trusts in and relies on frail man, making weak [human] flesh his arm, and whose mind and heart turn aside from the Lord.*
> 6 *For he shall be like a shrub or a person naked and destitute in the desert; and he shall not see any good come, but shall dwell in the parched places in the wilderness, in an uninhabited salt land.*
>
> *Jeremiah 17:5-6 AMPC*

In contrast, God proclaims blessings on those who put their faith in Him:

> 7 *[Most] blessed is the man who believes in, trusts in, and relies on the Lord, and whose hope and confidence the Lord is.*
> 8 *For he shall be like a tree planted by the waters that spreads out its roots by the river; and it shall not see and fear when heat comes; but its leaf shall be green. It shall not be anxious and full of care in the year of drought, nor shall it cease yielding fruit.*
>
> *Jeremiah 17:7-8 AMPC*

These verses from Jeremiah highlight the profound difference in outcomes based on where we place our trust. Trusting in human strength leads to a barren, unfruitful existence, while trusting in the Lord results in a life of vitality, resilience, and continuous growth, even in challenging times.

Since every curse from God is a withholding of His blessing, consequently, any other curse that a demon can produce through human efforts can be broken, canceled, and annihilated by a blessing from God.

This profound truth brings us to the heart of God's redemptive power. No curse is beyond His ability to reverse. When God chooses to bless, His blessings eradicate any curse. God's blessings hold the ultimate authority, whether the curse stems from disobedience, as mentioned in Deuteronomy, or the curse is brought on by malicious human actions influenced by demonic forces.

To understand how God employs blessings to eradicate curses that He sent, we must look at the nature of His grace and mercy. Through repentance and turning back to God, the flow of His blessings is renewed, breaking the chains of any curse. As we align our lives with His will, seek His face, and live in obedience, His blessings restore and protect us from future curses.

The story of Balaam in Numbers 23 underscores this principle vividly in Numbers 23:20. This verse illustrates that when God declares a blessing, it stands immutable, overpowering any curse. Whether dealing with generational curses, personal afflictions, or spiritual attacks, invoking God's blessings through faith, prayer, and obedience can dismantle any stronghold of darkness.

Thus, in every circumstance, we are invited to seek God's blessings as the ultimate remedy against all curses—finding freedom, restoration, and abundant life in His unchanging grace and love.

While not a single verse states strictly "who God blesses no man can curse" or "who God curses no man can bless," the concept is certainly present in the Bible, particularly in the Balaam/Balak narrative in the Book of Numbers, as mentioned earlier. The passages from Numbers 23:8 and 23:20 convey this idea effectively:

How can I curse those whom God has not cursed? How can I denounce those whom the Lord has not denounced?

Numbers 23:8 AMPC

> *Behold, I have received His command to bless [Israel]. He has blessed, and I cannot reverse or qualify it.*
>
> Numbers 23:20 AMPC

These verses show that God's blessings are irrevocable and cannot be undone by human or spiritual intervention. Similarly, when God curses, His judgment stands firm. This theme is echoed throughout scripture, emphasizing God's ultimate authority and sovereignty.

Blessings Prevent Curses

Blessings serve as a shield, preventing curses from taking root in our lives and breaking those already taking hold. If a curse is present in our lives, it indicates that we have met certain conditions that allow the curse to exist. To break the curse, we must align ourselves with the conditions necessary to receive God's blessings, which will nullify the curse.

Breaking a curse requires a specific blessing that directly counteracts the underlying cause of the curse. To remain free from curses, we must live according to God's Word and will, fulfilling the specific requirements for the blessing that destroys the curse. Doing so removes the cause of the curse and maintains a life of divine favor and protection.

> *1 Blessed is the man that walketh not in the counsel of the ungodly, nor standeth in the way of sinners, nor sitteth in the seat of the scornful.*
> *2 But his delight is in the law of the Lord; and in his law doth he meditate day and night.*
> *3 And he shall be like a tree planted by the rivers of water, that bringeth forth his fruit in his season; his leaf also shall not wither; and whatsoever he doeth shall prosper.*
>
> Psalm 1:1-3 KJV

Since *blessing* is biblically viewed as the opposite of *cursing* (Genesis 12:3, Romans 12:14), Psalm 1:1-3 provides a powerful blueprint for understanding how blessings serve as a protective barrier against curses. The passage begins by illustrating the actions of a blessed person—someone who avoids the counsel of the ungodly, refuses to stand in the path of sinners, and does not sit in the seat of the scornful. These choices reflect a conscious decision to distance oneself from the influences that lead to sin and, ultimately, curses. By steering clear of these negative influences, the individual is positioned to receive God's blessings, which creates a spiritual shield that prevents curses from discovering an entryway into such a life.

The focus then shifts to the blessed person's relationship with God's Law. The passage describes someone who delights in the Law of the Lord and meditates on it day and night. This constant engagement with God's Word forms the foundation of a life that is continually nourished by divine wisdom and guidance. Just as a tree planted by rivers of water is constantly supplied with the nourishment it needs to grow, a life rooted in God's Word is ceaselessly refreshed and sustained by His blessings. This ongoing connection to God's Law promotes spiritual growth and ensures that the individual remains resilient against any curses arising from either disobedience or sin.

The tree imagery in verse 3 further underscores the power of God's blessings to protect and sustain. A tree planted by the rivers of water is well-nourished and produces fruit in its season, with leaves that do not wither. This symbolizes a life of ongoing blessing—one that is prosperous. The cursed state of barrenness or failure finds no place in our lives when we're anchored in God's Word and receive His ongoing favor and protection. This metaphor reminds us that living according to God's Word produces spiritual health and an enduring shield against the curses that seek to disrupt and destroy our well-being.

Let's visit another part of Balaam's story in Numbers 22. He offers a profound example of how God's blessings serve as protection, preventing curses from laying hold of the lives of His people. Balaam, a prophet known for his ability to pronounce blessings and curses, was approached by Balak, the king of Moab, who was terrified of the Israelites. Seeing their numbers and knowing of their conquests, Balak sought to hire Balaam to curse the Israelites, believing that this curse would lead to their downfall.

However, as Balaam prepared to undertake the task, God intervened.

And God said to Balaam, You shall not go with them; you shall not curse the people, for they are blessed.

Numbers 22:12 AMPC

This verse highlights the aforementioned crucial principle: when God has blessed someone, no curse can succeed against them. Despite the pressure from Balak and the potential reward Balaam could receive, God's command was clear—His blessing on the Israelites rendered any curse powerless.

The significance of this verse extends beyond Balaam's immediate situation. It illustrates a timeless truth about the nature of God's protection. He shielded the Israelites from Balaam's curse because He had forgiven their wrongdoings, and they were now under His blessing.

[God] has not beheld iniquity in Jacob [for he is forgiven], neither has He seen mischief or perverseness in Israel [for the same reason]. The Lord their God is with Israel, and the shout of praise to their King is among the people.

Numbers 23:21 AMPC

This blessing of God's forgiveness was a spiritual barrier, making any curse unable to penetrate. The story continues with Balaam trying multiple times to curse Israel, only to find that each time he opened his mouth, God turned his intended curse into a blessing instead.

This narrative powerfully reminds us that God's blessings are not merely passive gifts but active forces that protect and preserve His people. When God declares someone blessed, that blessing stands as a formidable defense against any attempt by the enemy to bring harm. Balaam's experience underscores the pointlessness of cursing what God has blessed, reinforcing that aligning with God's will and receiving His blessings is the most effective way to remain free from curses.

Today, this story reminds us that when we walk in obedience to God and live under His blessing, we are safeguarded against the spiritual attacks that might come our way. God's blessing, as demonstrated in Numbers 22:12, is a reward and shield that ensures the enemy's plans are thwarted and that God's people remain in His divine protection.

But did the Israelites remain in God's protection?

The story of Balaam takes an even darker turn when he shifts from attempting to curse the Israelites directly to employing a more subtle and insidious scheme. After realizing that he could not curse what God had blessed, Balaam advised Balak to tempt the Israelites into sin through sexual immorality and idolatry. By luring them into compromising behaviors, Balaam knew they would provoke God's anger and breach His protection, causing them to lose His favor.

Balak followed Balaam's counsel, and soon, the Moabite women were seducing Israelite men, leading them into sexual immorality and the worship of baal of Peor. The consequences were severe: a devastating plague swept through the camp, claiming the lives of 24,000 people (Numbers 25:1-9). This tragic turn of events highlights how disobedience can open the door to curses that could have been avoided.

The story doesn't end with the plague, though. It reached a peak when an Israelite man named Zimri blatantly flaunted his disobedience by bringing a Midianite woman, Cozbi, into the camp. Aaron's grandson, Phinehas, in a zealous act of righteousness for God's sake, pierced Zimri and Cozbi with a spear, driving it through Cozbi's belly. (Numbers 25:8) Phinehas' act turned God's wrath, which ended the plague. Even though his actions immediately stopped the destruction, the damage had already been done.

This tragic event serves as a sobering reminder that while God's blessings protect us, disobedience can remove that protection, leaving us vulnerable to the enemy's attacks. Balaam's plan worked, not because of any curse he could pronounce, but because sin allowed the curse to take root due to God's removal of His shielding blessing. This real-life ancient account is an alarming illustration of how easily we can be deceived by subtle temptations and led astray, as compromises can have devastating spiritual and physical results.

> *Nevertheless, I have a few things against you: you have some people there who are clinging to the teaching of Balaam, who taught Balak to set a trap and a stumbling block before the sons of Israel, [to entice them] to eat food that had been sacrificed to idols and to practice lewdness [giving themselves up to sexual vice].*
>
> Revelation 2:14 AMPC

Today, this story serves as a warning: walking in obedience to God keeps us within the shield of His blessings, protecting us from hidden evil plans and those who target us. However, as Balaam's story proves, even the slightest rebellion can crack that shield, opening the door for curses to enter. Numbers 22:12 demonstrates how God's blessings serve as a protective force, safeguarding His people from curses. Maintaining God's care requires our constant vigilance against sin.

Deuteronomy 28—Blessing and Cursing

In Deuteronomy 28, God contrasts the blessings of our obedience and the curses of our disobedience. I will not delve into the debate about whether the blessings and curses in Deuteronomy 28 apply to us today. However, undeniably, many encouraging and inspiring sermons, blog posts, and bestselling books have referenced the blessings from this passage. These powerful messages, along with award-winning songs celebrated at the Grammy, Stellar, and Dove Awards, resonate with people who, by faith, successfully apply the promises of these blessings to their lives, trusting in God, Who promised.

The key to experiencing God's favor and protection lies in following His commands and living according to His Word. Every blessing is linked to a specific area of life, and the corresponding curse warns of the consequences of turning away from God. By understanding these principles, we are reminded of the importance of aligning our lives with God's will, ensuring His blessings flow into every aspect of our lives.

Deuteronomy 28:1-2 emphasizes the central requirement for receiving God's blessings: obedience. The passage states that if the Israelites diligently listen to the voice of the Lord their God, carefully observing all His commandments, then He will set them high above all the nations of the earth, and His blessings will come upon them and overtake them.

This obedience isn't just about outward conformity but a wholehearted commitment to living according to God's laws and principles. It requires a diligent, careful approach to following each aspect of God's commands, reflecting a deep devotion to His will. The promise is that if these conditions are met, God's blessings will not just be given but will overflow in every area of life. These stipulations underscore the importance of a life fully aligned with God's will as the pathway to experiencing His abundant blessings that prevent the curses mentioned later in Deuteronomy 28.

The first fourteen verses focus on the blessings that come from obedience to God's commands, while verses 15 through the end of the chapter detail the curses that result from disobedience. Many of the blessings in Deuteronomy 28 correspond to a curse, and together, they paint a vivid picture of the consequences of our choices. The following summarizes corresponding blessings and curses, highlighting God's requirements for living in alignment with His Word.

1. Blessed or Cursed in the City and the Field

Blessing: In verses 3-4, God promises that obedience will result in blessings both in the city and the field. This means that God's favor will be with you wherever you go, whether in urban environments or rural areas. Your family, work, and daily life will thrive under His blessings.

Curse: However, verses 16-17 describe the opposite for those who disobey. You will be cursed in the city and the field. This speaks to a life of frustration and fruitlessness, no matter where you are. The places where you seek to prosper will become sources of hardship and struggle.

2. Blessed or Cursed Baskets and Storehouses

Blessing: Verse 5 tells us that your basket and storehouse will be blessed. This represents God's provision for your daily needs—your food supply and resources will be abundant and sufficient. Everything will be overflowing, whether the pantry in your home or your long-term reserves.

Curse: In contrast, verse 17 states that the basket and storehouse will be cursed if you disobey. This means a lack of provision—constant need and insufficiency. Your efforts to store resources will be futile, leading to scarcity and lack.

3. Blessed or Cursed in the Fruit of Your Body and Livestock

Blessing: Verse 4 promises that the fruit of your body (your children), the produce of your ground, and the increase of your livestock will be blessed. Your family will thrive, your land will be productive, and your animals will multiply—symbolizing overall prosperity and growth.

Curse: However, verses 18 and 20 describe the curse that falls on those who disobey. Your children, crops, and livestock will suffer, representing a life of barrenness, both physically and materially. That which should bring joy and fulfillment will become a source of grief and disappointment.

4. Blessed or Cursed When You Come In and Go Out

Blessing: Verse 6 assures you that you will be blessed when you come in and go out. This speaks to God's protection and favor surrounding you in all aspects of life, whether you are starting a new venture or simply going about your daily routine.

Curse: Verse 19 warns that disobedience will result in curses when you come in and go out. Instead of protection, you will face danger and failure in all your undertakings. Anxiety and insecurity will replace the peace you seek in your comings and goings.

5. Victory Over Enemies or Defeat Before Enemies

Blessing: Verse 7 declares that the Lord will cause your enemies who rise against you to be defeated before you. They will come at you one way but flee seven ways, highlighting God's protection and deliverance, ensuring victory in every battle you face.

Curse: On the other hand, verse 25 reveals the curse of disobedience—being defeated by your enemies. Instead of victory, you will suffer defeat and humiliation, becoming a byword among the nations. Your battles will end in ruin, with no divine protection to shield you.

6. Abundant Prosperity or Drought and Famine

Blessing: Verse 11 promises abundant prosperity in all the work of your hands. God will make you prosperous in your family, livestock, and crops, leading to a life of plenty.

Curse: In contrast, verses 23-24 describe a curse of drought and famine. The heavens above will be like bronze, and the earth below like iron. Rain will be replaced with dust, representing total barrenness and failure to produce anything fruitful.

7. Established as God's Holy People or Destruction and Scattering

Blessing: Verse 9 highlights the ultimate blessing—being established as God's holy people, set apart for His purposes—the highest form of favor where God's name is glorified through our lives.

Curse: Verses 36-37 speak of the curse of being removed from the land and scattered among the nations. Instead of being set apart for God, you will face destruction, exile, and disgrace, living as strangers in foreign lands.

Sermon on the Mount Blessings

The Beatitudes, spoken by Jesus as part of His Sermon on the Mount (Matthew 5:1-12), are a series of declarations that begin with "Blessed are" and outline the attitudes and actions that God honors. These statements offer deep insight into how God dispenses blessings and the conditions required to receive them. Each blessing is tied to a specific attitude or heart condition that aligns us with God's favor. By meeting these conditions outlined by Jesus, we can rest assured that any opposing curse will be rendered powerless in the face of the blessings Jesus promised in the Beatitudes. Now, let's delve into the specific blessings Jesus shared in His sermon and explore the heart postures that unlock them.

1. Blessed with the Kingdom of Heaven: Poor in Spirit (Matthew 5:3)

To be blessed with the Kingdom of Heaven, Jesus tells us we must be "poor in spirit," meaning we recognize our spiritual poverty and complete dependence on God. Being "poor in spirit" is about humility, acknowledging that we cannot save ourselves or earn God's favor through our efforts. It is the foundation for receiving God's blessing because possessing a poverty of spirit opens our hearts to His grace. By humbling ourselves and admitting our need for God, we align ourselves with His Kingdom, where we find the riches of His mercy and inheritance.

2. Blessed with Comfort: Those Who Mourn (Matthew 5:4)

The blessing of comfort is promised to those who mourn. Mourning, in this context, refers to a deep sorrow over personal losses, sin, and the world's brokenness. When we mourn for our sins or grieve over the suffering in the world, it shows a heart aligned with God's compassion and righteousness. This type of mourning leads to repentance and a deeper relationship with God, which results in the blessing of divine comfort. God draws near to the brokenhearted and promises to heal and restore those who turn to Him in their grief.

3. Blessed with Inheritance: The Meek (Matthew 5:5)

Meekness is often misunderstood as weakness, but in the biblical sense, meekness refers to strength under control. Meekness means being gentle, patient, and submissive to God's will. The meek do not force their way into power or wealth; instead, they trust God's timing and sovereignty. In return, Jesus promises that the meek will inherit the earth. This blessing speaks to a future inheritance in God's eternal kingdom and the peace and contentment that come from living humbly and trusting God in the present.

4. Blessed with Fulfillment: Those Who Hunger and Thirst for Righteousness (Matthew 5:6)

To be blessed with fulfillment, Jesus calls us to hunger and thirst for righteousness, which is more than a casual desire; hungering and thirsting in the spiritual sense stands for an intense longing to see God's justice, truth, and holiness prevail in the world around us. Those who seek righteousness with such enthusiasm are promised satisfaction because God is faithful to meet the deepest spiritual desire of those who earnestly pursue Him. The blessing is that God will fill us with His righteousness, making us more like Him and satisfying our souls in ways the world never can.

5. Blessed with Mercy: The Merciful (Matthew 5:7)

Jesus said, "Blessed are the merciful: for they shall obtain mercy." (Matthew 5:7 KJV). The mercy Jesus speaks of isn't simply a fleeting act of kindness; it's a deep and abiding compassion that significantly reflects the heart of God. To be merciful is to extend forgiveness and grace, just as God has done for us. Mercy isn't about excusing wrongdoing; it's about choosing to forgive despite the wrong. Forgiveness is a powerful force that breaks chains and brings healing to those who receive it and those who offer it.

However, Jesus also issued a sobering warning about the limits of forgiveness in one specific area: blasphemy against the Holy Spirit.

> *31 Therefore I tell you, every sin and blasphemy (every evil, abusive, injurious speaking, or indignity against sacred things) can be forgiven men, but blasphemy against the [Holy] Spirit shall not and cannot be forgiven.*
>
> *32 And whoever speaks a word against the Son of Man will be forgiven, but whoever speaks against the Spirit, the Holy One, will not be forgiven, either in this world and age or in the world and age to come.*
>
> Matthew 12:31-32 AMPC

According to the original Greek meaning, blasphemy in this context of recorded scripture refers to slander, detraction, or speech injurious to another's good name. Specifically, it relates to impious and reproachful speech directed against the divine majesty of God. Therefore, blasphemy against the Holy Spirit involves a deliberate and conscious defamatory rejection of the Holy Spirit, attributing Him as an evil entity. This severe form of slander demonstrates a hardened heart that not only resists God but also defames His very nature, resulting in an unforgivable sin. This is an assertive reminder to approach God with reverence and an open heart, always mindful of our words and attitudes toward His Spirit.

6. Blessed with Seeing God: The Pure in Heart (Matthew 5:8)

To be blessed with the ability to see God in the situations we or others face, we must possess purity of heart. The purity of a heart surpasses mere external actions; it reflects an internal state free from corrupt desires, sin, and guilt. Those pure in heart seek God with sincerity and integrity while earnestly desiring to align their lives with His will. This purity opens the door to experiencing God's presence now and in eternity. The blessing of perceiving God's involvement in our circumstances results from cultivating a close, intimate relationship with Him, where His presence becomes increasingly evident in our lives, fostering ongoing purity in our hearts.

7. Blessed with the Title Children of God: The Peacemakers (Matthew 5:9)

Peacemakers actively seek reconciliation and harmony in broken relationships between people, humanity, and God. Jesus calls peacemakers "children of God" because they reflect the character of their Heavenly Father, the ultimate Source of peace. The blessing of being called children of God signifies that those who pursue peace are recognized as submissive members of God's family. By choosing peace and seeking what God desires, we gain recognition from both people and spiritual realms. Demonic forces will flee when we resist them, and we, instead, choose peace and all else God instructs, as promised in James 4:7.

8. Blessed with the Kingdom of Heaven: Those Persecuted for Righteousness (Matthew 5:10)

Those persecuted for righteousness are blessed with the Kingdom of Heaven (of the congregation of those who constitute the royal *city of God*). This blessing shows that following Christ and standing for righteousness often brings opposition and suffering. However, Jesus reassures us that persecution, for His sake, signifies being positioned to receive God's promised Kingdom. The reward for enduring persecution is the same as the first Beatitude: the Kingdom of Heaven. This blessing reminds us that no matter what we face on earth, we are citizens of a higher kingdom where God's justice and peace reign forever.

9. Blessed with Great Reward: Those Persecuted and Reviled for Christ's Sake (Matthew 5:11-12)

In this final Beatitude, Jesus expands on the concept of persecution. He emphasizes that those who are insulted, picked on, and falsely accused because of their association with Him are blessed. Jesus assures them their reward will be great in heaven. This blessing goes beyond enduring suffering—it promises eternal reward. The key to this blessing is remaining faithful to Christ despite opposition and slander. By enduring such trials for the sake of Christ, we align ourselves with the prophets who were also persecuted before us, placing us in the same spiritual lineage as those who faithfully served God. The blessing is not just in enduring the persecution but in the assurance of a heavenly reward that far outweighs any earthly suffering.

The Beatitudes show us that blessings are not random but conjoined to specific heart conditions and actions that reflect God's character. Each blessing serves as a form of protection and favor, shielding us from the curses of living contrary to God's ways. By living out the qualities Jesus declared in the Beatitudes, we align ourselves with God's divine order, positioning ourselves to enjoy His blessings and safeguarding our lives from spiritual and natural consequences of disobedience. Let's be studious to discover more blessings in the Bible and fulfill the requirements to receive those additional blessings that prevent curses from being woven into our lives.

God's promises of blessings and curses are evident from the story of Balak and Balaam, the accounts of Deuteronomy 28, and the Beatitudes. These scriptures mirror our own lives, revealing the outcomes of our choices. I pray that we will walk in wisdom and choose to meet the requirements necessary to receive God's blessings by being obedient to whatever He commands us to do, especially when we are faced with temptation.

Temptation comes for all of us because demons want us to stray down the road that leads to curses. Their goal is to make us complain and distrust God rather than arrive at the blessed destination of praising Him and having complete faith in His promises. Don't let temptation rob you of your opportunity to be blessed. Where are you being tempted today? Most often, when temptation suddenly rises in a specific area of our lives, it's a direct indication of where God intends to bless us. That temptation becomes a weapon formed against us, designed to lead us into disobedience, which displeases God. If we yield to it, we risk forfeiting the very blessing He had planned to add to our lives because we failed to remain in the state of obedience that the blessing required.

Remember, every moment of temptation is also an opportunity to strengthen our faith and walk in obedience. When we resist temptation, we safeguard our blessings and draw closer to God, who rewards those who choose His path. Stay strong, and know that God will be faithful to see us through.

A Curse in the New Testament

In the New Testament, the concept of a curse is conveyed through two primary Greek words, each with its distinct shade of meaning. To begin with, the Greek word *anathema* originally meant something set apart for God. However, its meaning changed over time, coming to represent something devoted to destruction because of its connection to evil. This term expresses the dire consequences of turning away from the gospel, as seen in Galatians 1:8-9, where Paul declares that anyone preaching a different gospel is to be *anathema*—utterly cut off from Christ.

In Galatians 3:13, the apostle Paul highlights Christ's profound act of redemption.

> *Christ purchased our freedom [redeeming us] from the curse (doom) of the Law [and its condemnation] by [Himself] becoming a curse for us, for it is written [in the Scriptures], Cursed is everyone who hangs on a tree (is crucified);*
>
> Galatians 3:13 AMPC

In this context, the term *curse* refers to one undergoing the appointed penalty of cursing, symbolizing the ultimate consequence and doom prescribed by the Law. On the other hand, *cursed* means to be exposed to divine vengeance and lying under God's curse, indicating the state of being accursed and abhorrent. Jesus took upon Himself the divine vengeance and condemnation meant for humanity by becoming a curse for us, thereby redeeming us from the Law's curse. He did this by dying on the cross, referred to in the verse as "hanging on a tree." This phrase references Deuteronomy 21:23, stating that a hanged man is cursed by God.

By willingly undergoing this cursed form of death, Jesus absorbed the curse that was meant for us, thus setting us free from its grip. This sacrificial act underscores the depth of God's love and the gospel's transformative power, demonstrating how Christ's substitutionary death frees us from the bondage of the Law and opens the way for us to live in God's grace.

Understanding these Greek nuances enriches our comprehension of the New Testament's approach to curses. It reveals a balance between recognizing curses as an existing and potent force and the overarching narrative of redemption and grace that Christ brings. In this light, curses are not merely punitive but serve a transformative purpose in God's plan for humanity.

Continued examination of Galatians 3:13 reveals a fundamental aspect of Christian belief regarding the redemptive work of Jesus Christ. This verse is rooted in the understanding that the Law, as given in the Old Testament, came with blessings for obedience and curses for disobedience. However, no one could fully keep the Law; therefore, all were under the curse of sin and its consequences.

In a conversational and emotional reflection, one might ponder, "Have I ever considered the weight of my words and actions in the light of scripture's teaching on curses? How does the reality of Christ becoming a curse for me change the way I view my redemption and relationship with God?"

Understanding the biblical definition of curses invites us to contemplate the gravity of our words and actions. It reminds us that the spiritual realm profoundly influences our physical world. As we delve deeper into the origins and meanings of these ancient words, we're reminded of the power of the spoken word and the importance of aligning our lives with God's will to avoid the consequences of a curse.

I sense the Holy Spirit prompting me that this is the perfect time to ask our Father, "Lord, do I have any unblessed areas in my life right now that are vulnerable to curses? Please reveal each area to me and the blessings I need to rid them from my life or the lives of my loved ones. In Jesus' name, I pray. Amen."

Generational Curses Today?

Generational curses can be incredibly perplexing, particularly because finding solid, clear evidence of them in the New Testament can be challenging. Many people view the principles of how God governs generations in the New Testament as more applicable to us in modern times, making reconciling the concept of generational curses as understood in the Old Testament more difficult.

Generational curses could be viewed as spells if we consider such curses as results of stories believed and acted upon, perpetuating harmful, recurring patterns of behavior or misfortune that plague families across generations. These afflictions are not punishments but consequences of sin that have not been addressed or repented of. In this context, generational curses aren't just external judgments from God but also internalized narratives that families continue to live out. Let's explore this concept further with biblical support.

One example of generational patterns perpetuated by belief and action is found in the story of Abraham, Isaac, and Jacob. In Genesis 12:10-20, Abraham lies about Sarah being his sister to protect himself in Egypt. His son Isaac repeats the same deception in Genesis 26:7-10 when he lies about his wife, Rebekah. Jacob, Isaac's son, continues the pattern of deception, particularly in his dealings with Esau (Genesis 27). This recurring pattern suggests that deception became a spell passed down through generations, a story that each patriarch believed and acted upon in moments of fear.

While this generational sin could be seen as a curse, it also fits the concept of a spell—a narrative that each generation accepted and enacted, perpetuating the same behavior. The story of deception became ingrained in their family's identity, shaping their decisions and interactions with others. This illustrates how generational curses can manifest as internalized stories that dictate behavior rather than purely external judgments from God.

In Exodus 34:7 KJV, God speaks of "...visiting the iniquity of the fathers upon the children, and upon the children's children, unto the third and to the fourth generation." This concept reinforces the idea that people pass down sinful patterns to the next generations and points to the importance of belief systems within families. If children grow up hearing and seeing the same sinful patterns, they may internalize these stories and act upon them, continuing the cycle. These generational curses can function as spells—stories believed and acted upon, perpetuating adverse outcomes.

The good news is that we can break these generational spells. Romans 12:2 urges: be transformed by the renewing of your mind. When we renew our minds and embrace God's truth, we can reject the harmful stories passed down and begin living out a new narrative based on God's Word. In this way, we can break the cycle of generational misfortune by replacing the old story with God's story of redemption, which fosters blessings. By bringing sinful patterns into the light and seeking God's forgiveness, we can break the cycle and set a new course for ourselves and future generations.

Curses Sent To and From

Understanding and holding onto the belief that when God blesses us, no one can curse us is crucial. This truth should be a foundational pillar in our faith, providing us with unshakeable confidence throughout our lives. Let's revisit the story of Balaam and Balak in Numbers 23:8, which illustrates this profound principle.

Balak, the king of Moab, hired Balaam to curse the Israelites, fearing their power and numbers. However, under divine inspiration, Balaam declared, "How can I curse those God has not cursed? Or how can I [violently] denounce those the Lord has not denounced?" (Numbers 23:8 AMPC) This powerful statement underscores the futility of any curse against those whom God has chosen to bless. Such a truth reminds us that God's blessings are sovereign and irrevocable.

No matter the opposition we face or the ill wishes of others, God's favor and protection prevail. Embracing this truth empowers us to walk in faith, knowing that His blessings shield us from all attempts to undermine His plans for our lives. Therefore, let us live with the assurance that His blessings are our steadfast defense, and no curse can prevail against His divine will and favor.

Embracing the truth that God's blessings protect us from any curse empowers us to live with confidence and peace. This assurance transforms how we respond to those who oppose or mistreat us.

Bless those who persecute you [who are cruel in their attitude toward you]; bless and do not curse them.

Romans 12:14 AMPC

In this scripture, the definition of the term bless is *to invoke (call upon God for blessings),* and the term curse is *to doom or summon evil on [someone].* Speaking blessings for our persecutors may be counterintuitive, especially when we're faced with hostility. However, such open-heartedness aligns perfectly with the understanding that God's favor is our ultimate protection. Because God's blessings protect us, we can freely and gladly bless our offenders, knowing we do not need to respond vengefully because their actions cannot harm us.

This act of blessing, rather than cursing, reflects our trust in God's sovereignty and justice. It demonstrates that we are not bound by the actions of others but are anchored in God's steadfast love and protection.

By blessing our persecutors, we break the cycle of negativity and open the door for God's grace to work in their lives and ours. This posture of grace and forgiveness not only honors God but also liberates us from the burden of bitterness. Our reaction of ease enables us to walk in the fullness of His blessings, confident that He will handle any injustice we face. In this way, Romans 12:14 calls us to live out our faith practically, embodying the profound truth that God's blessings safeguard us from curses, freeing us to extend His love even to those who oppose us.

Why We War

When considering that curses may be sent by someone to cause harm, a common response in modern-day Charismatic Christendom is to engage in what is known as spiritual warfare. Spiritual warfare is a Christian practice focused on resisting and combating the influence of evil supernatural forces. This concept is rooted in biblical teachings that acknowledge the existence of evil spirits or demons that can interfere with human life in various ways. Another phrase often used to describe this battle is *warring in the Spirit*.

But why do we engage in this supernatural conflict? What spiritual weapons do we have to stand firm in our battle against satan and his legion of demons?

How can we confidently know that we have triumphed over our adversary? And when is the right moment to strike back against our foe? The answers to these crucial questions are found in the following scripture.

> *No soldier when in service gets entangled in the enterprises of [civilian] life; his aim is to satisfy and please the one who enlisted him.*
>
> 2 Timothy 2:4 AMPC

The sole purpose of spiritual warfare is not to showcase the depth of our supernatural ability or to feed our passion for victory. Instead, the only purpose of spiritual warfare is to please God. That's why we fight, plain and simple—to delight God's heart through our unwavering faith and devotion during each battle. The divine arsenal bestowed upon us hinges on our obedience—a potent weapon that aligns us with God's will and purpose. Through our willingness to submit and our eagerness to obey, we unlock God's blessings, partaking in the abundance He has promised.

> *If you are willing and obedient, you shall eat the good of the land;*
>
> Isaiah 1:19 AMPC

The Bible, the Word of God, contains numerous verses that serve as authority to annihilate the curses and spells sent to destroy parts or the whole of our lives.

> *Your word is a lamp to my feet and a light to my path.*
>
> Psalm 119:105 AMPC

As a pastor, I gained profound revelation from God concerning Psalm 119:105. He revealed that every message I deliver should function as a lamp and a light. Just as a lamp positioned by a favorite reading chair illuminates the immediate surroundings, my sermons should help individuals understand their current spiritual state. Similarly, like a flashlight or a vehicle's headlights lighting the path ahead, my sermons should guide people toward their future in God. Each sermon must encompass where we currently stand with God and where He desires us to go. The light from God's Word, encompassing the

Holy Bible and His spoken revelations, inherently possesses the power to break spells. His specific revelations can disassemble even the most intricately woven curses used against His people.

A Causeless Curse

In 2000, I wrote my first book, *What Are You Doing After the Dance?* While I was seeking publishers, a major publishing company expressed significant interest. However, after thoroughly researching their pricing, I discovered that the upfront investment they required from me was substantial. My diligence at the same time made me realize I had all the necessary resources to self-publish. I moved forward independently, and soon after, aspiring authors began approaching me to help publish their books as well. What started as a self-publishing endeavor quickly became a small press publishing company.

I established Godly Writes Publishing over twenty-five years ago. I shared my passion for it with a familiar group of people, soliciting and hoping they would join me in prayer for the success of my business. However, during one of the public meetings, a person in the group who was very influential spoke out and told the others not to pray for me. His words carried a curse as they withheld the blessing of praying for me that I sought. He said, "If it's of God, it will succeed. If not, it will fail." I was shocked, embarrassed, and hurt that he would command the group not to pray for me, especially publicly, while I was present.

Why did he say such hurtful words to me? He was upset because earlier that week, I informed him that I was stepping down from my duties in his business to focus on my publishing venture. His words came from a place of anger, stemming from how he treated me after our initial conversation concerning my decision. I had offered two weeks' notice to give him time to find a replacement, but he rejected the possibility and insisted that I quit immediately.

Like the sparrow in her wandering, like the swallow in her flying, so the causeless curse does not alight.

Proverbs 26:2 AMPC

I didn't do anything to cause this curse to attach itself to me, so the curse was causeless and had no rightful claim over my business or my life. God had already blessed my project with His guidance and promised results of my obedience, ensuring that no curse could hinder the blessings He had set in motion. My company has been and will continue to be blessed. People from over 120 countries have been impacted through Godly Writes Publishing, and to God be all the glory!

Curses uttered without cause from the lips of humans will no more find and affect you as their intended target than a wandering sparrow or a swiftly fleeing dove will settle where they have abruptly directed themselves away from their perch. So, Christians who are the target of such meaningless curses directed at them are safe in the applied blood of Jesus from the intended effects the sender desires to occur. Being uncompromisingly obedient to God shelters us from becoming open to a curse's power to overtake any area of our lives.

In embracing this journey of obedience, we avoid the curses associated with disobedience and step into the abundant life that Jesus promises, a life marked by peace, joy, and fulfillment in God. This journey involves acknowledging our weaknesses, seeking God's forgiveness when we falter, and continually striving to live in a manner that reflects His love and holiness. Achieving freedom from spells and curses is not a one-time event.

Deliverance from demonic possession and oppression demands ongoing spiritual vigilance. Casting out demonic entities, including fear, confusion, or oppression, does not guarantee that the forces of evil will simply give up and leave the individual untargeted. True freedom from spells, curses, and demonic influence entails a continuous lifestyle of spiritual discipline and intentional living, requiring constant dependence on God's guidance, power, and protection. As we navigate this journey of obedience, we can find comfort in the promise specified in the following verse:

For no temptation (no trial regarded as enticing to sin), [no matter how it comes or where it leads] has overtaken you and laid hold on you that is not common to man [that is, no temptation or trial has come to you that is beyond human resistance and that is not adjusted and adapted and belonging to human experience, and such as man can bear]. But God is faithful [to His Word and to His compassionate nature], and He [can be trusted] not to let you be tempted and tried and assayed beyond your ability and strength of resistance and power to endure, but with the temptation He will [always] also provide the way out (the means of escape to a landing place), that you may be capable and strong and powerful to bear up under it patiently.

1 Corinthians 10:13 AMPC

God's love and mindfulness are evident in His not allowing demons to tempt us beyond our ability to resist. He knows the human condition well, and with each temptation, He provides an escape route—a way out that ensures we remain capable and robust enough to endure the trial and emerge victorious.

Furthermore, God never leaves us alone in the battle against temptation. His faithfulness guarantees that every trial, no matter how difficult or consuming, is something we can bear. He uses temptation as an opportunity to bless us, to show His provision, and to demonstrate His power. In these moments, we must remember His promise: He has already provided a way of escape.

Understanding this truth changes the way we perceive temptation. It no longer becomes a threat but an opportunity for growth. God's faithfulness is our assurance that with every temptation, He has equipped us to rise above it.

Many view temptation as a direct trial designed by demonic forces to challenge and disrupt our spiritual strength. When we look at the core reasoning for temptations, we discover they are trials that demons use to test the actual contents of our hearts for the validity of our commitment to God. Most temptations signify demonic awareness of an individual's craving for a specific need. Demons exploit this desire, hoping to steer the person into sin, negating potential blessings and creating openings for curses.

These tempting moments expose areas of our lives that may be longing for emotional, physical, or spiritual fulfillment. However, temptation doesn't solely highlight where we are weak. As I mentioned earlier, it also reveals the part of our lives God plans to bless. Because demons are also aware of our future blessings, they often use temptations to cause us to err by providing for ourselves instead of waiting for the blessings God has for us. Demons are well aware that once a blessing fulfills a precise part of our lives, every curse is forbidden to affect that area.

While this chapter highlighted the reality and power of both blessings and curses, the next chapter leads us to explore the transformative power of the gospel. If curses represent spiritual bondage and separation from God, the gospel is the key that unlocks freedom. Jesus, by becoming a curse for us, has nullified the power of curses for those who believe.

The gospel is not merely a message of salvation but also a demonstration of God's ultimate power over sin, death, and every form of spiritual oppression. Let's now examine further how the gospel breaks spells and curses, bringing divine protection and restoration into our lives. We will delve into the practical application of the gospel's power, ensuring that its truth remains the central pillar in every battle against darkness.

CHAPTER 3:

THE POWER OF THE GOSPEL

My Sister and Chick Tracts

Annette, my older sister, introduced me to Chick Tracts, pocket-sized Christian cartoon booklets that encapsulate the gospel message within engaging stories, culminating in a call to salvation and a prayer to receive Jesus as Savior and Lord. I was about seven years old when she first shared them with me, reading them aloud and explaining the messages. The creativity of Jack T. Chick, the late founder of Chick Tracts, struck me deeply. His ability to weave the gospel of Jesus Christ into relatable and impactful stories that could reach people from diverse backgrounds, regardless of religion, education, or profession, was genius.

These tracts initially frightened me, however, because I feared going to Hell. But once I understood that God graciously designed a plan for us to go to Heaven, I felt an urgent need to share this path and the tracts with everyone around me. The fictitious yet powerful narratives in Chick's tracts, with the gospel message seamlessly embedded, compelled me to live only for Jesus and to become a witness for Him. I began sharing the tracts at a young age as their stories instilled in me a lifelong commitment to evangelism, impacting lives across all ages. I owe my understanding of the gospel's transformative power today to the seeds planted by my sister through those impactful Chick Tracts.

Even today, when I browse through both new and old tracts, I am reminded of how powerfully convicting they were during my formative years, and that they continue to impact me now. Though I know I am a Christian, the thought-provoking way Mr. Chick presents the gospel in his stories often causes me to reevaluate my relationship with God. I never want to fall into the trap of thinking I've already "arrived" (Philippians 3:13). At the same time, I refuse to fall under a spell of doubting my salvation. Scripture clarifies that I have sinned if I know what is right to do and fail to do it. (James 4:17) The gospel message of Jesus Christ is unambiguous, and my goal is to give Him every moment of energy I have so He receives all the glory as I live to honor Him.

We must understand the source of our power to break free from the dark clouds of despair that loom over our lives. God has equipped us with the tools we need to perform these remarkable feats of strength and courage, and this power lies within the words we speak. However, the ability to use words that alter our destinies goes beyond mere utterances. In the next chapter, we will delve deeper into this concept and explore how the power of our words is rooted in a profound truth. For now, embedding the truth about the gospel's power, which extends beyond salvation is essential. By believing and knowing that what we say aligns with the truth, we gain the authority to break spells and curses successfully. This understanding will serve as a foundation for the transformative journey ahead.

The gospel, also called the good spell, is not merely the entry point into the Christian faith, it is the enduring force that sustains and empowers the believer's journey. The gospel of Jesus Christ has the power to shatter spells and curses, even those that seem deeply ingrained and unbreakable in our lives. No wonder Paul expressed his eagerness to preach the gospel. He knew the authority people would receive when they heard and accepted the truth. Paul declared the following:

> *15 So, for my part, I am willing and eagerly ready to preach the gospel to you also who are in Rome.*
> *16 For I am not ashamed of the Gospel (good news) of Christ, for it is God's power working unto salvation [for deliverance from eternal death] to everyone who believes with a personal trust and a confident surrender and firm reliance, to the Jew first and also to the Greek,*

> *17 For in the Gospel a righteousness which God ascribes is revealed, both springing from faith and leading to faith [disclosed through the way of faith that arouses to more faith]. As it is written, The man who through faith is just and upright shall live and shall live by faith.*
>
> Romans 1:15-17 AMPC

Growing Up in Faith

From a young age, the gospel of Jesus Christ took root in my life with profound depth. Growing up in church, the sermons on salvation and the realities of eternity shaped my early understanding. The thought of Hell's inescapable torment was a potent motivator, driving me to embrace the gospel not just as a one-time event but as a daily commitment.

This dedication became a natural part of my life, even in the halls of Holy Trinity Catholic School. With the support of my parents, who generously invested in my education and spiritual growth, I often found myself sharing my faith. My parents would alternate driving me and my friends—those whom I had gently persuaded of their need for a life devoted to Jesus—to my church, fostering a growing community bound by faith.

My enthusiasm for sharing the gospel was so evident that even my kindergarten teacher, Mrs. Dorothy Biering, affectionately dubbed me "Little Preacher." I vividly recall a classmate who suffered from daily bouts of vomiting after eating his lunch, a distressing ordeal for any child. Moved by a deep sense of compassion and at the behest of my teacher, I found myself by his side, laying hands on him as I had seen my pastor do, praying for his relief. Miraculously, his illness ceased from that day forward, a testament to the healing power embedded within the gospel.

This experience is just one thread in the rich tapestry of ways the gospel has manifested in my life. The good spell, the unending, transformative power of Jesus' love message and ministry, touches every aspect of our existence, offering salvation, healing, hope, and a daily pathway to live out His teachings. Each person's journey with the gospel uniquely portrays its life-altering impact, from dramatic healings to quiet moments of profound realization, showcasing the vast and tailored reach of God's grace.

The gospel's transformative power extends beyond our initial salvation because it permeates every aspect of the believer's life and is the ongoing source of God's power. We discover the genuine effectiveness of the gospel when we integrate it into our daily thoughts, words, and actions. The gospel empowers us to overcome sin, endure trials, and live a life reflecting Christ's character and love. The gospel is the wellspring of hope, the source of strength, and the guide to a life of purpose and meaning. Building on the revelation of the gospel's continuing power in our lives, we can look to John 1:12 for further insight:

> *But to as many as did receive and welcome Him, He gave the authority (power, privilege, right) to become the children of God, that is, to those who believe in (adhere to, trust in, and rely on) His name*
>
> John 1:12 AMPC

This verse highlights another dimension of the gospel's transformative power. The good spell (gospel) is an ongoing process of evolving into who God desires us to become in Christ Jesus. The gospel grants us the authority, power, and privilege to become the obedient, loving, forgiving, loyal, and empowered children God intends for us to be. Living according to the gospel is a dynamic, lifelong journey that unfolds as we believe in, adhere to, trust in, and rely on Jesus. Therefore, we can cancel any story that has brought a spell of negative characteristics or habits into our lives by making the story of the gospel our own by allowing Jesus to be the Lord of our lives.

I recollect being about nine years old when I gave my heart to the Lord. I grew up attending at least three church services weekly, from elementary school to several years after my college days. My custom was to pray, sing, and praise often in church and at home. Even though God used me to share my witness about Jesus at school and in my neighborhood, I wasn't allowing the effects of the gospel to revolutionize my life fully, and God made me well aware of my shortcomings, even as a child.

From my earliest memories, my mother often recounted that I was born battling yellow jaundice and asthma. She would describe, with a mixture of fear and tenderness, how she lovingly held me during those terrifying infant asthma attacks, whispering comforts as she desperately hoped for my breaths to steady.

The most harrowing episode occurred when I was eleven. During a severe asthma attack, the air simply refused to pass through my lungs; the struggle was so intense that I couldn't even muster a sneeze. The fear in my mother's eyes mirrored my panic as tears streamed down her face. In haste, my parents rushed me to the hospital, where the nurse immediately placed me inside an oxygen tent, a temporary sanctuary of air.

Left alone in the quietness of the hospital room, after the exits of doctors, nurses and the worried glances from my parents, I experienced a profound moment. In the stillness, a voice cut through the silence—a voice I instinctively knew was the Holy Spirit. He asked, "Are you ready to get serious yet?" In all sincerity, I responded, "Yes." It was a pivotal encounter, marking the first time I consciously remember hearing the Holy Spirit speaking directly to me—transforming my asthmatic battle into a spiritual awakening.

The power of the gospel in our lives is not static; it is active and progressive, compelling us to evolve from initial steps of faith to deeper adherence. In my journey, this meant advancing from simply sharing my faith and providing rides to church for classmates to wholeheartedly embracing my calling and preparing for a life pledged to ministry. As we embrace our identity as children of God, we tap into the divine resources available to us. We are empowered to live our lives to reflect the character and values of our Heavenly Father. God equips us to face challenges confidently, knowing that Jesus Christ, the King of Kings, loves, accepts, and supports us.

Moreover, the gospel's power in our lives extends to our relationships and interactions. As children of God, He calls us to be ambassadors of His love and grace, sharing the good news with those around us. The gospel's power is not just for our benefit; it exists to be shared to bring hope and transformation to a world in need.

Remaining Healed

One of the most influential revelations I've received from the Holy Spirit is that we cannot confine the power of the gospel solely to the moment of salvation; it is a continuous force that shapes our identity, empowers our lives, and impacts the world through us. As we delve deeper into the implications of this truth, we will explore how living in the light of the gospel can bring about a more profound, more intimate experience of God's love and purpose for our lives.

> 2 Now there is in Jerusalem a pool near the Sheep Gate. This pool in the Hebrew is called Bethesda, having five porches (alcoves, colonnades, doorways).
> 3 In these lay a great number of sick folk—some blind, some crippled, and some paralyzed (shriveled up)—waiting for the bubbling up of the water.
> 4 For an angel of the Lord went down at appointed seasons into the pool and moved and stirred up the water; whoever then first, after the stirring up of the water, stepped in was cured of whatever disease with which he was afflicted.
> 5 There was a certain man there who had suffered with a deep-seated and lingering disorder for thirty-eight years.
> 6 When Jesus noticed him lying there [helpless], knowing that he had already been a long time in that condition, He said to him, Do you want to become well? [Are you really in earnest about getting well?]
> 7 The invalid answered, Sir, I have nobody when the water is moving to put me into the pool; but while I am trying to come [into it] myself, somebody else steps down ahead of me.
> 8 Jesus said to him, Get up! Pick up your bed (sleeping pad) and walk!
>
> John 5:2-8 AMPC

Afterward Jesus findeth him in the temple, and said unto him, Behold, thou art made whole: sin no more, lest a worse thing come unto thee.

John 5:14 KJV

Jesus encountered the healed man in the temple and urged him to look at how wonderful it is to be healed. Jesus also instructed the man to stop sinning, or something worse could happen to him. We find a profound lesson and a stern reminder of the abiding impact of living a life aligned with the gospel, for a consistent change in our lives. This passage highlights more than just a celebratory miraculous event; it underscores the necessity of a sustained transformation in behavior and mindset. Therefore, as Jesus instructed, we should focus on the long-term journey of sanctification, growth, and bearing good fruit (what we produce for God), not just the immediate joy of healing or freedom in another area of life.

Jesus' words to the healed man are that healing and miracles are not merely celebratory events but starting points for a more profound, consistent reformation in our lives. The command to "stop sinning" is a directive toward continuous, conscious obedience to God's ways. It stresses that the true intention of the gospel is not just isolated moments of grace but the ongoing, daily determination to live out its teachings.

Through the continual practice of gospel principles, we find relief from falling back into destructive patterns that could lead to even more significant consequences. This ongoing transformation is a true testament to the gospel's life-changing power.

A lifestyle committed to the gospel proves conversion because it involves an active, daily decision to forsake the old ways and embrace a new path marked by righteousness and holiness. Such a lifestyle is potent because it consistently reinforces believers' commitments to God and deepens their spiritual growth. According to the gospel, this consistent living builds a robust, faithful testimony to the world, not just a single event but a lifetime of events that display God's transformative power and consistently give Him glory.

The Power to Forgive

> *21 Then Peter came up to Him and said, Lord, how many times may my brother sin against me and I forgive him and let it go? [As many as] up to seven times?*
>
> *22 Jesus answered him, I tell you, not up to seven times, but seventy times seven!*
>
> Matthew 18:21-22 AMPC

The gospel narrative brings to light the power of forgiveness, challenging the spell of bitterness and resentment that can take root in our hearts. Corrie ten Boom was born into a devout Christian family, and her journey is a remarkable testament to the power of forgiveness to break the spells and curses of bitterness and hatred. Ten Boom's life took a dramatic turn during World War II when she and her family hid Jews away from being arrested and imprisoned in concentration camps by the Nazis.

On February 28, 1944, a Dutch informant named Jan Vogel tipped off the Nazis about the Ten Booms' activities. As a result, at around 12:30 p.m. that day, the entire Ten Boom family was arrested by the Nazis. Sent to the Ravensbrück concentration camp, Corrie endured unimaginable suffering, yet she held onto her faith, finding solace and purpose in sharing God's love with her fellow prisoners.

Corrie ten Boom's faith faced its ultimate test after the war when she came face to face with a former Ravensbrück guard who extended his hand—seeking her forgiveness. At that moment, she stood before a man symbolizing the horrors she and her family suffered, including the "slow, terrible death" of her sister. This man, who had since become a professing Christian, might have directly tormented her loved ones in the camp.

Faced with a pivotal decision, Corrie encountered a crossroads: succumb to the spell of hatred that such dreadful memories could evoke or break that spell through the act of forgiveness. Invoking a strength beyond her own, she chose forgiveness—reaching out her hand in a gesture that broke the fetters of bitterness, liberating her heart from a potential lifetime of hatred.

Corrie ten Boom's ability to forgive, even in the face of such a personal atrocity, illustrates the life-changing power of the gospel. Her story serves as a beacon of hope, showing that forgiveness is not a sign of weakness but a powerful act of liberation. Through forgiveness, we can break the spells and curses that seek to keep us in bondage and behind barriers so we can step into the freedom and peace that God promises.

Metaphorically speaking, we can refer to a curse as a chain, symbolizing the binding and restrictive nature of curses that can hold individuals or even generations in a state of bondage and resentment, as in Corrie's case. We can refer to a spell as a wall, representing an obstacle or barrier that can block mental and physical progress or hinder someone's path to freedom and fulfillment, and in Corrie's situation, hatred. The hammer of forgiveness breaks the chains of curses, and we enter a life of true freedom.

> *And whenever you stand praying, if you have anything against anyone, forgive him and let it drop (leave it, let it go), in order that your Father who is in heaven may also forgive you your [own] failings and shortcomings and let them drop.*
>
> Mark 11:25 AMPC

This verse illustrates the deep connection between our ability to forgive others and our liberation. Holding onto grudges and resentment is like carrying a heavy burden that weighs us down, hindering our progress and joy. But when we choose to forgive, we release the person who wronged us and ourselves. This act of forgiveness is a decisive step toward breaking the curses of bitterness, anger, and hurt that can entangle our hearts.

If we are honest, forgiving people helps us more than it does our offenders. Forgiving repentant ones frees us from having to bear the weight of constantly mulling over how offenders are processing our grudges—a constant self-nagging that we can do without. At virtually every instance, we're more bothered by our unwillingness to forgive than our offenders are. I find that wrongdoers don't care about our grudges and are more likely to move past their faults, unbothered, while we aggravate ourselves with stressful feelings of harboring bitterness toward them. Forgive. Let it all go, and be free from the curse and sting of bitterness and resentment by letting God righteously judge your case.

Forgiveness and pardon are invitations for us to walk in the light of God's grace, experiencing the freedom and peace that comes from letting go and allowing His love to heal and restore us. As we embrace forgiveness, we open the door to a life marked by hope, transformation, and the boundless freedom found in Christ.

The story of Joseph in Genesis is a powerful example of forgiveness breaking a curse. Betrayed by his brothers and sold into slavery, Joseph faced numerous injustices that could have led to a life marked by resentment and curses. However, his choice to forgive his brothers and see God's sovereign hand in his circumstances led to the restoration and blessing of his entire family.

In our lives today, harboring grudges can act as a curse, binding us to past hurts and hindering our relationship with God. Always remember that by choosing to forgive those who have wronged us, we release ourselves from the nagging spell of resentment and open the door for God's healing and blessing. Forgiveness is not always easy, but it is a decisive step toward breaking curses and walking in the freedom Christ offers. So, when someone asks for your forgiveness, forgive them. Jesus taught us to pray for forgiveness for ourselves and said that God will forgive us as we forgive others. (Matthew 6:12, 14-15)

Challenging Societal Narratives

In a world where societal narratives often dictate our beliefs and behaviors, the gospel is a countercultural force that challenges us to reevaluate and transform our perspectives. Deeply ingrained in our culture, these narratives can shape our understanding of success, identity, and morality. However, the gospel invites us to view life differently, prioritizing God's values and truths over societal allowances and acceptance norms.

> *Do not be conformed to this world (this age), [fashioned after and adapted to its external, superficial customs], but be transformed (changed) by the [entire] renewal of your mind [by its new ideals and its new attitude], so that you may prove [for yourselves] what*

is the good and acceptable and perfect will of God, even the thing which is good and acceptable and perfect [in His sight for you].

Romans 12:2 AMPC

The power of the gospel to challenge society's narratives is evident in the early Christian community. The believers in Acts lived in contrast to the surrounding culture. Their God-centered lives included sharing their possessions, caring for those in need, and breaking down barriers set by ungodly collective efforts. Their actions were a direct response to the teachings of Jesus, who consistently challenged the status quo, whether in His interactions with the marginalized or His confrontations with the religious elite. This radical way of living was not just about being different for the sake of difference; it was about embodying the Kingdom of God on Earth.

Today, the gospel challenges us to question the stories that groups present as truth. It calls us to consider how we define success, view others, and make ethical decisions. As we allow the gospel to shape our thinking and actions, we become agents of change, reflecting God's love and justice in a world that desperately needs a reformation. Challenging commonly accepted standards is complex, but living out the full implications of the gospel in our lives and communities is necessary for true transformation.

Take a moment to ask yourself: "Am I living each day with the sole purpose of pleasing God, as Jesus taught? Or have I found myself more concerned with satisfying others? Do I let others' views, which often contradict the gospel of Jesus Christ, pull me away from fully following Him?"

Living Out the Gospel Narrative

When our lives boldly represent the gospel narrative, our example is an invitation to embody the teachings and model of Jesus in our everyday lives. Such a summons is about allowing the gospel's truth to shape our actions, decisions, and interactions with others. Otherwise, we'll become influenced by ungodly spells that will forcefully steer our lives in a direction we may very well not want to go because we failed to make godly, confident decisions. A commitment to love marks this journey of living out the gospel, serving and seeking justice, and reflecting the heart of God in a broken world as Jesus did. Our actions prove our dedication to love Jesus, just as He unashamedly told us how to demonstrate our love to Him.

> *If you [really] love Me, you will keep (obey) My commands.*
> John 14:15 AMPC

One key aspect of living out the gospel narrative is embracing a lifestyle of humility and service that Jesus instructed us to adopt. Jesus modeled this beautifully when He washed His disciples' feet, demonstrating that true greatness is found in serving others just as the lowest servants would wash the road-dusty feet of a home's guests. As we follow Jesus' example, He calls us to assist those around us with compassion and humility, whether through acts of kindness, volunteering our time, or advocating for the marginalized.

Another essential aspect in following the King of kings is pursuing justice and righteousness. The gospel narrative provides several examples of Jesus defending the oppressed and challenging systems of injustice. As we are His followers, He calls us to do the same—to be voices for the voiceless and to work toward creating a more just and equitable society.

> *Learn to do right! Seek justice, relieve the oppressed, and correct the oppressor. Defend the fatherless, plead for the widow.*
> Isaiah 1:17 AMPC

Cultivating a deep and personal relationship with God is a result of living according to the gospel message. This development can take many forms, such as setting aside dedicated time daily for prayer and meditation, studying the Bible to gain wisdom and insight, and seeking guidance from the Holy Spirit. For example, praying and asking for God's direction can help align our actions with His will when faced with a difficult choice. As we prioritize our relationship with God, we become more sensitive to His voice and better equipped to express a transformed life by the power of the gospel daily.

Moreover, living out the gospel leadings means intentionally sharing the good news with others, which doesn't necessarily require grand gestures or elaborate presentations. Often, the small, everyday interactions are what make the most impact, as when I would share the gospel message with my elementary school classmates. Such conveying of the gospel could be as simple as offering encouragement to a struggling coworker, inviting a neighbor over for a meal and authentic conversation, or volunteering at a local charity to demonstrate Christ's love in action. By allowing the gospel to permeate every aspect of our lives, we become powerful witnesses to its transformative power, drawing ourselves and others to experience the hope and freedom it offers.

Living out the gospel narrative protects against the influence of spells and curses. We fortify ourselves with divine armor by deepening our relationship with God and actively conveying the good news. This spiritual fortification empowers us to live our calling and insulates us from the destructive forces that might otherwise derail us. As we immerse ourselves in the truths of the gospel, we are equipped with the discernment to recognize and resist the subtle snares of darkness. This steadfast pledge to the gospel narrative ensures that no spell or curse can sway us from our divinely ordained path, enabling us to stand firm in the face of adversity and remain unshaken in our pursuit of God's Kingdom.

You may still wonder if or how we can live practically according to the gospel. Consider this: Jesus lived the gospel as an example to us. He was obedient unto death, kind, patient, willing to help, eager to teach the truth, defend the weak, and so much more. As our perfect example, Jesus' acts of love and honor for His Father, God, are easy to notice. Now, we have to show everyone that the gospel of Jesus Christ is still alive by allowing the living substance of His teaching to flow through our thoughts, words, and deeds.

Some days, I don't feel like a "strong Christian." Maybe my prayer time felt dry, I'm groggy from lack of sleep, or I'm impatiently waiting for an answer from God. Yet, the gospel of Jesus Christ speaks to all of these moments—and more. My belief in the good spell, the gospel story of Jesus Christ, anchors me in the truth that God's power is available to me regardless of what I feel. The gospel isn't something we rely on our emotions to experience; it's something we choose to believe and faithfully live out. No matter what I face—and I've faced plenty over nearly six decades—I find steady reassurance in my salvation because I believe the gospel of Jesus Christ is trustworthy, unshakable, and eternally true.

Ultimately, living out the gospel narrative is a lifelong journey that requires intentionality, sacrifice, and a deep reliance on God. It's a call to live a life radically different than following the world's standards, a life that shines the light of Christ into the darkness. As we commit to living from the gospel narrative, we become part of God's redemptive work in the world, bringing hope, healing, and transformation to those around us.

Counteracting Negative Narratives with Gospel Truths

In a world where negativity often clouds our perspective and erodes our sense of hope, the gospel offers a powerful antidote. Whether these pessimistic statements stem from communal pressures, personal insecurities, or past experiences, they can trap us in a cycle of negativity and despair. For example, a student struggling in school may internalize the story that she is not intelligent enough to succeed. At the same time, someone else might feel pressure from those around her to find a spouse to feel complete. However, the truths of the gospel can counteract these statements, reminding us of our identity, purpose, and value in Christ, as Jesus himself declared:

> *So if the Son liberates you [makes you free men], then you are really and unquestionably free.*
>
> John 8:36 AMPC

(Please remember that a negative narrative can only transform into a spell if believed.) One fundamental way the gospel counteracts pervasive pessimism is by affirming our identity as beloved children of God. In a world that often defines us by our failures or shortcomings, the gospel declares that we are fearfully and wonderfully made, created in God's image, and redeemed by the blood of Christ, meaning that a person struggling with addiction, for example, is not defined by their struggle but by their identity as a child of

God who is worthy of love and redemption. This truth empowers us to see ourselves through God's eyes, embrace our worth, and reject the lies that seek to diminish us. The apostle Peter beautifully captures this transformed identity in 1 Peter 2:9, where he writes,

> *But you are a chosen race, a royal priesthood, a dedicated nation, [God's] own purchased, special people, that you may set forth the wonderful deeds and display the virtues and perfections of Him Who called you out of darkness into His marvelous light.*
>
> 1 Peter 2:9 AMPC

For many years, I struggled under a spell of walking by sight, a tendency that manifested in two distinct ways. First, I often magnified problems in my conversations, reflecting a heart that already saw challenges as more significant than God's willingness to free me from the obstacles. This mindset stemmed from the uncertain nature of life's trials—we cannot predict which difficulties God will remove quickly or those that He will allow to linger as part of our growth.

Secondly, the timing of these trials further tested my faith. Not knowing when, if ever, my difficulties would end brought me to questioning God's specific promises, mainly when the good outcomes didn't materialize as swiftly as I had hoped.

Such impatience revealed a deeper issue: my reluctance to trust God over extended periods of my struggles. In my desire for immediate relief, I overlooked the spiritual growth that could be gained from enduring faith. Seeing my heart filled with impatience, fear, and frustration, God used these challenges to refine me. The Holy Spirit urged me to strengthen my faith and become unwaveringly patient—teaching me to trust in God's timing rather than fretting over the persistence of my problems. The following verse offers us valuable guidance on how to navigate trials effectively:

> *Rejoice and exult in hope; be steadfast and patient in suffering and tribulation; be constant in prayer.*
>
> Romans 12:12 AMPC

My breakthrough came when I patiently and prayerfully learned to trust in God's faithfulness rather than the reliability of my adversities. This was a profound lesson in spiritual maturity, as I realized that if God resolved the problem while I harbored doubts, my victory felt hollow. I succumbed to the spell of distrust instead of steadfastly trusting, praising, and worshiping God through the hardships. This journey taught me the importance of maintaining faith and patience, regardless of my circumstances.

Many evils confront the [consistently] righteous, but the Lord delivers him out of them all.

Psalm 34:19 AMPC

Knowing God as loving and caring assures us that His protective nature will defend us against wicked attacks. Furthermore, the gospel provides us with a purpose that transcends our undesired circumstances, reminding us that God calls us to be lights in the darkness, to love others as Christ loves us, and to make a difference in the world. Someone working in a mundane job can find purpose in treating their coworkers and customers with kindness and respect, knowing they're ultimately serving God through each daily interaction. God's purpose (original intent for our lives) gives us a sense of direction and meaning, counteracting the lie that our lives are insignificant or without impact.

The gospel also offers us hope that is unshakeable. When faced with difficulties like a health crisis, financial hardship, or the loss of a loved one, the gospel assures us of God's constancy and His promises for our future. When we are under the influence of the good spell, we know that no matter what we face, we can have confidence that God's sovereignty and His plans are always for our good. This hope enables us to rise above the depressive narratives and to live with resilience and peace, knowing that God's love and grace ultimately define our story.

Embracing the Blessings of the Gospel

The ultimate goal of breaking spells and curses is to be free from dark influences and to step into the fullness of God's blessings. We can only experience the power of the gospel through a committed relationship with Jesus Christ, which promises salvation and abundant life (John 10:10), peace that surpasses understanding (Philippians 4:7), and the fruit of the Spirit (Galatians 5:22-23).

To embrace these blessings, we must obey God's Word, cultivate a relationship with Him through prayer and worship, and allow the Holy Spirit to transform our hearts and minds. This is a journey of daily surrender, where we choose to live under the good spell of the gospel, experiencing the joy and freedom that come from being children of God.

Blessed be the God and Father of our Lord Jesus Christ, who has blessed us with every spiritual blessing in the heavenly places in Christ.

Ephesians 1:3 AMPC

Embracing the blessings of the gospel means discovering the depth and breadth of God's unmerited favor in our lives. The progression signifies recognizing that the gospel gives us access to a wealth of spiritual blessings, which can transform our lives from the inside out.

I discovered a new way God had favored my life with spiritual blessings after landing in San Jose, California, for a Supernatural Boot Camp I was conducting. The host pastor picked me up, and despite the very early start to my day and the resulting exhaustion, a conversation soon reinvigorated me. The pastor asked if I would speak with his daughter, Yvonne, who was struggling significantly with fear, to the point at which she barely left her room and never her home. A deep sense of compassion quickly replaced my tiredness. I consented to speak with her. As she spoke, each word came through tears, weighed down by depression, that I believed came straight from her heart.

Moved by the Holy Spirit, I asked her, "Will you come to the service this evening?" Her response was a heart-wrenching sob. She explained that she had seen me on the Christian television show, *Sid Roth's It's Supernatural*, discussing my books (*Understanding: All Success is Attained by It* and *The Supernatural Guide to Understanding Angels*). Seeing me on television had already established a godly and trusting connection for her.

Grateful for the exposure that lent me favor in her eyes, I encouraged her, saying, "I'm honored that my ministry touched you. Why don't you come tonight? Just sit in the front row, focus on me, and if at any point you feel overwhelmed, it's okay for you to leave." My instructions seemed to resonate with her, especially given her fear of public spaces, and she agreed, asking her father to bring her.

Yvonne later described this period as one of the darkest of her life, confessing that she had made countless excuses for her isolation. "I was imprisoned in my own home by my own understanding," she admitted, explaining her initial reluctance to leave her room and her need for reassurance over the phone that stepping out was safe.

She did come that evening, participated actively in the service, and continued to attend sessions for the rest of the weekend. When I later checked in with her father, he joyfully reported that she was helping in the church office daily and attending services regularly. Clearly, a significant shift had occurred, breaking the wall and chains of any spells and curses that had her bound.

Yvonne's story underscores a vital point: the desire for freedom is often the first step toward achieving freedom. Many individuals, including friends, family, and fellow churchgoers, may not even recognize the spells or curses influencing them, remaining trapped by their unseen bonds. Recognizing one's desire to break free from these constraints is crucial for liberation and transformation.

One of the gospel's most profound blessings is the gift of salvation, which assures us that Jesus saved us from sin and eternal separation from God and brought us into a relationship with Him. This blessing is the foundation of our faith, giving us an unshakeable sense of security and hope.

The prayer for salvation is at the end of this book, yet I also sense a strong leading of the Holy Spirit to place it here. If you don't know Jesus Christ, the Messiah, as Savior and Lord, or need to renew your relationship with Him, please use the following words to speak to God now, even if it's in a whisper. He's waiting for you:

Father God, I come before You now in the name of Jesus Christ. I confess that I am a sinner. Please forgive me and save me from all of my past sins. I know Jesus Christ is Your Son Who died for my sins and that You raised Him from the dead. Jesus, I invite You into my heart right now. Come in and live Your life through me so that I can please our Father just as You please our Father. I now believe that You have come into my heart and life. Father, I have asked and prayed for all these things in the name of Jesus Christ. Thank You for saving me and freeing me from the power of every devil. Father, I gave You my life. I don't have it any longer. I will live for You and You alone! In Jesus Christ's name, I pray, Amen! I AM SAVED!

By welcoming Jesus into your life for the first time or renewing your relationship with Him through prayer, you've taken a courageous step toward freedom from any spells or curses that may have held you captive. Yet, the journey to sustained freedom requires continual spiritual vigilance and engagement with God's truth. As you progress through this book, you'll uncover more profound insights into maintaining your liberty and walking in the fullness of God's blessings. Remember, the decision to follow Christ begins a transformative process that unfolds throughout your life.

Whether you just received Jesus into your heart or did so before this moment, you made the most critical decision of your life—giving yourself entirely to Jesus Christ. That decision marked the beginning of your freedom, and the walk of faith continues, step by step and day by day.

To help strengthen your journey, I've created the Shane Wall app, which is available on all major platforms. It's a quiet space designed to offer you biblically sound support, encouragement, and spiritual tools as you grow in Christ. Inside, you'll find exclusive teachings, guided prayers, and practical insights to help you remain free and walk in the truth that has just set you free.

Wherever you are in your faith journey, my passion is to help you continue growing and producing fruit through God's power in your life, for yourself and others. I invite you to explore the app at your own pace to experience the ongoing support God wants you to have beyond these pages.

And I will give you pastors according to mine heart, which shall feed you with knowledge and understanding.

Jeremiah 3:15 KJV

As a pastor of over 20 years, God has anointed me with the Holy Spirit and power and has given me a strong passion to see people discover and love their purpose. I am encouraged to help because I know how God has blessed me to realize who I am in Him, and I'd love to share more with you in the Shane Wall app, so we can continue to explore all that the Holy Spirit will reveal to us, together.

22 But the fruit of the [Holy] Spirit [the work which His presence within accomplishes] is love, joy (gladness), peace, patience (an even temper, forbearance), kindness, goodness (benevolence), faithfulness,
23 Gentleness (meekness, humility), self-control (self-restraint, continence). Against such things there is no law [that can bring a charge].

Galatians 5:22-23 AMPC

Another significant blessing accompanying your decision is the indwelling presence of the Holy Spirit. The Holy Spirit is our Comforter, Guide, and Advocate, empowering us to live lives that please and honor God. He endows us with spiritual gifts, deepens our understanding of scripture, and enables us to bear fruit that reflects the character of Christ. This divine assistance is crucial as you continue to learn about and overcome the spiritual challenges that once restrained you.

Furthermore, the blessings of the gospel include the promise of God's provision and care. We can trust in God to meet our daily needs, even when unsure of the specific resources He will use to fulfill them. According to Philippians 4:19 AMPC, we know that God will liberally supply (fill to the full) our every need according to His riches in glory by Christ Jesus. We are also confident that no matter the plot against us, God will never leave nor forsake us (Hebrews 13:5). This assurance allows us to live in peace and contentment amid life's challenges.

The gospel also blesses us with the privilege of being part of the body of Christ, the church, which connects us to a community of believers who support, encourage, and edify one another. This sense of belonging and unity is a beautiful reflection of God's active love and grace. For decades, "We are stronger together" has been an echoed affirmation of comfort and joy.

Christianity is ever-evolving with a need to discover innovative ways to connect with its communities and spread life-changing messages. One of the most intriguing trends is transforming sermon points, titles, or sound bites into Christian apparel, streetwear, and street fashion merchandise that resonates with congregants and enlarges any circle of believers.

A few years ago, I customized a ball cap that displayed the words *Ask Jesus He Answers*. Whether walking through airports or going about my day, this cap never failed to draw attention. People from diverse backgrounds would approach me with compliments, testimonies, or confirmations. Even John C. Maxwell, Inc. Magazine's #1 Leadership and Management Expert, couldn't help but remark, "I like your hat!" The responses I've received, ranging from "Yes, He does…" to "Amen," were always accompanied by warm smiles and a spark in the person's eyes, signaling a shared recognition of faith and a message that resonated deeply.

The widespread interest in the cap inspired suggestions for me to launch a clothing line, which I named Godly Writes. This line features a variety of Christian-themed phrases, offering a subtle yet powerful way to share faith. Christian apparel like this is a non-invasive method for witnessing on behalf of Jesus Christ, encouraging fellow believers, and sparking curiosity among those not yet acquainted with the gospel. It proves that sharing one's beliefs can be gentle and impactful, reaching others through everyday interactions.

Embracing the blessings of the gospel is about living in the fullness of what God has provided for us in Christ, which includes employing wise strategies to share the blessings of the gospel (good spell) with others. This way of life is about experiencing the joy, peace, and abundance that come from a daily walk rooted in the gospel. As we continue to embrace these blessings, we grow in our relationship with God and more effectively share His love with the world around us. While life as Christians isn't devoid of stress, we can access answers that protect our hearts from succumbing to chronicles of doom. These depressing narratives can lure us into various spells of undue frustration. By grounding ourselves in the truths of the gospel, we can navigate daily challenges without falling prey to such disruptive influences.

The gospel of Jesus Christ is a powerful force capable of breaking through the walls and chains of spells and curses that restrain us. The good news proclaims liberty to the captives and sets the oppressed free. The gospel offers us a new identity, destiny, and power to overcome the oppressive feelings that persist to hold us back.

> *Christ purchased our freedom [redeeming us] from the curse (doom) of the Law [and its condemnation] by [Himself] becoming a curse for us, for it is written [in the Scriptures], Cursed is everyone who hangs on a tree (is crucified).*
>
> Galatians 3:13 AMPC

The gospel's power to break curses is rooted in Jesus' sacrifice on the cross. He took the curse of sin and death upon Himself, offering us redemption and a way out of the curse's grip. His resurrection signifies the ultimate victory over every curse, giving us hope and assurance that we can overcome any emerging hardship.

> *But thanks be to God, Who gives us the victory [making us conquerors] through our Lord Jesus Christ.*
>
> 1 Corinthians 15:57 AMPC

In light of this truth, we can approach the topic of spells and curses with hope and assurance. When we encounter challenges or negative patterns in our lives, instead of focusing on the difficulties, we can turn our attention to God in prayer, seeking His guidance and deliverance. By aligning ourselves with His word and will, we are enabled to break free from any spell or curse and walk in the blessings of His covenant.

Along with the testimony I shared earlier about walking by sight, I had also developed a detrimental habit of consistently envisioning the worst-case scenario for any challenge I encountered. This approach began as a mental strategy to prepare for potential difficulties. I would mentally rehearse responses, crafting detailed plans to handle situations as effectively as possible. However, this method soon proved counterproductive, spiraling into a cycle of anxiety.

Each time I imagined a scenario, I prepared for it and convinced myself of its inevitability, which escalated my stress levels. I consciously developed this practice, not under the influence of a demon or any external force, but through my own perceptions, firmly believing that the scenarios I imagined would undoubtedly come to pass. Despite this, I recognize that devils often wield their power of suggestion, compelling us to accept any imagination as a reality more than any other conduit that casts spells on our lives.

To resolve my issue of self-inflicted anxiety spells, I aligned my approach with the same teachings I share in this book—focusing on the gospel's message of hope and trust in God. Instead of preparing for the worst, I shifted my mindset to expect God's intervention and guidance. I now trust that whatever His intervention will be is best for me. This mindset shift involves consciously replacing pessimistic predictions with praying and affirmations of faith through scriptures while seeking God's wisdom, understanding, and peace that surpasses all understanding to guard my heart and mind. (Philippians 4:7)

When faced with a potential issue, I now pause and pray, asking God for wisdom and strength, rather than immediately defaulting to creating and believing in catastrophic outcomes. Reacting immediately to every circumstance we face is optional. For the sake of our well-being, it would be wise to follow the guidance offered in the scripture below:

Understand [this], my beloved brethren. Let every man be quick to hear [a ready listener], slow to speak, slow to take offense and to get angry.

James 1:19 AMPC

This verse jolted my understanding and made me realize that immediate reactions to perceived threats are unnecessary, contrary to the vengeful urge to respond uproariously, which emerges from our human nature. Instead, the verse encourages us to intentionally delay our response, even when others might criticize us for being slow to react. This guidance helps curb the impulsive replies often fueled by our emotions, precisely the kind of reactions that spells and curses manipulate to fulfill their destructive purposes.

The joy of having instructive verses from the Bible as references is immeasurable, knowing the Word of God assures us that we can rely on God's authority and efficacy at all times.

By immersing myself in scriptures and surrounding myself with positive, faith-affirming messages, I gradually unlearned the habit of falsified, negative self-protection. Regardless of present circumstances, I cultivated a mindset that expects the best from God's plans. This shift alleviated unnecessary anxiety and strengthened my faith in God because I became even more reliant on His way and timing. This new track of dealing with the onset of problems keeps me rooted in the truth that God is in control and His outcomes are always for my ultimate good. Although I still face temptations to envision gloomy conclusions, I am now equipped with the knowledge and strategies to overcome lures each time, allowing me to enjoy and appreciate my freedom from the insistent impulses to surrender to anxiety attacks.

Embracing the gospel means embracing the reality that, once we're free, the spells and curses of our past no longer define us, nor can they cause limitations in our present. God's love, grace, and power define us. This truth enables us to rise above the circumstances that once held us captive and live with unshakeable boldness and confidence.

The gospel also equips us to help break the cycle of spells and curses in our families and communities. It gives us the tools to address generational patterns of sin and dysfunction, bringing healing and restoration to areas of brokenness, as I examined and mentioned in the previous chapter. The gospel breaks spells and curses within our families and produces positive actions that reverberate down the family line.

When the good spell of the gospel influences our families, positivity can permeate through generations. My father, born in 1932 as one of 14 children, cherished a vivid memory of his father. Every Sunday morning, without fail, his father would rise early to pray and sing loudly—an event his family came to expect and cherish. Although my father was typically a quiet man, he would occasionally burst into song, clapping his hands joyfully. He always began his day by kneeling beside his bed to pray, usually in a whisper. While he may not have been as outwardly expressive as his father in his prayers and songs, the legacy of praying and praise, deeply influenced by the gospel, never faded in his life.

The exuberance somehow bypassed my dad and passed directly to me, influencing my son, Joshua. He and I are known for our spontaneous outbursts of prayer, praise, and even impromptu preaching sessions at home. As we embody the truths of the gospel daily, we act as agents of transformation, disrupting the influence of spells and curses while being catalysts of the flow of God's blessings across generations.

Moreover, the gospel gives us a new perspective on our struggles and challenges. It teaches us that our purpose and meaning are never on hold, even during trials. Our experiences of overcoming spells and curses can testify to the power of the gospel, encouraging and inspiring others facing similar battles. Can you think of a testimony you can share with a family member or friend about how the gospel has delivered you from a spell or curse in your life? If so, I urge you to share your testimony to spread the gospel's power to transform lives beyond your own.

Living in the freedom of the gospel infuses our lives with definition and destiny. It anchors us in a grand chronicle of expectancy, liberation, and triumph. This ongoing, eventful dynamic calls us to live courageously, maintain our faith in God, and experience the fullness of His life within us. Central to this series of miraculous happenings is the gospel's power to break spells and curses, highlighting a vital tenet of the Christian faith. The crux of this message informs us of our supernatural abilities and resonates with the innate human longing to be empowered by God alone. As we fully embrace this truth and let it shape our existence, we find ourselves equipped to rise from any circumstance and conquer the world, unburdened by fear or doubt.

Yet amid all these things we are more than conquerors and gain a surpassing victory through Him Who loved us.

Romans 8:37 AMPC

Community: Breaking Curses to Foster Blessings

44 And all who believed (who adhered to and trusted in and relied on Jesus Christ) were united and [together] they had everything in common;

45 And they sold their possessions (both their landed property and their movable goods) and distributed the price among all, according as any had need.

46 And day after day they regularly assembled in the temple with united purpose, and in their homes they broke bread [including the Lord's Supper]. They partook of their food with gladness and simplicity and generous hearts,

47 Constantly praising God and being in favor and goodwill with all the people; and the Lord kept adding [to their number] daily those who were being saved [from spiritual death].

Acts 2:44-47 AMPC

The early church's communal living model underscores the critical role of brotherhood and sisterhood in our spiritual journey. Dietrich Bonhoeffer's leadership during the Nazi regime in Germany exemplifies the strength of the congregation in overcoming profound societal challenges. As a devout Christian pastor and theologian, Bonhoeffer rallied the Confessing Church, a movement resisting the Nazi state's control over churches. His faith-driven approach to social justice, rooted in Christian ethics and the collective power of a unified spiritual people, galvanized believers to stand against tyranny, showcasing the gospel's relevance in addressing and resisting earthly injustices.

Christian fellowship plays a crucial role in breaking spells and curses to foster blessings for all to experience. As believers unite in unity and prayer, we create an atmosphere where God's power is unhindered and operates with might. In the following verse, Jesus said,

> *Again I tell you, if two of you on earth agree (harmonize together, make a symphony together) about whatever [anything and everything] they may ask, it will come to pass and be done for them by My Father in heaven.*
>
> Matthew 18:19 (AMPC)

This verse emphasizes the power of agreement in prayer, a critical component in breaking spells and curses. During prayer, God informs us about what He wants us to do and who He wants us to be. Our intimate moments with the Creator of the universe are monumental for knowing our current situation and God's future expectations for our lives. Prayer is not a speech. Prayer is a conversation. When God speaks to us, He speaks through His Holy Spirit and never desires to be the only One speaking during prayer. He longs to converse with us to reveal powerful secrets to thwart the enemy's plan to cast potent, long-lasting spells and curses on our lives.

The story of Achan in Joshua 7 is a biblical example of the role of community in breaking curses. Achan's sin of taking forbidden spoils from the battle of Jericho brought a curse upon the entire Israelite camp. This curse manifested in a surprising defeat at the hands of the much smaller city of Ai, causing dismay and fear among the Israelites.

> *Israel has sinned; yes, they have transgressed My covenant which I commanded them. They have taken some of the things devoted [for destruction]; they have stolen, and lied, and put them among their own baggage.*
>
> Joshua 7:11 AMPC

Joshua, the leader of the Israelites, responded to this defeat by seeking God's guidance. The Lord revealed to him that the defeat resulted from sin within the camp. Joshua addressed the sin through the community's collective action. He called for a thorough investigation, eventually identifying Achan as the culprit.

> *And Joshua said, Why have you brought trouble on us? The Lord will trouble you this day. And all Israel stoned him and those with him with stones, and afterward burned their bodies with fire.*
>
> Joshua 7:25 AMPC

The resolution of the situation required the cooperation and obedience of the entire community. They followed God's instructions to remove the sin from their midst, which involved dealing with Achan, destroying the stolen goods, and purifying the camp. This collective act of obedience and justice was crucial in lifting the curse and restoring God's favor upon the Israelites.

After Joshua addressed the sin and God lifted the curse, the Israelites could advance and achieve victory in their next battle against Ai. This time, they followed God's commands faithfully, and their obedience led to success. The story of Achan serves as a powerful reminder of the impact of individual actions on the community and the importance of communal responsibility in addressing and breaking curses.

The role of all, in alignment with breaking curses, is evident in the story of Achan. It highlights the need for collective action, accountability, and obedience to God's commands to overcome challenges and restore blessings. The account serves as an example for factions (even nations) today, emphasizing the importance of unity and cooperation in addressing issues that affect a group's well-being. I cannot stress enough how being part of a faith-filled body of believers provides support, accountability, and collective prayer power to break spells and curses so we can all walk in God's blessings. Within this company, we can find encouragement, grow in our faith, and experience the transformative power of God's favor, authority, and success in life.

Churches are significant sectors around the globe. Yet, I'm puzzled as to why many people feel at ease separating Christian beliefs from community involvement outside church-related functions. The error of excluding Christian involvement from even non-governmental events is accepted within many sectors of society. Let's never abandon God to the outskirts of our gatherings, whether the events are Christian-oriented or not.

> *And He said to them, Go into all the world and preach and publish openly the good news (the Gospel) to every creature [of the whole human race].*
>
> Mark 16:15 AMPC

> *You are the light of the world. A city set on a hill cannot be hidden.*
>
> Matthew 5:14 AMPC

Jesus commanded us to go into all the world (Mark 16:15), making our social spheres prime venues for spreading the gospel through words and actions. We cannot turn our backs on the profound darkness that envelops many in our neighborhoods. I recall a preacher who humorously yet influentially admonished the global church, saying, "Jesus called us the light of the world, yet all we seem to do is go around blinding each other." His message underscores a critical observation: many Christians prefer to stay within their comfortable circles, exclusively shining their lights into the eyes of other believers rather than illuminating the dark corners of the world's arenas.

As the designated light of the world, we must cast our glow boldly into the shadows that pervade the excluded and often avoided areas of our cities and neighborhoods. Once the gospel of Jesus Christ has impacted a community, it can bind the believers together for the shared purpose of ridding itself of spells and curses, as in the accurate account of Achan.

Building on the lesson from the story of Achan, in fact, we can see how the gospel of Jesus Christ offers a glorious promise of freedom and protection from spells and curses. Just as the Israelite society came together to address the sin that brought a curse upon them, the gospel calls us into a spiritual wholeness, united by Christ's love and sacrifice. Through His death and resurrection, Jesus broke the ultimate curse of sin and death, offering us a new covenant of grace and redemption. In this covenant, we are freed from the bondage of curses and empowered to live a life of victory and blessing.

By embracing the gospel and living as one body with fellow believers, we fortify ourselves against the influence of unfavorable narratives and spiritual attacks. We are our brothers' and sisters' keepers. We need each other for strength, encouragement, and sometimes, even tough love. In Christ, we find the ultimate source of emancipation and protection, ensuring that no spell or curse can prevail against the power of His redemptive love shown to us and through us toward others.

Developing the Mind of Christ

> *4 Let each of you esteem and look upon and be concerned for not [merely] his own interests, but also each for the interests of others.*
> *5 Let this same attitude and purpose and [humble] mind be in you which was in Christ Jesus: [Let Him be your example in humility:]*
> *6 Who, although being essentially one with God and in the form of God [possessing the fullness of the attributes which make God God], did not think this equality with God was a thing to be eagerly grasped or retained,*
> *7 But stripped Himself [of all privileges and rightful dignity], so as to assume the guise of a servant (slave), in that He became like men and was born a human being.*
> *8 And after He had appeared in human form, He abased and humbled Himself [still further] and carried His obedience to the extreme of death, even the death of the cross!*
>
> Philippians 2:4-8 AMPC

Since the gospel that breaks spells and curses centers on Jesus Christ, by allowing His mindset to become ours, we safeguard ourselves against the snares of spells and curses, ensuring our freedom and protection from their grasp. Drawing inspiration from Philippians 2:4-8 calls us to emulate the all-encompassing perspective of Jesus Christ, where we find a profound blueprint for spiritual freedom and protection. Christ's example, characterized by humility, selflessness, and obedience, not only paves the way for personal conversion but also shields us from the ensnaring effects of spells and curses. By adopting

Christ's keenly focused outlook on our relationship to God and our fellow man, we engage in a process of inner renewal that aligns our spirits with the divine, fortifying us against the forces of darkness.

The first step in developing the mind of Christ is embracing humility. Jesus, despite His divinity, chose to take on the nature of a servant, placing the needs of humanity above His own. This humility disrupted the power structures of the spiritual realm, breaking the curse of sin and death. When we humble ourselves, acknowledging our dependence on God and prioritizing others' welfare over our desires, we mirror Christ's humility. This posture of humility safeguards against the pride and self-centeredness that often make us susceptible to spiritual attacks, including spells and curses.

Selflessness, another cornerstone of Christ's mindset, calls us to look beyond our interests to the needs of others. In Philippians 2:4-8, Christ's willingness to empty Himself for our sake reveals the power of sacrificial love. By embodying this selflessness, we participate in a rendering that counters the advancement of spells and curses often rooted in selfish desires and harm. Putting others first is a testament to the gospel's liberating truth, reinforcing our collective resilience against spiritual bondage and fostering an environment of mutual support and freedom.

Christ's obedience unto death, even death on a cross, exemplifies the ultimate submission to God's will. This obedience was the key to defeating the curse, offering us redemption and freedom. By cultivating an obedient spirit, ready to follow God's commands and embrace His plans for our lives, we align ourselves with the power of the gospel. This alignment ensures that our lives are grounded in truth and protected from the lies and deceptions that spells and curses represent. As we let the mind of Christ be in us, we are not only transformed but also equipped to live in victory, liberated from the chains of curses and the walls of spells to be empowered to walk in the fullness of God's blessings.

The process of developing the mind of Christ—embracing humility, selflessness, and obedience—equips us with the spiritual strength to overcome the deceptions that can lead us astray. By aligning our thoughts and actions with the example of Jesus, we safeguard ourselves from the traps of spells and curses, which often take root in areas of our lives where we feel unfulfilled or disconnected from God. One powerful testimony of this transformation comes from a member of the church I pastor, Jordan, who found himself under a spell rooted in a misunderstanding of what true pleasure in God means. His story is a profound reminder of how renewing our minds in Christ can break the chains that bind us and bring us into a deeper relationship with God. Allow Jordan's testimony to inspire you to embrace the true meaning of finding pleasure in God.

> *I'm 21 years old*, and a spell trapped me that emerged from my belief that God couldn't please me. I found myself in a dangerous place because I thought that, since I hadn't experienced physical pleasure from God, He had nothing to offer me. When I say "physical pleasure," I understand that before I gave my life to Christ, my perception of pleasure was deeply perverse. So when I began to deny my flesh, I started believing that God couldn't satisfy me because He wouldn't please me in the ways I was used to. This deception led me to stray further from God. Almost every time I faced temptation, I gave in because I thought if I wasn't getting pleasure from God, I had to find it elsewhere, especially in the ways I knew how to please myself.
>
> While under this spell, hearing from God, entering His presence, worshiping Him, and acknowledging His goodness in my life became difficult. This one lie corrupted my entire way of thinking. One night in prayer, I cried out to God, admitting that I didn't know how to receive pleasure from Him or whether the pleasure I sought was something He offered. I pleaded with Him to send someone to help me understand, as I couldn't hear His voice clearly.
>
> About 30 minutes later, I received a text from Pastor Shane Wall, my pastor, saying, "What's up, son?" Fear struck me because I realized this was the answer I had just prayed for, but I wasn't ready for it to come so quickly. I initially deflected the conversation, and shortly realized I couldn't miss this opportunity. I opened up to Pastor Shane, and at that moment, I received the key to breaking the spell.

Pastor Wall explained that I truthfully do find pleasure in God, but not the kind of pleasure I was used to. He showed me that pleasure in God isn't about physical sensations but spiritual fulfillment. I now realize that I find pleasure in His perfect Fathering, what He says to me, how He protects me, and how He faithfully loves me. I don't see God as a deadbeat dad at all. He cares for me and is merciful, kind, and patient with me. I also enjoy His presence, comfort, and peace. Now that I am free from this spell, I've experienced the true joy of what finding pleasure in God means.

Jordan's testimony beautifully illustrates the power of developing the mind of Christ, as we discussed regarding Philippians 2:4-8. As for many of us, Jordan's snare was the false belief that physical pleasure was the only obvious form of satisfaction, leading him into a dangerous place spiritually.

Trapped by this deception, Jordan found himself under a spell that distanced him from God, making hearing His voice, worshiping, or feeling His presence harder. However, just as Jesus' humility, selflessness, and obedience led to freedom from sin and death, Jordan's journey out of this spiritual bondage began when he embraced a strong aspect of the gospel's truth—God is our loving Father.

Through a simple text conversation, I reminded Jordan that we find true pleasure in God's spiritual presence—His peace, joy, and love—not in the physical gratifications of the past. This realization broke the spell that clouded his mind and restored him to a deep connection with God. As we, too, adopt the mind of Christ, we become equipped to break free from any spells or curses, allowing us to walk in the fullness of God's blessings and the freedom that only the gospel of Jesus Christ provides.

God wants to use you to break spells by way of the gospel. As in the next chapter, we explore revelatory methods I've successfully used to cause people to believe in the gospel of Jesus Christ, you'll be empowered and equally motivated to apply the good spell (gospel) successfully to the lives of others to see them live free from the demonic oppression that held them captive. It's just as simple to believe as it is to doubt.

CHAPTER 4:

HOW TO BELIEVE

The Power of Belief

In September 2008, my mother passed away. Her joy in giving left a lasting impression on me and sparked my love for surprising others with unexpected gifts. I praise God for my mom and honor her legacy of love. I recall the special moment she bought and presented me with a Bible. She wrote my name, her name, and the purpose of the gift in the space provided on the first page. Each time I revisit that first page, I am reminded of her motherly love for me, and as I'm immersed in all the pages of that Bible, I'm reminded of God's intense love for me.

I believe the Bible is the undeniable, expressed Word of God. It contains profound revelations that resonate deeply with me. The words inscribed within transcend mere text because I receive them as God's personal messages to me and everyone—the ultimate tool on earth I rely on that builds and shapes my entire belief system concerning life. Believing the gospel activates the good spell to affect our lives with all the blessings, miracles, boldness, and transformation that come from knowing and following Christ.

When we believe the gospel, that alone will release the power of God in us and through us, breaking every spell and curse of ours and those impeding others. This progression strengthens our faith, renews our minds, and equips us to walk in the fullness of God's promises. When we fully believe and live by the gospel, we experience freedom, healing, and abundant life resulting from being vitally attached to the truth of God's Word. The good spell is not just a message; it's the exceptional foundation upon which we build our lives, reshaping our hearts, actions, and future.

Whether spoken, internalized, or experienced, these are generally billions of people's daily thoughts: "I would believe the truth if I could convince myself it's unmistakably the truth. However, the challenge is that my current beliefs often create a barrier, causing my acceptance of what could be the truth to be difficult to believe." We hold on to specific ideas because they provide a sense of familiarity and security, even when they may be flawed. Only when we unleash ourselves from the beliefs holding us back can we embrace what will prove to be the truth.

What is belief, and how can we stop holding on to the familiar stories that shape our daily lives while quietly undermining our self-esteem and future?

Since belief is fundamental to successfully casting spells onto our lives and can cause us to live under curses unknowingly, what is vitally important is that we understand how belief comes to power in our lives. Our beliefs direct the course of our experiences toward either beneficial or harmful outcomes. Therefore, we must crucially understand how to harness our beliefs to achieve the best possible results—aligning with God's will for our lives and therefore having the astounding benefits that derive from God's love and care.

How to Believe

In the context of using belief to empower our lives through the gospel (good spell) of Jesus Christ, we define belief as *having firm, unwavering confidence in a concept or person*. How can we start ourselves and others on a path that will help us build that confidence?

Two critical steps are needed to help ourselves and others believe. First, we must ask God to guide us in a way that will reach us and others by conveying why spiritual belief enriches lives. Second, we then build our case using what we and others already believe.

In John 4:3-29, Jesus encounters a Samaritan woman at a water well and initiates a conversation with her by asking for a drink of water. This seemingly simple request becomes the foundation for a profound spiritual revelation. Jesus begins with what she already understands and believes—water quenches thirst. He uses this shared belief to open her heart to a more profound truth, offering her living water that quenches a different kind of thirst, one that is spiritual and eternal. By connecting His message to her everyday experience, Jesus makes the lesson accessible, relatable, and effective for her to believe.

The woman, intrigued by this living water, engages further in the conversation, leading to her recognizing Jesus as the Messiah. This masterful approach captures her attention and transforms her understanding, taking her belief in the necessity of physical water and elevating it to the eternal reality of spiritual satisfaction found in Christ.

This simple, relatable connection sets the stage for one of the most significant conversions recorded in the Bible, as the woman goes on to spread the news of Jesus throughout her community— becoming a bold witness for Him. Jesus' genius in this interaction demonstrates the power of meeting people where they are and building on what they already believe, to reveal more resonant spiritual truths.

In my Jesus Ministry Training online course, I teach this method of how to use a common item, like Jesus used water, to establish someone's belief in God and His purpose. Teaching thus transfers an ability from one person to another. That statement powers my passion for teaching and training others. When what we teach people causes them to believe the information shared, their lives change for the better. The testimonies I receive about their renewal fuel my passion to continue sharing and teaching others.

How Belief is Processed

How do people come to believe in anything? In other words, what is the process through which someone achieves the position of belief? A simple and accurate answer is that we achieve the condition of believing anything by exercising our power to choose. How, then, do we discover, receive, organize, and process all the information that causes us to decide on our choices?

In my first book, *What Are You Doing After the Dance?* I introduced a simplified process of how virtually each of us makes decisions, using the acronym T.I.D.A.R.:

- Time, over the course of events, will generate…
- Influence that causes us to make a…
- Decision, which will prompt us to take…

- Action that will always produce a…
- Result that will affect us and others.

Organically, the process of believing is rooted in our power to choose. This ability to choose is not random; a sequence of events and interactions that shape our perceptions and convictions influence our choices. The acronym T.I.D.A.R. illustrates how *time, influence, decision, action,* and *result* work in concert to guide our beliefs and actions.

Firstly, over time, the experiences we encounter and the information we absorb into our hearts become the references we use to make future decisions. Proverbs 4:23 (AMPC) states, *Keep and guard your heart with all vigilance and above all that you guard, for out of it flow the springs of life.* This scripture underscores the importance of monitoring the influences we allow into our hearts because they shape our beliefs. As we consistently expose ourselves to specific ideas or teachings, these influences take root in our hearts (minds), forming the basis of the belief system we'll use for each area of our lives.

Secondly, our decisions directly result from the influences we have accepted. Romans 12:2 AMPC exhorts, "Do not be conformed to this world (this age), [fashioned after and adapted to its external, superficial customs], but be transformed (changed) by the [entire] renewal of your mind [by its new ideals and its new attitude], so that you may prove [for yourselves] what is the good and acceptable and perfect will of God." This conversion is a choice to renew our minds according to God's Word rather than the world's influences. By immersing in the truth of scripture, we align our decisions with God's will, leading to actions that reflect His principles.

Finally, our actions, prompted by these decisions, produce tangible results in our lives and the lives of those around us. James 1:22 AMPC instructs, "But be doers of the Word [obey the message], and not merely listeners to it, betraying yourselves [into deception by reasoning contrary to the Truth]." This verse highlights the importance of acting on our beliefs. When we make choices grounded in God's Word, our actions manifest His will, producing results that bear witness to His faithfulness and power.

Understanding the T.I.D.A.R. process shows that our beliefs are spontaneous and shaped by our choices over time. By consciously choosing to immerse ourselves in God's Word and allowing it to influence our decisions, we align our actions with His will, leading to results that affirm our faith and glorify God. This intentional process enables us to believe by choice, grounded in the transformative power of scripture.

We can see the T.I.D.A.R. process in our earlier Bible story about how the Samaritan woman at the well came to believe that Jesus could provide living water, and that He was the Messiah. Throughout their conversation, time allowed Jesus' words to influence the woman's thinking, shifting her perspective from physical water to spiritual fulfillment. This influence led her to make the crucial decision to engage further with Jesus, asking Him to explain this living water.

Her decision prompted an action—she left her water jar behind to spread the news in her town. The result was profound, as her outlook underwent a reformation, and many others came to believe in Jesus through her testimony. This process demonstrates how T.I.D.A.R. can guide someone from initial disbelief to a life-changing encounter with Christ.

Believing God

Believing what we see is instinctual because it requires minimal cognitive effort to confirm what our natural senses perceive as reality. However, when we encounter an undesirable event or condition (which God does not desire for us), our brains are wired to accept it as the only reality, leading us to think we must endure this negative situation indefinitely. This perception needs to change.

Our understanding should be that if God does not want a particular occurrence to persist in our lives, our belief must shift immediately upon hearing God's will for our circumstances. This new belief aligns us with God's promises and His higher truth, enabling us to break free from the constraints of undesirable circumstances.

Romans 10:17 AMPC states, "So faith comes by hearing [what is told], and what is heard comes by the preaching [of the message that came from the lips] of Christ (the Messiah Himself)." This scripture highlights the importance of hearing and internalizing God's Word to build faith. Our faith grows when we hear God's promises and understand His will, empowering us to believe in outcomes beyond our usual perception or expectation.

Hebrews 11:1 AMPC further reinforces this by saying, "Now faith is the assurance (the confirmation, the title deed) of the things [we] hope for, being the proof of things [we] do not see and the conviction of their reality [faith perceiving as real fact what is not revealed to the senses]." This passage underscores that faith enables us to understand God's truth as the ultimate reality, even when it contradicts our physical experiences.

To illustrate, consider the testimony of a believer who faced a dire medical diagnosis of terminal metastatic liver cancer in 1981, Dolores "Dodie" Osteen, the mother of Joel Osteen, the pastor of Lakewood Church in Houston, TX. At only 46 years old, she was given just a few weeks longer to live by her physicians. She had lost a considerable amount of weight, was down to only 89 pounds, and her doctors said they could do nothing more for her. Dodie's miraculous healing from cancer is a compelling story of faith and perseverance. Refusing to accept this prognosis, she turned to her faith in God and the promises of healing found in the Bible.

Dodie began to immerse herself in scripture, reading and believing healing verses daily and praying fervently. She wrote letters to anyone she might have offended, seeking forgiveness, as she believed unforgiveness could hinder her healing. Despite the severity of her condition, she continued to live her life as if she had already received her healing, performing household chores and maintaining a positive outlook.

One of the critical aspects of her testimony was her unwavering belief in the power of God's Word. She consistently declared healing scriptures over herself, such as 1 Peter 2:24 AMPC, which states, "By His wounds you have been healed." Dodie saw the Word of God as her medicine, taking it in daily and allowing it to build her faith and trust in God's healing power.

Her faith and persistence paid off. Over time, she began to regain her strength and health. Today, decades later, Dodie Osteen is cancer-free and shares her testimony to encourage others facing similar battles. Her story is a testament to the power of faith in God, the importance of believing and speaking

God's Word over one's life, and standing firm in the miracles that can happen when one trusts in God's promises. She saw her situation through the lens of faith, looking to God for a miraculous turnaround. Over time, her condition improved significantly, demonstrating the power of aligning one's belief with God's actual intentions as seen in His declaration in scripture.

By consciously aligning our beliefs with God's promises, we open ourselves to His miraculous interventions and the fulfillment of His perfect will in our lives. This shift in belief is not just a mental exercise but a profound spiritual practice that brings God's Kingdom realities into our everyday experiences.

Faith or Sight

For we walk by faith, not by sight

2 Corinthians 5:7 KJV

Every Christian's fundamental decision is whether to walk by faith or sight. The path we take depends on whom we trust. As believers, we build our journey on the unshakable confidence that the One who promises us everything also possesses the power to fulfill His promises. Believing in things our senses and minds perceive as unreal or impossible is challenging, but our actions reflect our faith in God. Our deepest beliefs drive those actions. So, how do we strengthen our faith to trust God's every word instinctively?

We know that increasing and strengthening our faith in God is vital to our relationship with Him and understanding His ways. This message of faith is repeated in sermons, devotionals, and testimonies. Yet, believing in something we cannot see remains counter to our usual habit, especially when our natural inclination is to trust only what we perceive with our senses. This connection between belief and action is why faith is so crucial. Many become discouraged from multiple failed attempts to believe what He says, even while looking to God. We may never fully accept God's words until we build and maintain an unshakable faith in Him first.

We're all too familiar with the fatigue and weariness that can drain us mentally and spiritually, making us yearn for a shortcut or quick fix to boost our faith and overcome our weaknesses.

I have good news and even more good news. First, you don't need to do anything strenuous now; you can take time to rest and recuperate. Truthfully, you can. The belief that we must act swiftly in the face of problems often stems from the devil's persistent pressure. Demons are pushy and bossy, urging us to react based on our emotions instead of waiting for God's wisdom. However, the Holy Spirit is gentle, and Jesus is patient. He didn't command us to work regardless of our exhaustion. Instead, Jesus invites those of us who are weary and burdened to come to Him for rest, to transfer our troubles to Him, and to trust that He will handle them. Giving our problems to Jesus means we no longer carry those burdens ourselves.

This divine invitation to rest in Jesus is a profound reassurance. When we cast our anxieties and burdens onto Him, He liberates us from the constant strain of problem-solving on our own. Jesus knows our limitations and invites us to rely on His strength and wisdom. This approach provides relief and reinforces our faith as we learn to trust His timing and methods. As we embrace this trust, we can move forward with renewed strength, ready to follow His guidance and witness the fulfillment of His promises in our lives.

> 28 *Come to Me, all you who labor and are heavy-laden and overburdened, and I will cause you to rest. [I will ease and relieve and refresh your souls.]*
> 29 *Take My yoke upon you and learn of Me, for I am gentle (meek) and humble (lowly) in heart, and you will find rest (relief and ease and refreshment and recreation and blessed quiet) for your souls.*
> 30 *For My yoke is wholesome (useful, good—not harsh, hard, sharp, or pressing, but comfortable, gracious, and pleasant), and My burden is light and easy to be borne.*
> Matthew 11:28-30 AMPC

The other good news is that when we give our lives to Jesus, He willingly receives all of our future problems as well, and He is aware of that from the onset of our relationship with Him. We view problems as interruptions to our quiet and peaceful lives. Jesus views problems as opportunities for Him to get glory out of the lives given to Him—being the only One Who can produce amazingly unexpected victories for us. Now that we can relax when the time comes to act, let's explore further ways to strengthen our faith in God.

To believe something we don't see is challenging—nearly impossible. That's why we need faith. To believe anything without first having faith in the one whose words we want to believe is impossible. We can strengthen our faith in God by rising out of the mental sea of words that formed our belief that the worst is inevitable by submerging our minds into verses in the Bible that directly speak to our situations. Using the power of modern technology, we can search the internet for circumstance-specific biblical references. (I love the AMPC version of the Bible because it clarifies many vague/unclear words, including their original intended meanings in many verses.)

So, for example, one of the searches on Google or a free version of ChatGPT or Gemini could be: "What are verses in the AMPC version of the Bible that would help ease or rid my depression?" (You can replace *depression* with whatever you're experiencing. Even if you don't know a word that expresses your experience, you can describe your situation to the AI platform of your choice to receive very fitting results.)

After receiving the generated list, I would read the Bible verse results and then copy and paste them to my calendar to read and pray according to the verses daily—asking God to fulfill His promise for my situation.

Because you're worth the effort, when you do what I've just described, you can read and pray the scriptures each time thoughts of your circumstances come to mind, until you fully believe that God's promises directly relate to your specific situation and are your new reality.

Additionally, share one of the most impactful verses you found with a brother or sister who understands your pain and ask for their understanding of how the verse relates to your situation. I would be honest and explain what you admittedly believe your reality is versus what you want to believe God's reality is of your supposed problem.

As we continually remind ourselves of God's unbiased faithfulness throughout history and rehearse the relevant scriptural verses for our situations, we allow His promises to take root in our hearts. This practice builds our confidence in our Lord's nature as the loving Father He consistently proves to be.

Who Can Use God's Word?

Having delved into the essence of belief, we pivot to explore our role in wielding God's Word, the scriptures. So, what exactly is our relational stance with God when utilizing His Word? Understanding our positional relationship with God is crucial because accessing the promises in the Bible isn't merely a matter of claiming them at will; it hinges on our felt relationship with God.

As children of God, we embrace our primary identity as His beloved sons and daughters, and our fundamental posture is one of trust and dependence on our Heavenly Father. As children secure in their loving parents' promises, we approach the Bible with unwavering assurance that every word spoken by God is valid and that He's ever faithful to fulfill His declarations.

In this role, as His child, we cherish the scriptures as notifications of love that cause us to adore our Father's heart. His promises thus overwhelm us with the thoughtful and intricate details of His planned care for our lives. With intentionally designed parenting revealed in His heart's promises for us, trusting that He'll fulfill those guarantees according to His perfect timing and loving parental wisdom brings the comfort and relief we seek and expect in every circumstance. The Apostle Paul underscores this relational dynamic in his letter to the Philippians:

> *And my God will liberally supply (fill to the full) your every need according to His riches in glory in Christ Jesus*
>
> Philippians 4:19 AMPC

This verse captures our assurance as a child of God that He will provide abundantly for all our needs, according to the riches of His glory that He holds for our future fulfillment.

Furthermore, we are not passive recipients but active agents in God's Kingdom, akin to what could be termed supernatural attorneys. As believers, we leverage God's Word (His Law) in our lives and the lives of others. Just as a skilled attorney applies the law to secure favorable outcomes for her clients, we apply God's promises and principles to navigate challenges and gain victories.

Consider Sarah's testimony, a recent convert who experienced a life-changing transformation through the power of scripture. Struggling with financial hardship, Sarah stood on the promise of Malachi 3:10 AMPC: "Bring all the tithes (the whole tenth of your income) into the storehouse, that there may be food in My house, and prove Me now by it, says the Lord of hosts, if I will not open the windows of heaven for you and pour you out a blessing, that there shall not be room enough to receive it." Despite doubts and pressures, Sarah faithfully tithed and witnessed supernatural provisions that surpassed her expectations, confirming the reliability of God's Word.

In our faith journey, let's embrace the dual roles of childlike trust and spiritual advocacy, confident that God's Word is alive and active (Hebrews 4:12 AMPC), empowering us to walk in His assurances and impact our world for His glory.

Understanding Faith and Belief

The *Law of First Mention* is a principle used in biblical hermeneutics (the study of the principles of Bible interpretation). It suggests that the first mention of a concept or term in the Bible establishes an important pattern or foundation for understanding its subsequent use throughout Scripture. This method highlights significant themes and theological points that remain consistent within the biblical narrative.

The term *believe* and its derivatives first appear in the Bible during one of God's conversations with Abram, whose name God later changed to Abraham.

> *1 After these things, the word of the Lord came to Abram in a vision, saying, Fear not, Abram, I am your Shield, your abundant compensation, and your reward shall be exceedingly great.*

> 2 And Abram said, Lord God, what can You give me, since I am going on [from this world] childless and he who shall be the owner and heir of my house is this [steward] Eliezer of Damascus?
> 3 And Abram continued, Look, You have given me no child; and [a servant] born in my house is my heir.
> 4 And behold, the word of the Lord came to him, saying, This man shall not be your heir, but he who shall come from your own body shall be your heir.
> 5 And He brought him outside [his tent into the starlight] and said, Look now toward the heavens and count the stars—if you are able to number them. Then He said to him, So shall your descendants be.
> 6 And he [Abram] believed in (trusted in, relied on, remained steadfast to) the Lord, and He counted it to him as righteousness (right standing with God).
>
> Genesis 15:3-6 AMPC

In the sixth verse, the term *believe* refers to Abram's faith or trust in God's pledge that he would have a multitude of descendants despite his old age and his wife Sarai's barrenness at the time. This foundational moment in biblical history highlights the importance of faith and belief in God and sets a precedent that righteousness before God comes through faith. This theme is further developed and echoed throughout the scriptures, notably in the New Testament teachings of Paul regarding justification by faith.

This concept of belief, introduced with Abram, serves as a cornerstone for understanding the dynamics of faith and righteousness in the relationship between God and humans throughout the Bible. Belief underscores the idea that it is not merely human effort or adherence to the law that establishes righteousness but rather a sincere trust in God's character.

Understanding that we shouldn't use belief and faith interchangeably is essential; each serves a distinct purpose for us to practice separately. For example, we may say that we have faith in the Bible, God's Holy Word. Yet, Jesus encouraged us to place our faith in God. (Mark 11:22) The Bible's emphasis is indeed placed on having faith in God or Jesus Christ rather than having faith in Their words as a separate entity. When we wholly place our faith in God, we will believe whatever He says.

I remember when a close associate told me something a local community member said. I looked at the informant with a snide expression and announced, "For proven reasons, I have no faith in that individual, so there's no way I'm going to believe what he said." As you may have guessed, what the person said maintained his track record of sharing blatantly false information.

When we don't have faith in someone, we won't believe what he or she says. On the contrary, whoever we have faith in, we'll believe what the person says. It is also meaningful to understand that we can believe in a person we also have faith in. (John 14:1, Galatians 2:16, John 6:29)

Faith in God is about deep relational trust. That trust is not just believing God exists or acknowledging His sovereignty; it's about relying on His relational nature and character as the perfect Father. Faith is an unconditional surrender to God—always trusting in His goodness, power, and wisdom. Having faith in God is a commitment to a relationship with Him that shapes how we live, react to challenges, and embrace His plans for us.

Belief in God's words stems from this foundational faith. To believe in God's words is to accept them as accurate and a promise of the reality to come because we trust the One Who promises. Belief, then, is the natural outcome of faith—it is faith in action. When God speaks through scripture or the prompting of the Holy Spirit, our faith in God compels us to take His words and intentions seriously and integrate them into our lives.

Ntando's Spiritual Authority

The level of seriousness with which we accept God's words determines how confidently we'll faithfully incorporate His plans into the rest of our lives. Understanding and exercising our spiritual authority is crucial for breaking spells and curses effectively. God calls us as believers to recognize that Christ Himself has endowed us with authority, having conquered sin and death and given us the power to overcome the works of our enemies (all demons).

Behold! I have given you authority and power to trample upon serpents and scorpions, and [physical and mental strength and ability] over all the power that the enemy [possesses]; and nothing shall in any way harm you.

Luke 10:19 AMPC

This scripture promises protection and empowers us to combat spiritual forces that seek to bind us. By believing that Jesus has bestowed upon us His authority, we can confidently address and dismantle the spells and curses that threaten our spiritual well-being.

Consider the story of Ntando, a young man from Zimbabwe whose journey illustrates the transformation that comes from stepping into one's spiritual authority. Ntando grew up overly self-conscious and isolated due to a slight physical asymmetry of his ears, which he perceived as a significant flaw because of childhood teasing. This insecurity drove him to constantly wear hats to hide his perceived defect, particularly when he entered a larger high school where he feared increased judgment.

However, Ntando's life took a significant turn when he embraced his faith more deeply. He realized and wholeheartedly believed that his value and identity were not rooted in his physical appearance but in his spiritual heritage as a child of God. Despite his fears, this revelation formed when he joined the church choir, finding his voice literally and figuratively. The community and the act of worship helped Ntando see himself as God saw him—perfectly imperfect and wholly loved.

His participation in the choir not only improved his self-esteem but also placed him in a position to confront and reject the damaging spells—spoken words and beliefs—that had once held him captive. Over time, Ntando learned to appreciate his unique features and, surprisingly, discovered that his earlier fears had magnified what was a minor issue for others.

By applying the truth of God's Word to his life and stepping into roles that affirmed his worth, Ntando broke free from the spell of insecurity and self-doubt. His story is a testament to the power of spiritual authority from belief when aligned with the truth of the gospel and the support of a faith-based community.

However, the opposite is also true—when beliefs and words are rooted in negativity or hostility, they can lead to destruction. The story of the Edomites shows how their actions and words in opposition to Israel reached God's ears. What they believed and the choices they made ultimately led to God's judgment, revealing the consequences of believing, speaking, and acting against His people

Watch Your Mouth

> *For with the heart a person believes (adheres to, trusts in, and relies on Christ) and so is justified (declared righteous, acceptable to God), and with the mouth he confesses (declares openly and speaks out freely his faith) and confirms [his] salvation.*
>
> Romans 10:10 AMPC

> *34 You offspring of vipers! How can you speak good things when you are evil (wicked)? For out of the fullness (the overflow, the superabundance) of the heart the mouth speaks.*
> *35 The good man from his inner good treasure flings forth good things, and the evil man out of his inner evil storehouse flings forth evil things.*
>
> Matthew 12:34-35 AMPC

> *But whatever comes out of the mouth comes from the heart, and this is what makes a man unclean and defiles [him].*
>
> Matthew 15:18 AMPC

As we explore the power of belief, we recognize that what we hold in our hearts shapes our thoughts, actions, and words. Romans 10:10 reminds us that belief begins in the heart, and we express our belief through our confessions. But what we harbor in our hearts—whether faith or doubt, truth or deception—will inevitably flow out of our mouths, as Jesus teaches in Matthew 12:34. In Matthew 15:18, Jesus further emphasizes that what comes out of the mouth originates in the heart, revealing the actual spiritual condition within us. The words we speak truthfully indicate the undeniable evidence of what we believe.

Our words reflect the spiritual state of our hearts, and this connection between heart and mouth is vital to understanding how belief is formed and expressed. The transformation of our hearts is key because the mouth speaks out of the heart's overflow. What we confess with our mouths empowers us to influence our lives and those affected by our words. Therefore, as we learn to believe, we must also guard our hearts because by doing so, we will watch our mouths and see the good or bad we've spoken come to pass. We must hold onto and treasure God's impactful Word (the Holy Scriptures) in our hearts, cherishing His truth so that the words from our hearts align only with what God has spoken.

The Edomites

In Ezekiel 35, the prophet Ezekiel delivers a message from God to Mount Seir, representing the people of Edom, who were descendants of Esau and long-standing enemies of Israel. The passage, particularly from verses ten onward, reveals a powerful story about how concepts believed and words spoken by Edom's people would ultimately lead to their downfall. God warns them that their boastful declarations and hostile intentions toward Israel will come back upon them, turning their words into a curse that seals their own fate.

The land of Edom had long harbored resentment against Israel. Despite being relatives—descendants of the twin brothers Jacob and Esau—the animosity between them had festered for generations. The Edomites watched from their mountainous stronghold of Mount Seir as Israel faced devastation, and in their hearts, they rejoiced. They believed the fall of Israel would finally give them the long-awaited opportunity to seize the lands they had always coveted. Boldly, they declared, "These two nations and these two countries shall be mine, and we will possess them."

But the Edomites' words reached the ears of God. They didn't know that their beliefs, boastful statements, and plans of conquest would lead to their destruction. As they schemed and plotted, their words began to work against them. The same God who had promised to bless those who blessed Israel and curse those who cursed them (Genesis 12:3) was now preparing to turn Edom's spoken intentions into a curse upon themselves.

God's response to their words was swift and severe. He declared through Ezekiel that because Edom had said, "These nations will be ours," He would judge them accordingly. God would make Mount Seir a desolate wasteland, and the Edomites, who once plotted to occupy Israel's land, would instead be overrun by calamity and destruction. Their boastful words would not bring them the victory they sought but rather desolation and terror.

As Edom had rejoiced over Israel's misfortune, God would now make them a warning to other nations. The specific words that Edom had spoken, intending to curse and conquer Israel, became the chains that bound them to their doom. They would experience the same fear and devastation they had hoped to inflict upon Israel, and their pride would be their downfall. God's judgment was not only a consequence of their actions but also of their words. In their arrogance, they had underestimated the power of the spoken word and the justice of the God of Israel.

Speaking Blessings and Curses

The story of Edom in Ezekiel 35 serves as a stark reminder that the words we speak have weight and power. Just as the Edomites' words led to their curse, so too can our own words shape the reality we experience. Whether for blessing or cursing, our words matter to God as they can set the course for our future. As we embark on this chapter exploring the power of language, we are reminded in Scripture that what we say can align us and others with God's blessings or bring us down a path of destruction. James, the brother of Jesus, captures this truth with a piercing observation:

> *Out of the same mouth come forth blessing and cursing. These things, my brethren, ought not to be so.*
>
> James 3:10 AMPC

James emphasizes the contradiction that exists when blessings and curses flow from the same source—our mouths. He highlights the inconsistency of praising God while using the same tongue to speak ill of others (James 3:9), ultimately harming the world. This duality reveals the tension between our spiritual aspirations and our human weaknesses. The same tongue that declares God's goodness should never tear down, belittle, or curse. Whether speaking blessings or curses, the tongue reflects the condition of the heart and responds according to what we believe about those we are addressing.

In James 3:5, the apostle likens the tongue to a small fire that can set ablaze an entire forest. Though small, the tongue exerts immense influence over our lives and the lives of others, often shaping beliefs through words that people accept without question or verification. This verse causes us to recognize our responsibility concerning the words we choose to speak. Just as Edom's arrogant proclamations led to their downfall, so too can our words—spoken in moments of anger, frustration, or carelessness—create a reality we never intended. James challenges us to see the disconnect when our words don't align with our faith, reminding us to be consistent in our speech, using our words to build up rather than destroy.

This verse also points to a more profound spiritual truth: our words reflect our hearts. Jesus taught that out of the abundance of our hearts, our mouths speak. (Matthew 12:34) What we say reveals the beliefs stored inside us—love, peace, grace, bitterness, anger, or resentment. Psalm 119:11 encourages us to hide, store, and treasure God's Word in our hearts so that our thoughts, words, and actions remain free from sin. Therefore, the challenge of James 3:10 is not just about controlling our tongues but about allowing God to transform our hearts so that what flows from our mouths is always a blessing, never a curse.

James 3:10 reminds us of the inconsistency of allowing blessings and curses to come from the same mouth, challenging us to align our words with God's will. But this issue runs deeper than just our speech. In Luke 6:45, Jesus reveals that our words directly reflect what we store in our hearts:

> *A good man out of the good treasure of his heart bringeth forth that which is good; and an evil man out of the evil treasure of his heart bringeth forth that which is evil: for of the abundance of the heart his mouth speaketh.*
>
> Luke 6:45 KJV

This verse illuminates the powerful connection between our hearts and our words. The one who speaks curses has a heart to curse others. The one who speaks blessings has a heart to bless others. The question is about controlling our tongues and addressing the source—our hearts. The one who speaks curses harbors bitterness, anger, or envy, while the one who speaks blessings has a heart filled with love, peace, and grace. The beliefs we allow to take root in our hearts will inevitably overflow into our speech and actions.

Understanding this connection helps us see that the battle for controlling our words begins in the heart. To speak life, blessings, and truth, we must first cultivate a heart aligned with God's goodness of life, blessings, and truth. Therefore, as we continue exploring the importance of watching our mouths, we must also examine what we allow to grow within us. Are we filling our hearts with the Word of God to believe, or are we feeding our hearts what to believe that leads to cursing and negativity? The answer to this question will determine the ongoing nature of our speech and, ultimately, the path of blessings or curses in our and others' lives.

Jeremy Camp, a well-known Christian musician and singer-songwriter, has a powerful testimony that aligns with allowing God to shape our hearts, which, in turn, affects our words and our lives. Jeremy faced a test of faith when his first wife, Melissa, passed away from cancer shortly after their marriage. He has openly shared how he struggled with grief, anger, and questions about God's plan. In his moments of deep pain, he felt the temptation to speak words of despair and doubt. However, Jeremy allowed God to heal his broken heart through prayer and leaning on God's promises. As he surrendered his pain to God, his heart began to fill with hope and faith again.

This heart resurgence shaped Jeremy Camp's music and testimony. Instead of allowing bitterness and grief to dictate his words, he spoke life, sharing God's goodness through his music and testimony. Songs such as "I Still Believe," inspired by his journey, reflect how God can take even the most painful experiences and turn them into opportunities to bless others.

Jeremy's story beautifully illustrates the principle in Luke 6:45—that the mouth speaks out of the abundance of the heart. His journey reminds us that when we let God heal and renew our hearts, He empowers us to speak words of survival and blessing, even in the face of life's most significant challenges.

Profane, Curse, and Swear Words

Let no foul or polluting language, nor evil word nor unwholesome or worthless talk [ever] come out of your mouth, but only such [speech] as is good and beneficial to the spiritual progress of others, as is fitting to the need and the occasion, that it may be a blessing and give grace (God's favor) to those who hear it.

Ephesians 4:29 AMPC

Words carry more power than we often realize. From our everyday conversations to the sacred truths reflected in Scripture, what we speak can profoundly impact our lives and those of near and dear ones. The Bible reminds us repeatedly of the importance of watching our words, warning us that "Death and life are in the power of the tongue: and they that love it shall eat the fruit thereof." (Proverbs 18:21 KJV). Whether we know it or not, our uttered words can have lasting consequences—drawing blessings or curses into being. As we delve deeper into the origins of profanity and the usage of *curse words* and *swear words*, we'll discover how ancient beliefs about the power of language still resonate with us today. Our words have the potential to shape reality, making vital the development of wholesome, godly beliefs as we watch our mouths by selecting our words wisely.

Profanity is often called *curse (cuss) words* or *swear words* because of their historical and linguistic roots, which connect them to curses and oaths. Here's a breakdown of the origins:

1. **Curse Words:**

The term *curse* in this context originates from invoking a supernatural power to bring harm or misfortune upon someone. Historically, to curse someone meant to place an evil spell or wish ill upon them. Over time, words associated with these curses became known as *curse words*. These words were often used in anger or frustration, expressing the speaker's desire to bring harm or bad luck, akin to the practice of cursing someone in ancient times.

2. **Swear Words:**

The term *swear* comes from the act of taking an oath. In medieval and religious contexts, swearing involved invoking the name of God or sacred things in a promise or declaration. When people used sacred terms frivolously or in anger, it was considered blasphemous, hence the term *swear words*. These words were seen as profane because they violated the sanctity of religious oaths.

3. **Profanity:**

The word *profanity* comes from the Latin *profanus*, meaning *outside the temple or not sacred*. Originally, profane language referred to anything disrespectful toward sacred things or God. Over time, the word evolved to describe offensive language in general.

The origin of curse words and swear words traces back to religious and occult practices, where words held power, either to invoke harm (cursing) or to make sacred promises (swearing). Over time, these words lost their enchanted connotations but retained their offensive nature, which is why we still refer to them as we do today.

The power of words, whether used for harm or sacred promise, is undeniable. Just as negative words can leave a lasting impact, so can words that align with God's will bring life, hope, and renewal. This understanding brings us to the incredible influence of speaking words that God reveals—words that unleash the power to shift one's belief and courage in tangible ways.

Words Shift Belief

We've learned that spells and curses are deeply rooted in belief. Therefore, breaking a person's belief can break the spell or curse affecting them. One of my favorite groups for me to help break spells and curses is those serving in the food industry—waitresses, waiters, cooks, hostesses, managers, and others. I'm not entirely sure why God has given me a heart for those in this field, but I can speculate it may be because my father's side of the family was well-known for cooking and culinary skills. I've worked closely with them and have seen how the public has mistreated them repeatedly.

My uncle, Fred Wall, was the private chef for President Franklin Roosevelt while he was in office. My father was a cook and chef for various institutions, including the U.S. Army, several hospitals, Princeton University, and Claflin University in my hometown of Orangeburg, South Carolina, where he served for over 50 years. Hearing their stories, which spanned decades before my birth, gave me an endearing appreciation for those who love seeing people served well and satisfied with their food and beverage orders. Perhaps my close connection to my family's experience in food service is why God has used me to break the spells and curses of countless individuals in this industry across several countries. Even today, I have genuine compassion for those who serve in this field, giving their best daily.

In Philippians 2:15, 1 Timothy 4:12, and 2 Corinthians 3:2-3, Paul emphasizes that God called us to be godly examples for others in everything we do. I'm humbled when those dining with me are empowered to break spells and curses from others after observing God using me to minister to servers.

Our church hosted one of my favorite gospel singers, Keith Staten, formerly of the group *Commissioned*, for lunch at a restaurant after a Sunday morning service. About 10 of us were seated, and after the waitress introduced herself and took our drink orders, I asked if I could share something with her. She seemed slightly surprised by my question, but gave me her full attention. I simply said, "God told me to tell you to stop crying about it." Her jaw dropped, and with a trembling voice, she said, "Oh, my God! Oh, my God! Oh, my God!" She began to cry and became so overwhelmed that she had to leave the table immediately.

Keith said, "That's awesome!" because he appreciated that healing ministry moment and was inspired to minister to people that way, moving forward. After a few minutes, another waitress introduced herself and took our order. The first waitress eventually returned and gave a brief testimony. Sometimes, all that's needed is one sentence of encouragement, instruction, or prophecy to break a spell from someone's life.

As the saying goes, "How do you know if someone needs encouragement? They're breathing."

Everyone needs encouragement. Paul's reference in 2 Corinthians 5:20 relates that Jesus is no longer on Earth, so we are His representatives. Let's make ourselves available and willing to share words that shift someone's belief from an evil spell's lies to the gospel's truth. The Holy Spirit will use us to bring inspiration and solutions to those who are suffering. The joy they experience as a result is reward enough when they give God all the glory for the broken spells and curses in their lives.

After attending a pastor's church service near Columbia, SC, I went out to eat with members of the congregation. This time, the person I ministered to wasn't a food industry worker, but a United States Olympian who had been a guest at the church that morning. God gave me a Word of Knowledge for her—a spiritual gift I am often given by the Holy Spirit that allows me to speak insight into another person's life, often without prior knowledge of their situation.

As is my custom, I asked the pastor if I could share what God had revealed to me. He said, "Sure!" I turned to her and said, "All God told me to tell you is that it's not your fault." She immediately began to cry, exclaiming, "You don't know! You just don't know! You just answered a prayer I asked God last night!" I was sincerely humbled that God would use me; the woman even called me her angel for delivering that message. Though she knew I wasn't actually an angel, I was honored to serve as a messenger of God's love, which shifts our belief from confusion to the truth that brings clarity.

I also recall two young women facing crucial certification exams that would determine their professional advancement. The overwhelming fear and anxiety nearly crushed both. They felt as if these tests would defeat them. Each was under a heavy spell of doubt, convincingly believing they might fail. They appeared as though the weight of these exams had paralyzed them, stripping them of their confidence. Their fear was noticeable, and the thought of not succeeding nearly broke their hearts.

In both cases, the Holy Spirit gave me words to break the spell of defeat that had taken hold of them. I said, "Don't let the test intimidate you. The test is just trying to see what you know." This simple truth began to shift their perspective, lifting the oppressive weight they had carried.

Years later, the Holy Spirit added to the previous revelation when the second young woman came to me, trapped in the same spiral of fear about her exam. I told her what I said to the first, and then added, "God wants you to pass the test, not just scrape by with the minimum score. Just as a vehicle passes a store on its journey, you are to pass this test and continue toward the future God has for you." Tests are simply moments on our paths, not the end of the road.

I encourage you today to stop merely taking the test of life that you're facing and instead pass it because your life doesn't end at this test. Pass this test and move forward to be certified, licensed, and approved for what God has already prepared for you to accomplish. The spell of doubt may plague you, with you thinking, "I don't believe I'm ready to pass this test." But let me remind you—God equips you for every challenge He places before you. You are more than ready, and as you pass this test, you step into the greater purpose God has waiting for you. The test is not the end; it's a doorway to the next level of what He has called you to do.

I once encountered a young man I knew while he was working at Walmart. I knew him through his father, a well-respected pastor in our city. I told him he would be a preacher, and his reaction was immediate—his face twisted in disgust. I don't know what story or spell he believed about his life that made him feel so upset by my words. After he responded with a profanity-laced expletive and walked away, I stood shocked by what had just occurred. Today, he has a beautiful family and has been the senior pastor of a church for several years. We've since laughed multiple times about that moment at Walmart.

I believe you have this book because God wants to use you to break the spells and curses gripping someone else. Do you see how simple it was for me to speak just a few words that helped break the spells off those young women and the young man? You can do the same. The good spell, the powerful story of the gospel of Jesus Christ, is still active and working through men, women, boys, and girls worldwide. By allowing the Holy Spirit to inspire our words, we can speak living words to transform condemning beliefs into verified God-ordained truths that bring freedom, healing, and a renewed trust in God's plan for the lives we encounter daily.

CHAPTER 5:

PRACTICAL STEPS TO OVERCOMING BONDAGE

Lisa's Battle with Fear

Lisa's heart pounded as she scrolled through the news headlines on her phone. Each story screamed of impending doom—economic collapse, political unrest, natural disasters, and global pandemics. A wave of nausea washed over her as a familiar tightness gripped her chest.

She glanced at her husband, David, who sat across the room peacefully reading a book. How could he remain so calm? Didn't he see what was happening in the world? Didn't he feel the same impending dread that threatened to consume her?

"David," she called out, her voice trembling, "Did you see this article about the new virus? It's supposed to be even worse than the last one!"

David looked up from his book, a mix of concern and gentle amusement crossing his face. "Lisa, honey, you must take a break from the news. You're letting these stories get to you again."

"But it's real! These things are happening!" she protested, her anxiety rising.

David sighed, setting his book aside. "I know, but we can't live in fear, Lisa. We have to trust God."

Though Lisa knew he was right, her mind continued racing with worst-case scenarios, each one more terrifying than the last. She felt as if a dark cloud had settled over her, threatening to steal her joy and peace.

We must remain vigilant as news media, social media, and other outlets often cast spells on us without our consent or awareness. Instead of fearing imagined or projected outcomes, we must rely on God's Word and pray about the current events unfolding in our world.

Jenna's Struggle with Comparison

Miles away, Jenna scrolled through her Instagram feed, battling her feelings of inadequacy. Each image presented a carefully curated snapshot of perfection—smiling faces, exotic vacations, designer clothes, and impeccably decorated homes. A familiar pang of envy tightened her chest.

Why didn't her life look like that? Her job felt mundane, her apartment cramped, and her social life practically nonexistent. Everyone else seemed to be living the dream, while she felt stuck in a rut.

She caught her reflection on the phone's screen, her face suddenly appearing far from glamorous. A wave of self-doubt surged over her.

"I'm not good enough," she thought, the familiar lie echoing in her mind. "I'll never be as successful, beautiful, or happy as they are."

The phone slipped from her hand, landing face down on the couch. Jenna buried her head in her hands, overwhelmed by despair.

As she sat there, the Holy Spirit reminded her of Psalm 139:14 KJV, "I will praise thee; for I am fearfully and wonderfully made: marvellous are thy works; and that my soul knoweth right well." Slowly, Jenna began to realize that her worth didn't depend on how she measured up to others but on the truth that God uniquely crafted her. With each reminder of this verse, the grip of comparison began to loosen, and Jenna felt a new sense of peace about her journey.

Mark's Battle with Past Mistakes

Across town, Mark wrestled with the heavy burden of his past mistakes. Years ago, he had made choices that deeply hurt his family, damaged his reputation, and left him feeling broken and unworthy.

Although Mark had asked God for forgiveness and knew in his mind that God had forgiven his errors, the memories of his past still haunted him. They whispered accusations, robbing him of joy and peace.

"You're a failure," the inner voice hissed. "You don't deserve a second chance. You'll never escape what you've done."

Mark closed his eyes, desperately trying to shut out the message, but the accusation persisted, weaving a web of guilt and shame that threatened to suffocate him.

At that moment, the Holy Spirit brought to his mind 2 Corinthians 5:17 KJV, "Therefore if any man be in Christ, he is a new creature: old things are passed away; behold, all things are become new." As Mark meditated on this truth, he realized that his identity wasn't tied to his past but was anchored in Christ's redemption. The spell-ridden wall of shame started to weaken as he was able to break through, and a strong sense of freedom welled up in him, reminding him that God had already given him a fresh start.

Recognizing the Battle

These stories, though fictional, reveal the very real spiritual battles raging within the hearts of believers, whether in your own experience or the lives of those around you. While each may face unique challenges, the difficulties all share a common thread: the pervasive influence of negative thoughts and deeply ingrained beliefs that can hold us captive in a spell. The relentless enemy seeks to exploit our vulnerabilities, using deception and untruths to weave narratives of fear, inadequacy, and condemnation.

Scripture reminds us, "For we wrestle not against flesh and blood, but against principalities, against powers, against the rulers of the darkness of this world, against spiritual wickedness in high places" (Ephesians 6:12 KJV). We should not confine spiritual warfare to biblical times; it's an ongoing reality for every believer.

> *Be sober, be vigilant; because your adversary the devil, as a roaring lion, walketh about, seeking whom he may devour:*
>
> 1 Peter 5:8 KJV

The Battlefield of Our Thoughts

The fiercest spiritual battles often occur in the mind, which Scripture frequently equates with the heart. Unlike the physical brain, the mind operates in the spiritual realm. The mind is often called the seat of our thoughts, emotions, and beliefs. The enemy, cunning and deceptive, understands the power of our minds to influence us with thoughts to shape our reality. Proverbs 23:7 relates that our lives are the sum of our hearts' thoughts. If satan can control our thoughts, he can influence our actions, relationships, and ultimately, our destiny.

I remember working for a Toyota/Mazda dealership, selling new and used vehicles. I did so well that I even outsold the used car sales manager. One seemingly ordinary day, one of my supervisors approached me and informed me that they had to terminate my employment due to a lack of customers coming onto the lot. "We don't have enough sales to go around," he said apologetically. It was the old "last hired, first fired" situation.

Being fired surprised me, and I felt discouraged. Worrisome thoughts flooded my mind regarding finding suitable employment. What if I couldn't find another job? How would I support myself? Would I ever succeed again? These anxious thoughts threatened to overwhelm me as the enemy whispered lies meant to choke out God's truth.

Maynard, a kind gentleman who worked in the body shop department, encouraged me one day outside the showroom. He said, "You don't belong here. God has more for you because you have more to do for Him. Just watch what happens when you leave this place—you'll see." His words inspired me, and in just a few moments, they began to dispel the spell of fear I had been under. He was right. After I left that job, God's power utterly broke the spell because I believed the words He gave Maynard for me. God blessed me and placed me in supervisory roles and other positions where I earned more money than ever.

How to Be Free from Unforgiveness

The human heart, fragile and susceptible to pain, can easily fall into the enemy's traps when wounded by betrayal, injustice, or unmet expectations. Like a seed sown in fertile soil, an offense can quickly take root, growing into bitterness and resentment. We might find ourselves clinging to past hurts, replaying offenses, and nursing wounds that refuse to heal. These responses, while understandable, can have devastating consequences for our spiritual well-being by transforming us into susceptible hosts for a harsh spell to affect. Scripture warns us about the danger of allowing bitterness to fester:

> *Looking diligently lest any man fail of the grace of God; lest any root of bitterness springing up trouble you, and thereby many be defiled;*
>
> Hebrews 12:15 KJV

The enemy often disguises his lies as legitimate grievances by whispering thoughts of justifications for our pain. We might even believe God Himself condones our bitterness, mistaking the voice of offense for the voice of the Holy Spirit. Yet, God's Word teaches that a human's wrath does not produce God's righteousness (James 1:20). When we allow an offense to dominate our thoughts and emotions, we elevate that wound to a position of authority in our lives, ultimately and effectively making it an idol.

Just as a poisonous plant can contaminate a garden, spreading toxins and choking out life, unforgiveness poisons our souls, stunts our spiritual growth, and corrodes our relationships. When we harbor unforgiveness, that grudge takes root in our hearts, growing into bitter irritation and animosity. This unrelenting spite prevents us from experiencing God's peace and joy and creates barriers between us and others, making forming genuine connections or maintaining healthy relationships complicated.

Over time, unforgiveness isolates us, leaving us trapped in a prison of our own making, unable to move forward and truly live the abundant life God has planned for us. The Gospel of Jesus Christ has been made available to us through God's loving grace. We can take the following steps to be free from not forgiving those who have apologized for their offenses against us.

1. **Acknowledge the Hurt:** Begin by honestly acknowledging the pain you've experienced. Denying or ignoring the hurt only allows unforgiveness to grow deeper roots. Instead, bring your pain before God, who understands your suffering and offers healing (Psalm 34:18).

2. **Pray for God's Help:** True forgiveness is often beyond our human ability, but with God's help, a genuine forgiving of others becomes possible. Ask the Holy Spirit to help you release the offense and heal your heart toward the person who wronged you (Matthew 5:44). Pray

for the strength to let go of the animosity and to see the offender through God's eyes.

3. **Choose to Forgive:** Forgiveness is a decision, not a feeling. We may not feel like forgiving. Even after forgiving our offenders, there's no promise we'll feel any better. Still, when we choose to obey Jesus's command to forgive the repentant (Luke 17:3-4), we invite His power to work in our inmost parts (hearts, souls, and spirits). Remember that forgiveness doesn't mean excusing or justifying the wrongdoing, but releasing the offender from any debt they owe you. Also, reflect on a point I made earlier: forgiveness frees us from wondering how our grudges affect the ones we refuse to forgive—a needless, bothersome burden we place on ourselves.

4. **Replace Bitterness with God's Word:** Counteract the negative thoughts and emotions associated with unforgiveness by immersing yourself in God's Word. Meditate on scriptures that speak of God's forgiveness, love, and grace, allowing His truth to replace the lies that unforgiveness tells you (Ephesians 4:31-32).

5. **Release the Offender to God:** Entrust the person who hurt you to God's justice and mercy. Romans 12:19 reminds us that vengeance belongs to God, not us. By releasing the offender into God's hands, you free yourself from the burden of carrying the offense and allow God to handle the situation according to His perfect wisdom.

6. **Seek Reconciliation (if possible):** While reconciliation may not always be feasible or safe, be open to it if the opportunity arises. Reconciliation doesn't mean you must restore the relationship to its former state; it does mean allowing God's grace to restore any brokenness so we can move forward in peace (Romans 12:18).

7. **Remember Christ's Forgiveness:** Always be mindful that Jesus forgave us when we didn't deserve it. His willingness to forgive our sins should inspire us to extend that same grace to others (Ephesians 4:32). When you understand the depth of Christ's love and forgiveness, you'll find it easier to release others from their offenses. And maybe we're not right in being angry. Perhaps the offense is trivial, and we're just being picky. When we say "Oh, never mind. I refuse to let this situation consume any more of my peace…" sometimes the anger resolves.

Following these steps, we can break free from unforgiveness and open ourselves to God's healing, peace, and blessings. Let's begin to experience the freedom of letting go and allowing God's love to flow through us and transform our hearts.

Unlearning Negative Patterns

Negative thought patterns can be like quicksand—the more we struggle, the deeper we sink. Replaying past hurts or dwelling on worst-case scenarios can pull us into fear, anxiety, and despair. I shared that I had many times when I constantly dwelt on negative thoughts, trapped in a cycle of stress and worry. I felt like a spell had been cast over my mind, keeping me stuck.

The enemy seeks to establish strongholds in our minds through repetitive negative thoughts. If left unchecked, these thought patterns become deeply ingrained, shaping our perceptions and influencing our emotions and responses to life's challenges.

The Apostle James offers a powerful strategy for combating negative patterns: "Let every man be quick to hear, slow to speak, slow to take offense and to get angry" (James 1:19 AMPC). By intentionally pausing, we create space to interrupt the cycle of negative thoughts and invite the Holy Spirit to guide our actions. This verse is a practical blueprint for breaking the cycle of destructive thoughts and behaviors that spells often use to trap us. Listening quickly and intently to what is said and then waiting until the prompting of the Holy Spirit opens our hearts to understand others and the situations around us is better than reacting impulsively. This approach allows us to hear God's voice more clearly, even in challenging circumstances.

Remembering that by pausing before speaking, we can filter our words through the lens of wisdom and grace, we can avoid rash responses that could escalate conflict or reinforce negative beliefs. This pause in speech helps us guard our tongues from speaking curses, doubt, or negativity over ourselves and others.

Being slow to take offense and anger allows us to assess situations more objectively, freeing us from the emotional traps the enemy often sets. When problems arise, taking a break at the onset will enable us to invite the Holy Spirit to intervene, guiding our thoughts and actions with His peace, patience, and understanding. This intentional pause becomes a moment of divine intervention, in which God's truth can replace lies, and His love can diffuse anger, malice, or fear. Though faithfully practicing this discipline is not easy in each circumstance, when executed, we create an environment where the Holy Spirit can actively shape our responses and transform our minds in alignment with God's will.

Waging War on the Enemy's Lies

The Christian life demands active engagement in spiritual warfare. The enemy employs deception, lies, temptations, and accusations to weaken our resolve. But, as Paul reminds us, even though we are in the flesh, we do not wage war according to our flesh (2 Corinthians 10:3). We fight our spiritual battles with the divine power God provides, not with our mere physical strength.

God equips us with spiritual armor to withstand the enemy's assaults (Ephesians 6:11). This armor includes the belt of truth to combat deception, the breastplate of righteousness to protect our hearts, and the shield of faith to extinguish fiery darts of doubt. The helmet of salvation guards our minds, while the sword of the Spirit—the Word of God—is our offensive weapon against lies and other ungodly words sent against us, including spells and curses. As we consciously wear this armor and wield such weapons, we stand firm against the enemy, empowered to break free from his attacks and walk in victory.

None of the responses at our disposal is more potent than the sword of the Spirit—the Word of God (Ephesians 6:17 AMPC). The Psalmist declared, "I have hidden Your word in my heart, that I might not sin against You." (Psalm 119:11 KJV). Internalizing Scripture enables us to counter the enemy's lies, dismantle strongholds, and stand firm in faith.

Our New Reality

Making ourselves wholly available to God begins as we apply these spiritual disciplines—renewing our minds, rejecting lies, embracing forgiveness, and engaging in spiritual warfare. The strongholds that once held us captive crumble, and the chains of bondage break. As we obey God's way of how our lives are designed to live, the enemy's attempts to instill fear and doubt lose their power, and forgiveness becomes a defining characteristic of our softened hearts.

This journey of personal reinvention is a lifelong pursuit resulting from a continuous process of yielding to the Holy Spirit's work. As we fix our gaze on Christ, immerse ourselves in His Word, and seek His guidance, we experience the abundant life He offers—free from the enemy's ensnaring spells.

Johnathan's Story

This kind of transformation isn't theoretical—it's real, tangible, and happening in the lives of people just like you. At our church, I've witnessed firsthand how God's power can completely reshape a person's life when they're ready to surrender, obey, and walk in the truth. One such testimony is from Jonathan, affectionately known as "Chop." He has attended the church I pastor for a year. His life was bound by addiction for decades—until the Holy Spirit broke through and brought him into a new reality. His following testimony glorifies God most uniquely.

First and foremost, I thank God for His extraordinary patience and mercy, for repeatedly sparing my life through countless trials. Today, I'm sharing my story only because God graciously granted me multiple second chances, pulling me time after time from the brink of destruction caused by life-consuming addictions.

My most devastating battle was with opioids. When fentanyl first appeared in my town, the drug was disguised as a common pharmaceutical painkiller. What I expected to be an ordinary, busy workday almost became my last when I unknowingly overdosed on what I believed was Percocet, only to discover later that the pills contained a dangerously high dose of fentanyl. What could have easily turned me into another tragic statistic instead became a moment of divine intervention—God chose otherwise. His hand reached down in mercy and saved me.

My survival is also due to the steadfast prayers of my grandmother, a devout Christian woman whose faithfulness continues to echo in my life. After surviving that terrifying ordeal, I remember earnestly thanking God for His mercy. In that sacred moment, He clearly spoke to my heart, reminding me that my life still had purpose. He assured me that He never demanded perfection from my life to receive His loving patience. Instead, He wanted me to grow to live a life of obedience—urging me to boldly share what He had done in my life.

Miraculously, I was completely unharmed and back at work the next day—a testament to God's supernatural care. After a few months of attending Shane Wall's church, hearing the powerful messages and teachings inspired by the Holy Spirit, my heart experienced a profound awakening. I realized that while I had attended church for decades and knew much about Jesus, I didn't honestly know Him intimately. Like the expert in the law from Luke chapter 10, my heart sincerely asked the Holy Spirit, "What must I do to inherit eternal life?"

Reflecting upon my journey, I have come to realize that many people I've known did not get a second chance like I did. This humbling truth echoes in the words of an old Southern Baptist hymn my grandmother frequently sang:

"Trust and obey, for there's no other way to be happy in Jesus, but to trust and obey."

I'm learning that fulfilling God's purpose requires trusting Him wholeheartedly and obeying without hesitation. As I dive deeper into

Scripture and daily communion with God, He continues challenging me to become a better man—a devoted husband, nurturing father, loyal friend, compassionate boss, and supportive coworker.

One of Shane Wall's sermons profoundly impacted me, addressing the kind of fruit we produce in our lives—either fleshly or by the Holy Spirit. Examining myself, I realized that daily sins had imprisoned me, particularly a crippling marijuana habit I'd relied on for 30 long years. I doubted freedom from this bondage was even possible, but when I truly placed God first, He shattered those chains that bound me.

God gradually revealed my true purpose through reading His Word, praying earnestly, and interceding for others. He showed me the undeniable truth that my salvation is rooted entirely in His boundless mercy—I could never earn Heaven on my own merits. Yet, this is possible through faithful and essential obedience to His Word. Jesus graciously expects and lovingly requires my submission, guiding me daily into a life pleasing to Him. This disciplined life in Christ is why my freedom from marijuana is evidence of God's power to deliver us from spells that secretly control our choices for coping mechanisms. The following verses became a powerful beacon for me:

> 6 Let no man deceive you with vain words: for because of these things cometh the wrath of God upon the children of disobedience.
> 7 Be not ye therefore partakers with them.
> 8 For ye were sometimes darkness, but now are ye light in the Lord: walk as children of light:
> 9 (For the fruit of the Spirit is in all goodness and righteousness and truth;)
>
> Ephesians 5:6-9 KJV

With each passing hour, I understand more deeply that my time on earth is shortening, compelling me to daily learn and embrace what pleases God. Thank You, God, for Your relentless mercy and the gift of redemption. Truly, through Christ, I am free.

Johnathan's testimony reminds me of the words of Jesus in Matthew:

You, therefore, must be perfect [growing into complete maturity of godliness in mind and character, having reached the proper height of virtue and integrity], as your heavenly Father is perfect.

Matthew 5:48 AMPC

Jonathan's story illustrates what Jesus meant by calling us to perfection—growing continually in spiritual maturity, character, and virtue, reflecting our Heavenly Father. The command to be perfect isn't a harsh demand but an empowering invitation. It's God's loving call for us to mature daily, progressively shedding old habits and ungodly spells that once trapped us. Jonathan's life demonstrates that the path to true freedom lies in complete dependence upon God, embracing His merciful grace, and faithfully following His guidance. Like Jonathan, we can confidently walk toward perfection, knowing that as we trust and obey, our lives become vibrant testimonies of God's transforming power.

CHAPTER 6:

WALKING IN FREEDOM

Understanding Freedom

In the Bible, the Apostle Paul warned us that in the last days, oppressive and troublesome times would come, marked by a breakdown in moral values and devotion to God. Scripture reveals that people will become self-centered, lovers of money, and arrogant, and will prioritize personal pleasure over loving God:

> *1 This know also, that in the last days perilous times shall come.*
> *2 For men shall be lovers of their own selves, covetous, boasters, proud, blasphemers, disobedient to parents, unthankful, unholy,*
> *3 Without natural affection, trucebreakers, false accusers, incontinent, fierce, despisers of those that are good,*
> *4 Traitors, heady, highminded, lovers of pleasures more than lovers of God;*
>
> 2 Timothy 3:1-4 KJV

Too often, many of us are uninterested in faithfully serving God. Serving Him doesn't feel like a genuine desire, but more like an obligation that inconveniences how we'd rather conduct our lives. Our minds drift away from our God-ordained purpose and remain fixated on worldly pursuits that distract us from His expressed intent for our lives. We often experience weariness and direct the blame toward the expectation of faithful devotion to the Lord. While trying to manage challenging circumstances, an undisturbed focus on God usually leads to boredom or disinterest, particularly when we crave and seek immediate comfort by rushing to find pleasure for ourselves outside of God's will and provision.

The enemy cunningly offers substitutes for God—pleasures and distractions that falsely promise freedom. These alternatives deceive people into thinking they can find more liberties apart from God. Many don't want to live this way, but the lure and addiction to worldly pleasures make breaking away complicated.

We know the feeling of relaxing at home when Sunday service, Bible Study, a small group, or prayer service occurs. So, for many, choosing to do whatever they want seems like true freedom. But God wants to free us from everything that makes us feel freer than being with Him. Being unshackled begins in our minds, and understanding that can break the chains that bind us to false beliefs about independence.

Jesus said, "If ye continue in my word, then are ye my disciples indeed; And ye shall know the truth, and the truth shall make you free." (John 8:31-32 KJV)

Confusion and misguided efforts result when we act on what we don't fully understand. Also, if we operate in opposition to God's will, our deeds become sinful practices. Knowing the truth but refusing to live by it leads to spiritual bondage. Scripture warns us:

So any person who knows what is right to do but does not do it, to him it is sin.

+++James 4:17 AMPC+++

When Jesus addressed the Jews who claimed to have never been enslaved, He made it clear that sin itself is a form of slavery:

Whosoever committeth sin is the servant of sin.

+++John 8:34 KJV+++

In ancient Israelite culture, enslaved people were bound to their enslavers and could not secure their own emancipation. Only through the master's decision or the authority of his son could the enslaved be released from bondage. Jesus used this cultural understanding to explain a profound spiritual truth.

Just as those in physical slavery in Israel relied on the master or his son for delivery from bondage, we, spiritually enslaved to sin, are entirely dependent on Jesus, the Son of God, to liberate us. He has the authority to declare undeniable freedom for all who give their lives to Him:

If the Son therefore shall make you free, ye shall be free indeed.

John 8:36 KJV

True freedom comes only through Christ, Who breaks the chains of sin that enslave us and grants us release from the spells and curses that control our lives. When Jesus declares that those He sets free are "free indeed," He points to a more intense liberation—spiritual freedom from the power and consequences of sin. Freedom from feeling and believing we're powerless can only be experienced when we live by the gospel of Christ—the power of God that will last until Jesus returns.

The Apostle Paul further emphasizes that our obedience determines our spiritual allegiance and whether we're free through Christ or bound by devils. If we choose sin, which leads to death, or obedience to God, which leads to righteousness, the decision reflects who truly rules over us:

Do you not know that if you continually surrender yourselves to anyone to do his will, you are the slaves of him whom you obey, whether that be to sin, which leads to death, or to obedience which leads to righteousness?

Romans 6:16 AMPC

But thanks to God, we have been set free from sin and are now called servants of righteousness. A profound difference exists between being bound to serve and being free to serve. As servants of righteousness, we are not forced into submission; we willingly serve because we are free in Christ.

Sin remains the only act that permits the enemy to bind us. Sin comes from the devil, and "He that committeth sin is of the devil" (1 John 3:8 KJV). But thanks to Christ, the very reason He came into the world was to destroy the works of the devil and release us from sin's grip.

To remain in the freedom Christ has given us, we must stand firm:

> *Stand fast therefore in the liberty wherewith Christ hath made us free, and be not entangled again with the yoke of bondage.*
>
> Galatians 5:1 KJV

Remaining free requires diligence and the constant choice to walk in obedience, rejecting the lure that would draw us back into bondage. Absolute freedom is discovered in a life aligned with God's truth, through faithfully walking with Him daily.

Real-life circumstances provide tangible examples of what wholeheartedly understanding and attaining freedom means.

Trying to be Free

The syringe glistened under the dim light of the streetlamp, beckoning Marvin with its deceptive promise of temporary escape. He knew he shouldn't give in, but the craving gnawed at him, demanding satisfaction.

As he removed his backpack and placed it on the old wooden bench in the alley, his eyes caught sight of the worn Bible tucked in the corner of his bag—a gift from his mother, a fading reminder of the faith he'd abandoned years before. Guilt twisted in his gut, leaving a bitter taste in his mouth.

"I know, God, but just once more for a real-good-feel-good…" Marvin mumbled, his voice hoarse, his hand trembling as he reached for the syringe. "…then I'll get clean. I promise." The addiction, a vicious spell, had taken root in Marvin's being, whispering seductive promises of relief while tightening its grip on his soul. But this time, something shifted. The repeated lie—that the exhilarating sensation from the drug would satisfy him—suddenly tasted stale, like biting into a piece of fruit that looked ripe but was rotten to the core.

Anger flared up as he stared at the syringe, realizing for the first time that heroin's grip was weakening. Even though this was his last needle—his last chance for a quick high—he shocked himself by hurling it onto the pavement and stepping on it, shattering it into pieces. The heroin mixture slowly oozed into the street's drain. "This isn't my last time using this mess…" Marvin muttered with a gentle sob, watching it disappear. "The last time I shot heroin, three days ago, was the last time I'll ever do it!"

Marvin's story, a reflection of many, reveals the insidious nature of spells—often disguised as solutions, but leading only to deeper bondage. The weight of sin—whether manifested in harmful habits, toxic patterns, or the consequences of past mistakes—can feel like an inescapable burden, shackles that bind us. Fear, shame, or resentment grips our hearts, whispering lies that convince us freedom is out of reach. But the truth is, freedom results from the life-giving choices we make.

The human experience, marred by our fallen nature, often traps us in bondage to destructive desires, the enemy's deceptions, and the consequences of our actions. Yet, amid the uncertainty of our lives, the gospel of Jesus Christ shines as a beacon of truth, offering a path to genuine freedom. The reality of the gospel is a powerful force, ready and able to shatter the shackles of sin, silence the enemy's lies, and lead us into the glorious liberty of a life transformed by God's grace.

A Desperate Cry for Freedom

Let's explore what walking in the freedom Christ has purchased for us through His sacrifice means. We'll examine the crucial role of obedience and recognize the effects that mark a resurrected life of strength and encouragement on our journey to liberation.

Before we proceed, let's remember this: the gospel is not merely a transaction for eternal salvation; it is a continuous force of betterment in our lives. It is a life-giving force that reshapes us from the inside out, tearing down strongholds, renewing our minds, and empowering us to walk in the fullness of Christ's freedom. Authentic freedom isn't passive, but an active pursuit—a daily surrender to the truth of God's Word and a commitment to walking in obedience to the way, the truth, and the life revealed through Jesus Christ.

Jesus said to him, I am the Way and the Truth and the Life; no one comes to the Father except by (through) Me.

John 14:6 AMPC

Recall the testimony of my childhood asthma attack and the question posed by the Holy Spirit: "Are you ready to get serious yet?" This encounter, profound in its simplicity, revealed an eternal truth: walking in obedience to Christ is not merely a matter of preference or convenience; it is the sole path to authentic and lasting freedom that our hearts, souls, and human spirits crave.

Jesus Christ is not merely one path among many; He is the singular and exclusive path to salvation and a Father-to-child relationship with God. He is not simply a representation of truth; He is the embodiment of Truth itself. The life He offers is not an imitation of abundance; it is the essence of abundant life, characterized by purpose, joy, and an intimate bond with our Creator. To turn away from Christ is to reject the Way, to abandon Truth, and to forfeit the very Life for which we were created.

When I was a teenager, I developed a habit of selfishness that I both despised and indulged in. My desire to satisfy myself at the expense of others became overwhelming, especially as I witnessed the negative impact of my actions on those around me. Even something as simple as finishing an entire bag of my favorite snack before anyone else could ask me to share it with them became an unhealthy obsession. Though I repented each time, I repeatedly fell back into the same behavior, feeling trapped in a cycle of guilt and indulgence.

The conviction of my misbehavior grew unbearable as my selfish tendencies infiltrated other areas of my life, such as reducing prayer and Bible reading time to engage more with entertainment. Also, I would fail to do homework and chores satisfactorily to have free time to do whatever I please.

One night, in complete desperation, I pleaded with God to take my life while I slept. I made sure to repent again before that prayer, as I wanted the assurance of going to Heaven. The grip of selfishness felt so powerful that I genuinely believed I could never break free while still alive. When I woke up the following day, I was angry with God for not granting my request for death.

Realizing that God intended for me to live and confront my hidden sins, I chose to have an honest conversation with Him to understand why I couldn't shake this selfishness. During that conversation, God revealed that my selfishness stemmed from a lack of trust in His ability to provide for all my needs and desires. He lovingly fathered me through that moment, showing me that much of what I sought was outside His will and that He would provide all that was necessary and healthy for my life.

This divine revelation He shared illuminated my heart. I felt compelled to write a song based on that conversation, which I recorded in 2008, just months before my mother unexpectedly passed away. The CD was titled *Conversations with God*, and the song, inspired by my commitment to Him, was aptly named *Not in This Place Again*. Some of the lyrics I expressed are:

> *It was awkward taking my first steps*
> *I can run now, but still there are things to perfect*
> *I'm sorry. Please forgive me, Lord*
> *I've known better, and I should be much further up the road*
> *That's why I say*
> *Not in this place again will You find me*
> *Not in this place; if it wasn't for Your grace*
> *I'd be misplaced and left without a trace*
> *Not in this place (LORD); if it wasn't for Your grace*
> *I'd be erased and gone without a trace*
> *Not in this place again will You find me*

I sincerely asked God to forgive me, even though I'd previously requested forgiveness. I just wanted to be free from that spell of selfishness and the misery it caused me. God then freed me as I replaced selfishness with giving. Jesus said it's more blessed to give than to receive (Acts 20:35). I'm blessed because God gives me more than enough for myself so that I can freely share with others—a lesson I learned decades ago. Another valuable lesson I learned is that if God doesn't supply it, it's because I don't need it. I trust God to provide everything I need, and I must discipline myself to be satisfied with my gracious gifts from God. As Paul said,

> I know both how to be abased, and I know how to abound: every where and in all things I am instructed both to be full and to be hungry, both to abound and to suffer need.
>
> Philippians 4:12 KJV

The appeal of compromise, the temptation to blend the world's ways with the principles of the Kingdom, is a subtle snare that can easily entangle believers. We may find ourselves attempting to straddle two opposing realms, clinging to God's promises while indulging in patterns of thought and behavior contradicting His Word. Such compromise, though often rationalized as a harmless pursuit of a balanced life or a desire to avoid extremes, inevitably leads to spiritual inharmoniousness and a growing vulnerability to the enemy's deceptions.

Believing false doctrines that cater to our flesh instead of God's truth:

Amelia found solace in the warm embrace of the yoga studio, drawn to its messages of mindfulness, self-love, and inner peace. The gentle stretches and soothing meditations brought a sense of tranquility she'd never experienced before. But as the instructor spoke of tapping into her "inner divinity" and the "universal energy" connecting all things, a disquieting feeling began to stir in her heart. These teachings clashed with her deeply held Christian beliefs, yet the allure of peace and acceptance was strong.

As weeks turned into months, Amelia found herself questioning the strict doctrines of her faith as, to her, the Bible's words were harsh and judgmental compared to the inclusive spirituality of the yoga studio. She craved the freedom to explore a more personalized, less-restrictive path to God.

But this new path, paved with good intentions and a longing for inner tranquility, began to lead her away from the solid foundation of truth she once knew. Prayer felt ineffective, fear crept back into her life, and the God she once loved felt distant and impersonal.

One evening, as Amelia sat alone, she felt an overwhelming emptiness despite the moments of peace she experienced at the studio. She had a flash of realization that all the "inner divinity" she had been pursuing fell short of truly satisfying her soul. In desperation, she picked up her Bible, long forgotten on the shelf, and began to read. The words of Jesus in John 14:6 KJV echoed in her heart: "...I am the way, the truth, and the life: no man cometh unto the Father, but by me."

Tears streamed down her face as she realized how far she had strayed from the Truth. She fell to her knees, repenting and crying out to God for guidance. As she prayed, a deep sense of rest and clarity washed over her—far greater than anything she had experienced at the yoga studio.

Amelia rededicated her life to Christ at that moment, abandoning the false doctrines she had embraced. She returned to her church, surrounded herself with godly mentors, and began rebuilding her relationship with God on the solid foundation of His Word. No longer seeking an "inner divinity," Amelia found her true identity and purpose in Christ alone. The peace she now carried wasn't momentary; it was the eternal peace that surpasses all understanding, rooted in the presence of the Holy Spirit.

Amelia's journey reminds us that the allure of false teachings may be strong, but the truth of God's Word is mightier. God's Word is always waiting to lead us back into His loving embrace.

Chasing Dreams or God's Purpose?

The stage lights glared down on an empty microphone, the silence in the auditorium heavy with anticipation. Backstage, Ben paced nervously, his heart pounding in his chest. Five minutes until showtime, the headliner, his best friend and musical partner, Jake, was nowhere to be found.

"Where is he?" Ben's manager, Mark, barked into his phone, his voice laced with panic. "The crowd's becoming restless! This concert is sold out! What am I supposed to tell them?"

Ben slammed his fist against the wall, his frustration boiling over. "This is all my fault," he muttered, his voice filled with self-recrimination. He remembered the countless nights spent dreaming of musical stardom, the relentless pursuit of gigs, the compromises he'd agreed with to "make it big"—concessions that had strained his relationship with God and led Jake down a destructive path of addiction.

He'd ignored the warning signs, the whispers of reality, the gentle nudges to re-evaluate his priorities. He'd been so focused on his own ambition that he'd failed to see his friend's struggles and spiritual decline. Now, facing the empty stage, the silent microphone, and the impending disappointment of thousands of fans, Ben felt the question pierce his heart like a shard of glass: "Is this what God told me to do?"

After the disastrous concert night, Ben felt an overwhelming sense of failure and conviction. Sitting in the empty auditorium, he realized how far he had drifted from God's purpose in his pursuit of fame. In that stillness, he cried out to God, repenting for placing his ambitions above his calling, realizing that he wouldn't have even needed ambition if he'd just followed God's will for his life. Ben understood that God supports His will, not man's.

With a renewed sense of humility, Ben decided to step away from the music industry to seek God's direction. Over time, God restored his heart, and Ben began using his musical gifts to lead worship in his church again, prioritizing God's glory over his own. His story became a testimony of how surrendering our desires allows God to redirect our lives toward His perfect plan, bringing true fulfillment and joy.

Though the identities in these scenarios are protected, they illustrate real-life struggles that honest people have shared publicly. Whenever we attempt to modify God's truth to reflect our own desires, preferences, or circumstances, we inevitably stray from the path of actual freedom and find ourselves ensnared once again in the chains of bondage. Whether we embrace practices that cater to our fleshly appetites, prioritize our ambitions over God's calling, or allow the pain of past experiences to shape our beliefs about God's character, we are, in essence, rejecting the Lordship of Christ and choosing to live according to our flawed human wisdom.

But as the apostle Paul warned the Galatians, embracing false teachings or relying on our righteousness always leads us to deception and despair. If we don't receive God's story for our lives, whoever does believe that story will receive the miracle the story provides. Think about that—the exact breakthrough, healing, and deliverance you've been praying for might be given to someone else simply because they were willing to embrace the truth you rejected. Not that God is punishing us or withholding blessings, but rather that He honors faith and obedience. He longs to pour out His goodness on those aligned with His will and ready to receive. That's the good you too can be given when you walk the path God has set forth for you.

The Scriptures abound with promises of blessing for those who obey God's commands. Let us consider a few examples of these promises, which testify to God's faithfulness and desire to pour out His goodness upon those who align their lives with His will.

> *1 Blessed is the man that walketh not in the counsel of the ungodly, nor standeth in the way of sinners, nor sitteth in the seat of the scornful.*
> *2 But his delight is in the law of the Lord; and in his law doth he meditate day and night.*
> *3 And he shall be like a tree planted by the rivers of water, that bringeth forth his fruit in his season; his leaf also shall not wither; and whatsoever he doeth shall prosper.*
> Psalm 1:1-3 KJV

> *1 Blessed are the undefiled in the way, who walk in the law of the Lord.*
> *2 Blessed are they that keep his testimonies, and that seek him with the whole heart.*
> *3 They also do no iniquity: they walk in his ways.*
> Psalm 119:1-3 KJV

> *24 Therefore whosoever heareth these sayings of mine, and doeth them, I will liken him unto a wise man, which built his house upon a rock:*

> *25 And the rain descended, and the floods came, and the winds blew, and beat upon that house; and it fell not: for it was founded upon a rock.*
>
> *26 And every one that heareth these sayings of mine, and doeth them not, shall be likened unto a foolish man, which built his house upon the sand:*
>
> *27 And the rain descended, and the floods came, and the winds blew, and beat upon that house; and it fell: and great was the fall of it.*
>
> Matthew 7:24-27 KJV

Often in those challenging moments of testing, our faith is refined, and we experience the liberating power of obedience. When we align our will with God's will, even when it is costly or painful, we partner with Christ in His mission to demolish the enemy's works in our lives and the world around us. Walking in obedience, we actively break strongholds, dismantle curses, and set free the captives. What the enemy intended for our destruction becomes, through yielding to Christ, the catalyst for our release.

In its relentless pursuit of self-gratification and autonomy, the world system offers counterfeit versions of freedom, enticing us with the promise of unrestrained liberty to live as we please and believe as we choose. Yet, true freedom, the freedom that liberates us from the bondage of sin and the tyranny of our desires, is found only in faithful submission to God's will, truth, and the eternal life offered through Jesus Christ.

The Evidence of a Life Genuinely Freed

When we wholeheartedly embrace the path of obedience, surrendering our desires and aligning our lives with God's will, we experience spiritual freedom and a profound alteration that permeates every aspect of our being. This conversion is not a fleeting emotional experience or a temporary surge of motivation; it is a lasting change rooted in the power of the Holy Spirit and evidenced by His results in our lives.

How can you recognize the signs of this transformed life? By its unmistakable results:

> *22 But the fruit of the Spirit is love, joy, peace, longsuffering, gentleness, goodness, faith,*
> *23 Meekness, temperance: against such there is no law.*
>
> Galatians 5:22-23 KJV

David, a pastor from Ohio and a dear brother in Christ, called me one day, asking for prayer regarding his campaign for city mayor. As we prayed on the phone, the Holy Spirit revealed a vision to me, which I shared with him: "I see you becoming the mayor." We both rejoiced over this encouraging word!

After the election, David called back to inform me that he had lost. I could sense the hurt, disappointment, and confusion in his voice as he said, "You told me you saw me being the mayor." A spell-like wave of fear and shame started to overwhelm me, but I responded, "All I know is what the Holy Spirit showed me. My brother, it's not over until it's over." David reassured me that he wasn't blaming me or trying to make me feel bad, and we ended the conversation positively.

A few months later, David called with an incredible update: the elected mayor had been caught engaging in illegal activities and was subsequently removed from office. As a result, David was appointed as the new mayor. We celebrated together, and I reminded him of what I had said, "It's not over until it's over!" This experience demonstrated how the Holy Spirit cultivates patience and confidence, enabling us to wait on the Lord's perfect timing.

When we read the list of the fruit of the Holy Spirit, do we see that list of spiritual fruit as a heavy burden—a set of strict rules to obey? Or does it inspire us with a vision of the beautifully reshaped life awaiting us on the other side of obedience? These aren't just spiritual 'to-dos; they are narrative descriptions of who we're becoming in Christ!

Patience empowers us to lovingly parent a strong-willed child, even when their tantrums test our every nerve. Kindness compels us to serve the poor and marginalized, not out of obligation but from hearts overflowing with compassion. Gentleness guides us to restore, not condemn, a fallen brother or sister, offering grace instead of judgment. Self-control equips us to tame our tongue and temper, choosing words of life instead of letting anger or frustration dictate our speech. We can call this type of discipline: walking in the radiant freedom of the gospel life!

We must remain vigilant, however, recognizing that the enemy relentlessly opposes our pursuit of spiritual growth. He seeks to distract us from the path of righteousness and justice, tempting us to believe such endeavors are hopeless, burdensome, or the responsibility of others. Yet, as our understanding of genuine freedom deepens, we recognize that lasting passion marks a life transformed by the gospel of Jesus Christ. This life reflects God's heart for the oppressed, those who believe they're insignificant, and the lost. As ambassadors of Christ, we are called to be agents of His love and grace in a world that desperately needs both.

God's Plan Vs. My Plan

Though marked by moments of victory and breakthrough, walking in freedom has its challenges. Just as a child learning to walk will inevitably stumble and fall, we will also experience seasons of struggle, doubt, and weariness as we navigate the path of obedience and patience.

Intrinsically, I'm a planner and like to plan far in advance because I detest the last-minute rush to do anything. In my relationship with God, I've found that He's unwilling to give me a "heads up" about how particular situations will work out. If I can say it this way, faith seems to be a part of God's love language, which he receives and takes pleasure in.

> *But without faith it is impossible to please him: for he that cometh to God must believe that he is, and that he is a rewarder of them that diligently seek him.*
>
> Hebrews 11:6 KJV

Faith is pleasing to God. So, when I seek to know the outcome or timing of an event directly from Him, I often don't receive the information I desire. My plans stall, my inspiration wanes, and I am left relying on the information God chooses to reveal on a need-to-know basis.

I won't hide the fact that I've faced plenty of frustration, both in and out of prayer, often finding myself in a similar position to Jesus when He asked the Father for a different path than the one set before Him. Jesus, in His humanity, didn't want to endure the brutal crucifixion awaiting Him. Yet, He concluded His plea by surrendering to God's will, saying, "Father, not my will, but Thine be done." This prayer has become my frequent response when asking God for specifics that remain unknown to me.

God continues to remind me that He is the God of the unknown. As long as my faith rests in Him, that is all I need. I know He loves me unconditionally and has compassion for me, as expressed in Psalm 103:13 AMPC: "As a father loves and pities his children, so the Lord loves and pities those who fear Him [with reverence, worship, and awe]." I can find peace knowing He cares for me far better than I ever could.

Rather than letting a spell of anxiety control me when I don't receive the information I seek from God, I focus on His faithfulness in every other circumstance. I reflect on how He has always delighted me with how He works things out. I've learned that dwelling on the problem only adds stress. Within the past 24 hours, the Holy Spirit asked me, "How can you be anxious about anything God will do for you? Remember, He is Almighty and loves you more than anyone else ever could. What is there to fear when God Himself is in control? He's the King of the Universe, and He loves you!"

The freedom I experience these days brings peace, allowing me to rest knowing that the Lord's plans and timing are always perfect for me. While I still desire more details from Him, I can now wait calmly and patiently for His response, even if that response comes in the form of a miracle—one He performs without giving me any prior insight into what He will do.

CHAPTER 7:

OVERCOMING FEAR AND ANXIETY SPELLS

In today's world, fear and anxiety seem ever-present. From global pandemics to personal struggles, the weight of fear can feel overwhelming, casting a spell over our minds and hearts. However, Scripture is clear: *perfect love casts out fear* (1 John 4:18). Yet, for many believers, breaking free from fear and anxiety spells requires more than just knowing this truth. Long-awaited freedom requires practical instructions that produce undeniable results, and I look forward to how empowered you'll become to knowingly overcome fear and anxiety when this chapter ends.

Breaking the Spell of Fear

Fear is a powerful force, but it has no place in the life of a Christian believer. By wisely operating in God's love, the truth of His Word, and the power of faith, we can break free from the spells of fear and anxiety that seek to hold us captive. The enemy may try to cast fear over our lives, but we have the authority to reject it and walk in the freedom that Christ has purchased for us. We must comprehend how to believe, take authority, dismiss fear, and walk in Christ's freedom.

By putting on the armor of God, confessing His Word, and trusting in His love, we can overcome fear and live in the peace and confidence that comes from knowing we are His. Let's choose faith over fear, truth over lies, and freedom over bondage as we walk in the victory that is ours in Christ.

Breaking the Cycle of Fear

The Apostle John declares that perfect love expels fear. But what does this mean in practice? The love John refers to is not merely human love, limited and conditional. The divine love of God, complete and mature, reaches its fullest expression in us when we wholly trust Him. Fear cannot coexist with this love because fear is rooted in punishment, while God's love assures us of grace and protection.

What, then, is perfect love? The term *perfect* refers to something *brought to its end, finished, lacking nothing necessary for completeness*. Love encompasses *affection*, which is *fond attachment and devotion*. Once we know that God loves us, when our dependence on Him faithfully meets His abundant supply, we will never have room in our hearts for fear. Love's nature is to fill hearts to their full capacity. While that kind of fullness may seem unattainable, God's assurance that we can rely on His love stands firm because He has faithfully proven to countless souls that He keeps every promise.

God's perfect love is a powerful force of provision, rescue, sacrificial giving, and more. The following Bible stories illustrate how God's love meets people's needs in ways that surpass human capability or expectation.

John 3:16: A Love That Sacrifices

In John 3:16, we see the ultimate example of God's perfect love. God's love was so profound that He sacrificed His only Son, Jesus, to save humanity. This sacrificial love was given without condition, ensuring that anyone who believes in Jesus would not perish but have eternal life. God's love seeks to restore and redeem, reaching down to meet humanity at the point of its greatest need. His perfect love isn't bound by what we can offer in return; instead, it overflows with grace, offering salvation even when we are still lost.

The Red Sea: A Love That Rescues

When the Israelites were trapped between Pharaoh's army and the Red Sea, God's love intervened with a miraculous escape route. Exodus 14 describes how God split the sea, allowing His people to cross on dry land. This act of love wasn't just a rescue, but a demonstration of God's faithfulness and protection over His people, even when all seemed lost. Through this miracle,

God's perfect love showed that He would go to any lengths to secure the safety of those He loves, reinforcing their trust in Him and leading them forward, free from fear.

Feeding the 5,000: A Love That Provides

In Matthew 14:13-21, Jesus saw the crowd that had followed Him and felt compassion—recognizing that they were hungry and could faint along the way without nourishment if they were sent away. Moved by His love for them, He told His disciples not to send the crowd away and instead performed a miracle that multiplied five loaves and two fish to feed more than five thousand people. This story of God's perfect love demonstrates that He provides for spiritual and physical needs. Jesus' love is attentive, seeing the real needs of the people and moving to fill those needs abundantly.

He sees your needs. Your trust in Him and obedience to His commands will release miraculous provision, just as He did in the true accounts of Scripture for those who followed Him in faith.

These stories reveal God's perfect love in action—a love that sacrifices, rescues, and provides, so God's devotees do not need to fear because God lovingly cares for His own. Whether we need salvation, are in a crisis, or simply require provision, God's perfect love is powerful, steadfast, and sufficient to meet us right where we are—at the point of our need.

When perfect love enters our hearts, it casts out fear. But how does love drive fear away? It does so by virtue of its territorial right and sheer authority. The question isn't so much about how love casts out fear; instead, it's about how we bring love fully into our hearts. Once perfect love fills our hearts, fear is immediately expelled.

How, then, do we attain the love that drives out abiding fear, and in what way does love cast fear away?

To attain the kind of perfect love that expels abiding fear, one must first draw close to the source of that love: God Himself. This isn't a love rooted in mere sentiment or human affection; it's divine and transformative, a love that overflows from God into our hearts. The Apostle John tells us, "We love Him, because He first loved us." (1 John 4:19 AMPC). Recognizing God's love for us and accepting it allows us to grow in our love for Him, which is the beginning of perfect love.

When we truly believe in God's love for us and allow it to become the foundation of our lives, His love dismantles our fears. We no longer see challenges, difficulties, or even suffering as things to fear but as situations in which God will care for and protect us from, in all conditions, even to utter destruction, because He loves us. Trust in God builds, and fear loses its grip on our hearts as we faithfully dwell in His love.

Often, we may feel that the circumstances we endure are a form of punishment from God. However, if we've obeyed His Word, we can trust that our righteous Father would not punish us without cause. The Bible is filled with verses that remind us we will face challenges and hardships. Jesus never promised a life without problems, but He did encourage us:

> I have told you these things, so that in Me you may have [perfect] peace and confidence. In the world you have tribulation and trials and distress and frustration; but be of good cheer [take courage; be confident, certain, undaunted]! For I have overcome the world. [I have deprived it of power to harm you and have conquered it for you.]
> John 16:33 AMPC

God, our Father, loves us, and in this divine love is no room for the punishment or dread that fear suggests (1 John 4:18). Perfect love and fear cannot coexist, and when perfect love grows within us, abiding fear is forced out of its space in our hearts.

The love of God expels fear by displacing it. Fear is as darkness in a room; when invited into that place, the light of God's love forces the darkness to retreat because light and darkness cannot coexist. Similarly, as we deepen in God's love (1 John 4:16-21), His truth and presence shine within us, and fear must leave. This love assures us that, come what may, we are safe in God's hands. The more we understand and believe that God sincerely loves and perfectly cares for us, the more secure we feel, knowing that nothing—neither life nor death, angels nor demons, present nor future—can separate us from His love (Romans 8:38-39).

We must understand that love is a spirit, not a physical substance that can be stored in our pockets or purses. Likewise, fear is also a spirit. Since anything spiritual must be governed by the one who controls it, we look to God so His Spirit can guide us regarding how to love. The Holy Spirit also instructs us on how to grow in love until it reaches perfection (1 John 4:18). Conversely, fear is stirred by the influence of demons, who seek to instill various types of fear within us.

For God hath not given us the spirit of fear; but of power, and of love, and of a sound mind.

2 Timothy 1:7 KJV

This verse from 2 Timothy reminds us that fear is not from God; instead, He has given us power, love, and a sound mind, which drives out the effects of many spells. This divine combination equips us to reject fear and live in freedom. But what makes both love and fear such powerful influences in our lives?

While love and fear may share certain qualities, their effects on us are strikingly different:

Similarities
1. **They grow through attention**: The more we focus on either love or fear, the stronger their influence becomes in our lives.
2. **They shape our perspective**: Both love and fear can change how we see the world and others, influencing our decisions and actions.
3. **They're contagious**: Love and fear can be passed from one person to another, spreading through relationships and communities.
4. **They affect relationships**: Both love and fear profoundly impact how we relate to ourselves and others, often causing us to have confidence in or suspicion of our closest connections.
5. **They motivate actions**: Love and fear can prompt us to act, whether by helping someone out of compassion or avoiding an individual due to anxiety.

Differences

1. **Love brings peace; fear brings distress**: Love instills a sense of calm and security, while fear introduces worry, anxiety, and agitation.
2. **Love unites; fear divides**: Love fosters unity, connection, and harmony, while fear often isolates, creating distrust and separation.
3. **Love encourages vulnerability; fear promotes self-protection**. Love allows us to be open and vulnerable, whereas fear causes us to shield ourselves from unsubstantiated perceived threats.
4. **Love inspires courage; fear inspires avoidance**: Love motivates us to take risks and face challenges, while fear often compels us to avoid what seems uncertain.
5. **Love is selfless; fear is self-preserving**: Love moves us to focus on others' well-being, even at a personal cost. Fear, however, usually keeps us focused on self-preservation and avoiding discomfort.

These distinctions help us see how cultivating love, especially spiritually, can transform us in ways that fear cannot. Love enables freedom, whereas fear often results in a limiting mindset and actions, often under the control of a spell or curse. These distinctions also help us understand that as we allow perfect love to grow within us over time, it will naturally expel any fears that reside in us or attempt to take hold of us.

Unhealthy Fear of God

For many people, even Christians, the lingering fear is that God may allow them to face more hardship or an undesirable outcome lurking in the shadows. This uncertainty is similar to the discomfort of having a bird suddenly fly into your home. You may love watching birds from your kitchen window, enjoying them in their natural habitat, but you certainly don't want one flapping around in your living room. So, you do everything possible to guide it back outside, to cast it out of your home. With the same determination, love casts out fear from our hearts.

Make no mistake—love is not a fragile emotion that sways with our feelings or is quickly demolished by momentary desires. Love is a powerful force, so potent that it moved God to give His only begotten Son to die for a world often indifferent or disobedient to Him. True love wields a strength that destroys hatred, fear, depression, and many other spell-binding burdens, as Scripture proclaims that love is as strong as death:

> *Set me as a seal upon thine heart, as a seal upon thine arm: for love is strong as death; jealousy is cruel as the grave: the coals thereof are coals of fire, which hath a most vehement flame.*
>
> Song of Solomon 8:6 KJV

We know that death can affect us in devastating ways, leaving impacts that linger for decades. In the same way, love, being just as mighty, can empower, heal, and affect us on profound, lasting levels. When love is strong and enduring, it overcomes every fear, disarming the power of dread and anxiety. The strength of perfect love doesn't merely push fear to the background; perfect love drives fear out entirely, leaving no space for the negative emotion to take root, because perfect love fully occupies our inner being. This kind of love doesn't fade with changing emotions or circumstances; it is as constant as God, Who *is* Love.

As I neared the end of one problematic life battle, God told me more frequently that He loved me. When He shares His love for me, I often say, "You love me." I want Him to hear me affirming His words from my heart. Sometimes, I'll add, "You love me, Lord, and I love You, also!" I've often sensed that He increased His expressions to comfort and assure me that He was with me, caring for me perfectly through the trial—and He indeed was!

His love filled me with the confidence that, regardless of what I faced, being filled with His perfect love would carry me through to victory. Even when fear tried to approach me, the proverbial "No Vacancy" sign confronted the unpleasant feeling each time.

Since God is omniscient, all-knowing, and all-wise, He already knows how and when we will respond to Him with love. Yet, the Holy Spirit showed me that although God foresees our acts of love, praise, worship, or kindness, these don't move His heart until we express them. God cannot be intimate with His knowledge; He only experiences intimacy when we love Him through our thoughts, words, and actions.

When our love reaches full maturity, we'll know it because we'll believe, deep down, that God loves us and would never allow the enemy to succeed in ways that God Himself doesn't define as victory. Confidence in His love causes it to flow into and from our lives, transforming how we love others. We will find ourselves loving wholeheartedly, freely, genuinely, and naturally, reflecting God's unconditional love for all.

Have you ever heard someone say—and truly mean it—"I didn't care if I died because I was exhausted with life and wanted it to end"? They might even say that if someone had put a gun to their head, they'd welcome them to go through with it because of their fear-ridden life. I've been there myself. When I was exhausted and afraid, there was no space left in me for life. But when I became filled with God's love, I had no room for exhaustion and fear. I was amazed at the strength that emerged within me once I accepted God's love and allowed it to fill me.

I realized that exhaustion had masked the strength hidden deep within me. God's perfect love became a freeing force, with the Holy Spirit reassuring me, "You're fine. God has already worked everything out for you; you're simply waiting to reach that moment when the provision is ready." What a gracious and patient God and Father we have!

Recognizing the Spell of Fear

Fear doesn't emerge out of nowhere. It is often introduced through a story, a situation, or an experience that plants the seeds of anxiety in our hearts, which is a spell. For example, hearing bad news about the economy or a troubling medical diagnosis can trigger fear. But fear is not simply an emotion—it's a spiritual force that takes hold of us when we believe a story contrary to God's Word.

Again, 2 Timothy 1:7 teaches us that God has not given us a spirit of fear. If fear doesn't come from God, where does it come from? It comes from the enemy (satan and his demons), who seek to cast spells of fear over our lives. These spells often manifest through the media, social websites, adverse reports, or even the words of others who speak fear into our circumstances. When we entertain these stories and allow them to shape our beliefs, we open the door for fear to take root.

Fear is a master of disguise. It can morph into countless forms, whispering lies, distorting reality, and holding us captive in its shadowy grip. As we journey together through this chapter, let's unmask the many faces of fear, recognizing them as spells that need to be broken by the power of God's truth and love:

Common Stories and Faces of Fear:

- **Fear of Failure:** The presentation slides blurred before her eyes, her carefully rehearsed words dissolving into incoherent phrases. The boardroom, filled with the expectant faces of her colleagues and superiors, suddenly felt like a gladiatorial arena. She was the condemned, about to be devoured by the lions of judgment. Her carefully crafted career, her hard-won reputation, and her dreams of advancement all hung insecurely in the balance, threatened by the crippling spell of failure. Her mind raced, a torrent of what-ifs: "What if I forget everything I've prepared? What if they ask a question I can't answer? Not good enough… going to fail… everyone will know…" Her palms were slick with sweat; her breath caught in her throat, and her voice trembled as she began to speak. "I can't do this," she thought, a wave of nausea rising in her chest. "I'm going to fail."

- **Fear of the Future:** Another wedding invitation arrived in the mail, the delicate script mocking Emily with a reminder of her unfulfilled longing. At 35, she felt the pressure of societal expectations, the whispers that her time was running out, the dread that she'd be alone forever. "Will I ever find love?" She wondered, her heart a fragile whisper in the silence of her empty apartment. "Will I ever experience the joy of marriage and family?" The anxiety about the future, a persistent ache in her soul, cast a shadow of doubt over her dreams, making her question God's plan and her worthiness of being in a beautiful, lasting relationship. The clock's ticking seemed to amplify her anxieties, each passing day a stolen opportunity, a reminder of what she feared she might never have.

- **Fear from the Past:** The fireworks boomed, a clamor of celebratory thunder that ripped through the night, triggering a flood of felt memories he couldn't escape. John, a decorated war veteran, gripped the edge of the picnic table, his knuckles white, his jaw clenched tight. The backyard barbecue, a scene of laughter and carefree revelry, felt like a battlefield, with every sudden noise and flash of light presenting a potential threat. "Get a grip…," he thought, his mind replaying images he couldn't erase: the deafening roar of explosions, the blinding flash of gunfire, the screams of fallen comrades. In an effort to reassure himself, he pondered, "You're safe now. You're home." But the spell of yesterday's threat of death, woven from the trauma of war, held him captive, turning a simple gathering into a mental screen of flashbacks, a relentless reminder of the battles he still fought within.

- **Health Anxieties:** Every cough, every ache, every twinge sent a jolt of fear through Stuart's body. He scoured medical websites, his mind racing with worst-case scenarios. Each new symptom, a fresh thread in the tapestry of worry, was tightening its grip on his peace. He imagined tumors lurking in the shadows, his body betraying him, his life slipping away. The world, once a vibrant landscape of possibilities, now seemed a minefield of potential threats, each stalking him around the corner, waiting to strike. The doctor's words, "We need to run more tests," echoed in his mind, fueling the ceaseless rush of his worst fear, reshaping a simple checkup into a terrifying descent into the unknown.

- **Fear of Rejection:** The text message sat unread on her phone, a blinking cursor mocking her hesitation. She longed to pour out her heart, to confess her feelings to the man who had captured her affection, but the fear of rejection, a cold hand squeezing her chest, held her back. "What if he doesn't feel the same way?" She agonized, her mind conjuring up images of his laughter, dismissive words, and the crushing blow of his indifference. "What if he laughs at my vulnerability? What if my heart, already so fragile and exposed, is shattered beyond repair?" The spell of rejection, a guarded fortress, had enclosed her heart, trapping her in a prison of silence and unanswered love.

- **Fear of Success:** The promotion letter lay on his desk, the crisp paper symbolizing achievement and a gateway to a new level of responsibility. But instead of excitement, a sensation of nausea overwhelmed him. He stared at the words, each of which was a weight pressing down on his chest. He thought, "I am just not ready for this…," his mind swirling with doubts. Images of long hours, impossible deadlines, and the intimidating weight of expectations flooded his mind. What if he couldn't handle the pressure? What if he failed, letting down his colleagues and his family? What if his success was fleeting, a momentary flicker before the inevitable crash? The fear of success, an unexpected shadow, threatened to eclipse the joy of his accomplishment, tempting him to stay small and safe, hidden from the scrutiny and expectations that came with stepping into his potential.

- **Fear of the Unknown:** The moving boxes, stacked high in the living room, ridiculed her for their emptiness. The new city, a blank page in her life's story, filled her with excitement and dread. She stood in the center of the room, surrounded by the remnants of her old life, her heart a tangled knot of apprehension. Would she find friends in this new place? Would she be successful in her new job? Would she ever feel at home in this unfamiliar environment, so different from everything she'd ever experienced? The spell of the unexplored, a swirling vortex of uncertainty, pulled at her, threatening to unravel the threads of her courage and faith.

- **Fear of Making the Wrong Decision:** The two paths stretched before her, each a fork in the road, a doorway to a different future. One path promised familiarity and a sense of security. The other beckoned with adventure, risk, the potential for great reward, along with the possibility of failure and regret. Which one should she choose? The weight of the decision hung over her, a heavy burden that threatened to crush her spirit. What if she made the wrong choice? What if she took a step in the wrong direction and found herself lost and alone, unable to retrace her steps or undo the consequences of her decision? The fear of making the wrong decision, an incapacitating force, kept her frozen at the crossroads, unable to move forward, trapped in the agony of indecision.

Do these scenarios seem far-fetched? Believe it or not, they are just a glimpse into truthful experiences people face worldwide, and many real-life stories of parishioners I know have been far more intense. You likely have serious, accurate accounts of fears you've faced, perhaps even more drastic than those shared here. Fear often strikes when "bad things" happen and when we encounter unexpected "good things."

When we experience pleasantries repeatedly, we may fear that trouble is lurking around the corner. When I was a little boy, some middle-aged and elderly folks would say, "Things are going very well right now, so something bad must be about to happen." That belief isn't just superstition or a protective mindset—it's a spell. The moment fear begins rewriting the narrative of blessings, twisting peace into anxiety, we're no longer operating in faith—we're under the influence of a spiritual distortion designed to distract us from trusting God.

Most, if not all, of these examples and mindsets fall under Fears of the Unknown. As I shared in an earlier account, God, our Heavenly Father, is the God of the Unknown. He sees what we cannot, knowing the end from the beginning. While fear feeds on uncertainty, God's perfect love assures us that His plans for us are inherently good, even when the details remain unseen. This assurance doesn't promise a life without unknowns or even supposed "dips," but it does mean we can trust God completely, despite the shadows of unpredictability. By His love, He guides us through every mystery we encounter.

As believers, God called us to live, accepting His narrative as the only plan for our lives. When fear knocks on the door of our hearts and minds, we must quickly reject it. This discipline requires a deep faith in God's perfect love and a commitment to His truth rather than the enemy's lies. Fear thrives on the stories society trains us to believe, but if we entertain the enemy's falsehoods, we unknowingly give power to his influence over our thoughts and actions.

Spells are designed to undermine our faith in God by sowing seeds of fear, doubt, and confusion. Whose words and impressions we choose to believe ultimately determines where we place our faith. That's why the enemy works tirelessly to shift our trust away from God. Whether through subtle lies, fear-inducing stories, or the opinions of others, the goal is to shift our faith away from God and toward circumstances, human reasoning, or even ourselves. But when we fix our eyes on God and embrace His Word as the ultimate truth, we dismantle the falsehoods designed to weaken our faith and can live fully in the freedom He provides.

A spell functions much like a car's ignition, sparking an action that sets everything in motion. Once it has done its job, the ignition is no longer active, but the motor continues running. Similarly, spells ignite a narrative that, for better or worse, compels us to act in a way that feels natural, often becoming ingrained behavior over time. For any of us, fear-induced behaviors can become so habitual that we perceive them as a necessary part of our everyday lives. However, this behavior can be changed by "switching off" the kindling of fear. The following section explores how to turn off this proverbial switch and regain control over our lives.

The Power of Love Over Fear

Fear thrives in environments where love is absent or misunderstood. Fear gains a foothold when we are unsure of God's love for us, whispering falsehoods about our worth, our future, God's intentions toward us, and His ability to protect us. However, when we embrace the reality of God's unwavering love, fear loses its power. God's love is the only genuine love in existence, and it's experienced through an intimate relationship with God. The Apostle John reminds us, "There is no fear in love; but perfect love casteth out fear: because fear hath torment. He that feareth is not made perfect in love." (1 John 4:18 KJV). This isn't just any love—it's a mature, complete love gained from an intimate relationship with God.

Understanding God's love gives us peace and the courage to confront fear without being overcome. Just as light dispels darkness, God's love expels fear, giving us a sense of security and calm. In practice, we don't have to be humbled by fear's influence because God's love and promises are more potent than any threats the enemy can bring. Through God's power within us, we can recognize and face fear head-on without allowing it to define our subsequent actions.

Fear wants to dominate our thoughts like a spell, urging us to react impulsively. However, the truth is that fear doesn't stand a chance when we understand how much God loves us. God's love is a shield around us, protecting us from the false narratives the enemy tries to push upon us. Fear pivots out the door as we immerse ourselves in God's love. Fear can knock, but it cannot enter or even stay long enough to continue knocking at our doors.

I remember driving in my hometown of Orangeburg, SC, during the day. I was going to our state's capital city, Columbia. I was driving on Columbia Road to the highway we typically use to travel to Columbia. As I drove, I saw a few deer run across the road in front of a young lady driving an SUV on the opposite side of the road. The deer surprised her, and she missed them by maybe six inches. After that occurrence, I avoided using Columbia Road at night, and I didn't want to travel that road during the day either, fearing that deer in the woods bordering it might decide to leap out in front of my vehicle.

A spell of fear gripped me because I believed I'd heighten my chances of being in an accident by traveling on that road. I decided to stop taking that road because of what never happened to the young woman. Did you catch what I just said? I feared that an accident, which never happened to the other driver, would occur in my case. Even though she was unharmed, I mulled over the fact that she could have been in an accident. The possibility alone caused unwarranted fear in me.

The Holy Spirit enlightened me to view this event for what it was—a spiritually successful attempt to cast a spell on me. I resolved to trust God's love for me and claim I will be safe on Columbia Road.

I live in South Carolina, where deer are relatively abundant near roadways. In my driving experience, I hadn't had an accident involving a deer. The newness of this experience startled me, and I believed that the disturbing moment I witnessed would one day become my own.

If only to break the spell of fear, I was determined to drive on Columbia Road as a testament to God's delivering power. Now, I take that road when it's faster to Columbia from where I am in my hometown. I am free from that spell, and that incident doesn't replay in my mind when I take that road. I received my freedom by refusing to believe the story that I would be in a car accident due to any deer that might wander or dart into the roadway. I don't remember the last time I received a traffic ticket, so I'm a careful and watchful driver. I just got myself all worked up over nothing.

Fear's Spell-Binding Nature

People and even demonic forces often attempt to cast spells that trigger fear, typically through discouraging news, unsettling rumors, or even well-meaning advice that plants seeds of doubt. For example, we might hear that we won't be able to pay our bills or that we'll fail to achieve a particular goal. These stories cast shadows on our faith, tempting us to worry about finances, health, relationships, or any other aspect of our future. But these fears are essentially spells—they have no rightful claim over us and don't have to become our reality.

The enemy's tactic is to tell stories that provoke fear. All demons know we live under their power once we believe their stories. But God's Word assures us differently. For instance, in Psalm 84:11 AMPC, we are assured that "...No good thing will He withhold from those who walk uprightly." This promise, anchored in God's love, starkly contrasts the enemy's fear-inducing lies.

At the moment of temptation, when we feel fear, we must recall that sensing fear doesn't automatically indicate we are afraid. As spiritual beings, we often sense the sudden approach of fear, discouragement, frustration, and other spell-binding sensations. However, sensing fear doesn't mean it controls us. We can strongly sense the spirit of fear and still choose to walk by faith—trusting God's loving ways to protect and defend us.

When we trust in God's love, fear loses its grip. We recognize that nothing happens to us outside of God's sovereign control, and nothing can thwart His plans for our lives. At its core, fear is a story we don't have to believe.

Stories That Feed Fear

Fear always begins with a story. Whether it's a news report, a diagnosis, or a personal setback, fear feeds on the narrative we choose to believe. Have you ever driven down a road and suddenly seen a car veer toward you? If fear arises, it stems from the story we tell ourselves at that instance: "I'm about to have an accident!"

We are constantly fed stories through media, social interactions, and even our habitual inner dialogue. People design stories to cast spells of fear. For example, we might hear a story about economic collapse and fear losing our jobs, homes, or financial stability. The more we listen to, believe, and dwell on these stories, the more they shape what we'll accept as our reality.

But as believers, we are called to a higher story—God's story. This call to believe is why Romans 8:6 tells us that the mind ruled by the flesh leads to death, but the mind governed by the Spirit leads to life and peace. Fear takes root in us when we allow the stories of this world to control our minds. But when we allow the Holy Spirit to guide our thoughts, we are filled with peace, regardless of the circumstances.

Rejecting Fear-Based Spells

One of the enemy's most effective strategies is to lure us into collecting stories that reinforce our fears. This entrapment can happen subtly, such as saving social media posts or news articles that feed our anxieties. We may begin to develop a collection of fear-based narratives that shape our perception of the world.

For example, many people unknowingly save, like, comment on, or share TikTok videos or other social media content that aligns with their fears and anxieties. Instead of using God's Word as their guide and defense against worry, they use these fear-inducing stories to justify their feelings and actions. In doing so, they are collecting spells—stories that have the power to bind them to fear.

But the Bible offers a different approach. Psalm 118:8-9 KJV reminds us: "It is better to trust in the Lord than to put confidence in man. It is better to trust in the Lord than to put confidence in princes." When we place our confidence in God, we break the power of fear-based spells. We choose to live under the truth of God's Word, not the ever-shifting narratives of the world.

Are you in the habit of driving through unfamiliar neighborhoods and knocking on random doors just to see what strangers have to say about life? Probably not. That's certainly not my practice either. I once posed this question to our Sunday morning congregation. Then I shared something the Holy Spirit told me: Stop aimlessly scrolling on social media—swiping past post after post, video after video, until something catches your attention. More often than not, what grabs our attention is frivolous, offering nothing meaningful, encouraging, or biblically sound.

If wandering into random homes to listen to the unfiltered thoughts of strangers isn't a part of our everyday behavior, then neither should scrolling through social media to absorb the unknown-sourced opinions and worldviews of people we don't even know. We already face enough battles against common spells and curses—why possibly and willingly invite more demonic influences of fear, doubt, and deception into our lives?

The Power of Confession

One of the most effective ways to overcome fear is by confessing God's Word over our lives. Romans 10:10 KJV says, "For with the heart man believeth unto righteousness; and with the mouth confession is made unto salvation." What we speak matters. If we continually confess fear, doubt, and defeat, we reinforce those things in our lives. But when we confess faith, hope, and God's promises, we activate the power of His Word to work on our behalf.

Some time ago, after a long day of work, I would drive to an old, dilapidated building and shout. No, I wasn't there to relieve stress—I was exercising my faith. I'd lean toward the front window, find a small opening, and declare boldly, "You belong to The Feast of the Lord! You belong to The Feast of the Lord!"

The Lord had shown me that this building would become the next location for the church I pastored, The Feast of the Lord. I started the church in my family room at home, and God blessed us to outgrow it quickly. Soon, we began renting a space downtown, which served us well but came with challenges.

For every Sunday service and Tuesday evening Bible Study, church members would drive to my house in the country, located on a crater-ridden dirt road, to load and unload heavy speakers and other equipment needed for the services.

The setup and breakdown were exhausting, and the congregants remained faithful. God was preparing us to move to a higher level.

Owning a building enabled us to reach a wider audience and operate with a higher level of excellence. But by earthly standards, the idea seemed impossible. People thought I was crazy. Young people filled our congregation; at the time, only a few members had full-time jobs. Financially, the prospect of purchasing a building looked unattainable.

Every logical reason in the world told me we shouldn't even try. I didn't have the money, and the church certainly didn't have the resources, so why even look? But I refused to doubt. I had a Word from God, a good spell (story) that we would have our own building, and that Word was all I needed. So instead of worrying, I prophesied. As the Lord led me, I spoke life into that building daily. I didn't make declarations based on wishful thinking or personal ambition—I only declared what God said.

People told me I was rushing. They said this wasn't the time. But I knew what I heard from the Lord, so I pressed forward without second-guessing. I didn't need confirmation from my circumstances or approval from others because I had faith in God. Faith at its highest level doesn't require external validation—it believes God's Word alone and doesn't mind openly declaring what God said.

Today, I am in awe of what God has done. We hold services in that building, which is completely debt-free. When we have great faith in God and confess what we genuinely believe, He, in response, does great things for us. Had I wavered, I would have been held captive by the opinions of my circumstances rather than the promise of my God.

> *What I tell you in darkness, that speak ye in light: and what ye hear in the ear, that preach ye upon the housetops.*
>
> Matthew 10:27 KJV

When God speaks, and we confess our belief because we believe what He said, we must cast away all circumstance-based decision-making.

Confession is not just a one-time event; it's a daily practice. The more we speak God's Word, the more we train our hearts and minds to believe God's truth. And as we do this, fear loses its grip on us, and faith in God grows and rises with the benefit of confident boldness within us.

Overcoming the Fear of Failure

Many people struggle with the fear of failure. They are afraid that they won't measure up, will make mistakes, or disappoint others. This fear can be paralyzing, preventing them from taking steps of faith and pursuing God's plans for their lives.

But God's Word assures us that we don't have to fear failure. Philippians 4:13 KJV declares, "I can do all things through Christ which strengtheneth me." This verse reminds us that our ability to succeed does not come from our own strength, but from Christ's strength working in and through us.

> *For a righteous man falls seven times and rises again, but the wicked are overthrown by calamity.*
>
> Proverbs 24:16 AMPC

Even if we make mistakes or face setbacks, we can trust that God is with us and will guide us through every challenge. Failure is not final for those who trust in God. He gives us the strength to recover, learn from our mistakes, and keep moving forward in faith.

Moses' journey is a prime example of how the fear of failure can hinder obedience to God's call. When God commissioned Moses to confront Pharaoh and lead the Israelites out of Egypt, Moses immediately focused on his personal inadequacies. He protested, "O my Lord, I am not eloquent… but I am slow of speech, and of a slow tongue." (Exodus 4:10 KJV). His fear was rooted in his limitations—he was concerned about how he would be perceived, whether he would fail to communicate God's message, and how the people would respond.

However, God had already planned to support Moses' obedience by working miracles that exceeded his expectations. Moses had no idea that his rod would become a serpent that devoured the magicians' snakes, proving God's power over Egypt's sorcery. He couldn't have predicted the ten devastating plagues that would force Pharaoh's hand. He had no foresight that in the span of just one night, the Red Sea would part before him, allowing him and the Israelites to walk on dry ground while their enemies drowned afterward.

At the moment of Moses' calling, God revealed none of this to him—God simply asked for his obedience. We may never know how often we have feared failure and complied with that fear, thereby missing the opportunity to experience God's power firsthand and for the benefit of others.

One benefit of complete obedience to God is that it activates His intervention. When Moses finally submitted to God's command, despite his insecurities, God performed wonders that silenced his doubts and proved His divine backing. Moses wasn't just stepping out to "try and see" if things would work—he was walking in a calling that God had already equipped him for, even though the evidence of that equipping was unseen until he obeyed. Be encouraged when God gives you a command because He doesn't lose, nor will you.

Fearing failure means focusing on the abilities we're comfortable with—believing we can accomplish something in our strength. Yet, when God calls us, He doesn't expect us to rely on ourselves. He expects us to trust Him. By God's authority, we must break the spell of fearing failure so He can work with us (Mark 16:20 KJV), confirming His call through the supernatural evidence He produces to accompany our acts of obedience to Him.

Breaking the Spell of Social Fear: Kaitlin's Story

Kaitlin, a young woman who attends the church I pastor, lived under this spell for over a year. She sent me a powerful testimony about how God used me to help her break free through the gifts of a Word of Knowledge (knowing specifics only by the Holy Spirit's revelation) and a Word of Wisdom (receiving God's supernatural wisdom for successfully applying knowledge). I pray that as you read her story, you will experience the same freedom she did.

For some, the fear of speaking up, being noticed, or simply existing in a room full of people can be paralyzing. It's not just a minor discomfort—it's a spell that binds, convincing its host that their voice is insignificant, that their presence doesn't matter, that silence is safer.

I know this because I lived under that spell.

I struggled with fear and anxiety around people, especially strangers. Specific thoughts constantly ran through my mind:

"What if I say something that isn't received?"

"What if they don't like me?"

"I have something to share in this Bible Study, but I don't want people to think I talk too much."

I would consistently have these and other thoughts around people, especially strangers. These thoughts were rooted in fear and anxiety.

I didn't like talking to people unless they initiated the conversation, and even then, I kept my responses brief. I avoided small talk, and if I was in a group setting, I sat quietly, disengaged. Even when I thought I had something valuable to add to the conversation, I second-guessed myself, convinced that my words weren't necessary.

My anxiety grew to the point where I would welcome any excuse to leave social gatherings. As a delivery driver, I receive random orders on my phone and would eagerly await a notification to escape the group settings. I had no objective reason to feel uneasy in these warm and friendly environments, but I often just wanted to get out.

What I didn't realize was that I was under a spell—one that was working against God's purpose for me.

THE SPELL OF SILENCE

I wasn't merely shy—I was deliberately avoiding people. I had built a habit of shutting myself off and withdrawing from moments that God designed for me to share what He had placed in my heart. Even in lighthearted conversations, I was absent. If people laughed at a joke, I barely reacted. My mind was somewhere else—anywhere but in the moment.

As much as I longed to be a powerfully effective minister and leader, God couldn't fully use me if I remained under the spell of believing that my involvement didn't matter, even when the Holy Spirit prompted me to speak.

Looking back, I see how selfish I was. Several people said I have a beautiful personality, but I didn't feel like sharing it. I see myself in a clearer light now than ever before. I wasn't in a fight-or-flight state—I was in freeze-or-flight.

Then one night, everything changed.

I prayed a simple but desperate prayer: "God, take everything from my heart that is not like You." I didn't know it yet, but my breakthrough was on the way.

A WORD FROM GOD

My pastor told me that the Holy Spirit revealed I was under a spell—one that made me avoid people, one that made me disengage, one that kept me trapped in silence. He made me aware that how we treat those who belong to Jesus, even those whom I may have considered the least, is also how we treat Jesus. Then, he shared a verse with me that changed everything:

> *I was a stranger and you did not welcome Me and entertain Me, I was naked and you did not clothe Me, I was sick and in prison and you did not visit Me with help and ministering care.*
> Matthew 25:43 AMPC

This verse hit me like a ton of bricks. I was shocked and convicted. I never wanted to treat Jesus like that.

I had never really noticed this verse before, but as soon as I read it, I felt something break inside me. I now clearly see that my heart wasn't open to intentionally cherishing every opportunity to be used by God to welcome and show hospitality to others, and in doing so, I was treating Jesus the same way.

I suddenly saw my behavior for what it truly was—not just introversion or shyness, but rejecting and hiding from the very people Jesus had placed in my life. And because of that, I was rejecting Him.

BREAKING FREE

After the conversation with Pastor Shane, when he shared what the Holy Spirit revealed to him about my behavior, the spell was broken, and my mindset shifted. I told him what he shared created something in me because I felt different. The case wasn't that something left me or something entered me—the impact was as if his words from the Holy Spirit had created, shifted, rearranged, or adjusted something deep within my heart, as though He unlocked something that had been trapped.

I hadn't realized that my behavior was rooted in fear or that it had such a firm grip on me and was holding me back from fulfilling God's purpose for my life. I understand now that I cannot have love and fear simultaneously. If I'm to be entirely filled with God's love, I can have no vacancy for fear.

> *There is no fear in love; but perfect love casteth out fear: because fear hath torment. He that feareth is not made perfect in love.*
>
> 1 John 4:18 KJV

With God's revelation implanted in me that day, I will no longer allow unsubstantiated fear or concern over others' reactions and opinions to hold me back. I will continually pray to be filled with and wholeheartedly act according to God's love for people, allowing His love to guide my every interaction.

I had to act on this revelation. I couldn't return to being disengaged and shrinking away from social settings, so I started small, learned, and changed my ways from there. My fear of others' reactions or opinions gradually vanished, and today, I'm sharing out of my love for them. Loving people takes my focus off my and others' thoughts, and keeps me thinking about caring for people because that's how I'm also treating Jesus.

Now, I'm engaging in conversations with both those I don't know and those I'm more familiar with, whether discussing food, education, travel, or spiritual topics. I speak first instead of waiting for someone to start a conversation with me. Instead of dodging interactions, I lean into them. I talk to strangers. I laugh at jokes. Also, I don't just tolerate social settings; I genuinely enjoy them. I can honestly reveal that I am fully present and ready for God to use me at any time.

God wants me to be myself and use my personality for Him. My pastor often shares that God anoints individuals and uses their personalities. That truth has stuck with me.

Love has overtaken fear in my prospective relationships. Instead of asking myself, "What will they think of me?" I now ask, "How can I show love to those around me?" Instead of hiding, I step forward, knowing that every time I engage with someone, I'm loving them and Jesus. I'm free from the spell of avoidance and refuse to return to that bondage ever again.

YOUR FREEDOM AWAITS

Fear was a spell that convinced me that my presence didn't matter, that my voice wasn't important, and that hiding kept me safe. If you've ever struggled with a fear of speaking up, a fear of rejection, or a fear of simply being seen, know this: You don't have to stay bound.

Since being freed from that spell, I understand that I could have never experienced freedom in that area of my life if I hadn't first acknowledged the captivity, believed in the possibility of freedom, and sincerely desired to be free.

> *38 And when did we see You a stranger and welcomed and entertained You, or naked and clothed You?*
> *39 And when did we see You sick or in prison and came to visit You?*
> *40 And the King will reply to them, Truly I tell you, in so far as you did it for one of the least [in the estimation of men] of these My brethren, you did it for Me.*
>
> Matthew 25:38-40 AMPC

I will continue to love people actively, and in doing so, I will simultaneously show love to Jesus. I chose to step into love, engage with others, and break free from the fear that held me hostage. Now, I feel free because I am free.

Battling What to Believe

Believing that spells and curses are so powerful that they require an army of angels, weeks of fasting, or other extreme measures reveals that fear has successfully cast its spell—a deception that convinces us that evil will destroy us before the power of God will protect us. We habitually expect harm from evil more readily than trusting God's love to keep us safe. Another way of viewing the belief system of fear and anxiety is that we instinctively place more faith in the ability of a spell to hurt us than in God's power to prevent or block a weapon's attempt against us.

> *No weapon that is formed against thee shall prosper; and every tongue that shall rise against thee in judgment thou shalt condemn. This is the heritage of the servants of the Lord, and their righteousness is of me, saith the Lord.*
>
> Isaiah 54:17 KJV

The mindset of believing in evil's power over God subtly shifts our trust away from Him and strengthens fear's grip on our hearts. Instead, we must learn to believe—quickly and almost effortlessly—that God's power will defeat the power of evil. Now is the time to remove ourselves from the spell of fear and stop trusting that demons will work tirelessly to harm us while hesitating to expect God to devastate and destroy the works of the devil.

> *The Lord is my light and my salvation; whom shall I fear? the Lord is the strength of my life; of whom shall I be afraid?*
>
> Psalm 27:1 KJV

No matter how strong spells and curses appear or how much havoc they've already wreaked, God's might is an unstoppable force. He can break and destroy any spell or curse with ease. All we need to do is place our faith in His power rather than fear the enemy's schemes. We demonstrate our faith in God by refusing to act on the fear that torments us and instead acting on our faith in Him by waiting for His command before moving forward.

Believing God over devils requires living faith, not dead faith (James 2:26). Dead faith hesitates, doubts, and demands proof before believing and obeying. But living faith moves in obedience—fully trusting that God will act without our seeing evidence of Him working. When we obey because we have faith in God, we will see in the natural realm what God will do supernaturally for us and those we pray for. Just as Moses had no clue how God would deliver Israel until he fully obeyed, we, too, will not always know how God will intervene. But one thing is sure: He always does what is needed when we act in faith.

Overcoming the Fear of the Unknown

One of the most common fears is the fear of the unknown. We worry about the future, what might happen, what someone may say in retaliation, and other unknowns beyond our control. But Jesus gives us a sobering reminder:

> *So do not worry or be anxious about tomorrow, for tomorrow will have worries and anxieties of its own. Sufficient for each day is its own trouble.*
>
> Matthew 6:34 AMPC

This verse gives me little comfort because it seems Jesus is telling me to refrain from worrying about what could happen tomorrow until tomorrow comes, and then to worry about it. I know Jesus doesn't want us to worry at all, because when tomorrow comes, He still expects us to have faith. In Matthew 6:24-33, Jesus explains that God takes perfect care of His own.

Nobody worries about the past because we are very familiar with what has happened. We worry about what we don't know—details concerning the outcome of our situation in the future. Though God calls us to live one day at a time, we are still called to trust Him with our future. When we try to control everything or constantly worry about what might happen, we rob ourselves of the peace that comes from relying on God. Instead of focusing on the uncertainties of the future, we should focus on God's faithfulness in the present.

Instead of wasting time saying, "I'll be so glad when I can get some peace..." or "I'll be so glad when this is over..." or any other statement expressing frustration about time, we can choose to be glad today about tomorrow. Let's not postpone having a joyous day because we choose to spend today worrying about tomorrow's unknowns. As I mentioned in a previous discussion, we can take comfort in knowing that our God is the God of the unknown. We may not know what tomorrow will bring, but we know Who brings every tomorrow, and He loves and cares deeply for us.

When we read the Bible, believe God's Word, pray according to that belief, and align our thoughts and actions accordingly, we will thank God today for how well He has already prepared us for tomorrow's situations. Faith doesn't focus on tomorrow's worries. Faith sees the God of today and tomorrow as a loving Father Who will never leave or forsake us in our troubles. Trusting in God's sovereignty allows us to rest, knowing that whatever comes, He is already there, working all things together for our good.

We must be careful not to exalt anything we believe that is against what God already knows (2 Corinthians 10:5), because if we believe in something God doesn't know to be accurate, we are under a spell of deception. That deception convinces us that our perception is more reliable than God's omniscience. Our limited opinion places our trust in human reasoning rather than God's perfect and exact knowledge, causing us to walk in uncertainty and fear rather than faith.

True peace comes when we surrender our understanding to God's truth, trusting that when we encounter the beginning of a trial, He is very much aware of the end and that His plans for our victory are already underway. Even when we are uncertain about the future, let us keep our minds fixed on God's love and promises. Then, we'll experience a peace that surpasses understanding.

Thou wilt keep him in perfect peace, whose mind is stayed on thee: because he trusteth in thee.

Isaiah 26:3 KJV

And the peace of God, which passeth all understanding, shall keep your hearts and minds through Christ Jesus.

Philippians 4:7 KJV

Living in the Freedom of God's Love

Ultimately, living in the freedom of unwaveringly knowing and confidently resting in God's love breaks the spells of fear and anxiety. When we understand how deeply and perfectly God loves us, fear loses its power to confuse and torment us about the circumstances we encounter.

There is no fear in love; but perfect love casteth out fear: because fear hath torment. He that feareth is not made perfect in love.

1 John 4:18 KJV

This freedom doesn't mean we will never face challenges or difficult circumstances. But it does mean we don't have to face them alone or in fear. When fear and anxiety attempt to take root in our hearts, we must remind ourselves of God's proven love for us. We must choose to believe His promises over the lies of the enemy and stand firm in the truth that we are loved, protected, and cared for by our Heavenly Father.

Yes, reminding ourselves to believe and stand firm is difficult unless we act in accordance with the teachings of the Holy Scriptures. Just as a play or movie producer follows a script that tells each actor and actress what to say and do, the Scriptures tell us what to say and do. God always does His part perfectly—He is both the Producer and the Star of our lives. Our role is to trust Him, follow His Word, and stay aligned with His direction. When we live according to God's script, fear loses its grip, and we walk confidently in the peace and assurance that comes from knowing He is in control. God makes the end of the 'good spell' story of our lives victorious!

ALTAR CALL AND PRAYER FOR SALVATION

Our Lord Jesus said,

All whom My Father gives (entrusts) to Me will come to Me; and the one who comes to Me I will most certainly not cast out [I will never, no never, reject one of them who comes to Me].

John 6:37 AMPC

Dear Father, I know you will save the one who prays the following prayer according to Your most holy, just, and righteous will for this precious life. I ask, pray, and thank You in the name of my Lord and Savior, Jesus Christ!

If you are a sinner or you want to renew your relationship with God, please pray the following prayer and receive Jesus Christ into your life this very moment. He's waiting for you. He's the only way to Heaven, and looks forward to being the primary part of your life here on Earth.

Father God, I come before You now in the name of Jesus Christ. I confess that I am a sinner. Please forgive me and save me from all of my unrepentant sins. I know Jesus Christ is Your Son, Who died for my sins, and that You raised Him from the dead. Lord, Jesus, I invite You into my heart and life right now. Come in and live life through me so that I can please our Father just as You please our Father. I now believe that You have come into my heart and life. Father, I have asked and prayed for these things in the name of Jesus Christ. Thank You, Father, for forgiving me for all of my sins, for saving me, and freeing me from the power of every demon. Father, I have given you my life—I no longer have it. Use me, and I will live for You forever! In Jesus Christ's name, I pray, Amen! I AM SAVED!

DAILY PRAYER FOR DAILY POWER

You are asking for these things that are mandatory for today (the next 24-hour period):

"Father, in the name of Jesus Christ, I come before You now. I believe that by requesting the following, I will receive all that I ask for immediately. Thank You, Father, so very much for allowing me to come, request, and receive all these great things from You, through my Lord, Jesus Christ, and by the power of Your Holy Spirit.

Father, it is my only desire to perfectly please You today in all that I think, every intent of my heart, all that I say, and with every action I take—and I will please You in all these ways. Strengthen me where I am weak, pick me up from where I have fallen, and place me where You want me to be for Your glory only! Father and Lord, I inquire and require all of the following. So, in the name of Jesus Christ, give me…"

1. The blood covering of my Lord, Jesus Christ. (John 6:53, 54, 56; Romans 5:9; Ephesians 1:7, 2:13; Colossians 1:14; Hebrews 10:19, 13:12)
2. The anointing of the Holy Ghost and power. (Acts 10:38)
3. Your holy, awesome, and divine presence and heavy glory, on me and upon all to whom I minister. (Luke 2:9; Acts 3:19; 2 Cor 3:18)
4. The greatest sensitivity to Your Holy Spirit that I can have and to personally know Him very well. (John 14:17; Romans 8:26; 1Cor. 2:11; 1 Cor. 12:8-13; Ephesians 3:5; Hebrews 5:14)
5. Wisdom and Understanding (Proverbs 4:5-7)

6. Confidence (Acts 28:31; Ephesians 3:12; Hebrews 10:35)
7. Your original intent for each situation I encounter and for those to whom I am to minister. (Jeremiah 29:11)
8. The revelation of everything You want to be destroyed in my life and in the lives of those to whom I am to minister. (Romans 6:6; 1 John 3:8)
9. The ability to freely release and how to impart Your divine, conquering, and destructive power in my life and in the lives of all to whom I minister. (Acts 1:8; Romans 1:11, 8:37)
10. The ability to yield to Your sweet Holy Spirit for all mighty and overpowering transfers of Your power from You, through me, to all to whom I minister. (Romans 6:13)
11. Your power, present to heal today, and the release of Your mighty healing power through me, so that I will glorify You. (Luke 5:17-26)
12. Your healing virtue, through me, to all who believe and to those who seek help for their unbelief. (Mark 5:30; Luke 6:19; Mark 9:24, Acts 5:15, Acts 19:12)
13. The great increase of Your Kingdom's supernatural power in my life. (1 Corinthians 4:20)
14. The supernatural position of authority You have for me. (Luke 10:19)
15. Supernatural thoughts. (Romans 12:2; Philippians 4:8)
16. Very keen accuracy in the gifts of the Spirit that the Holy Spirit desires to be in my life. (1 John 2:27; 1 Corinthians 12:11)
17. Knowing specifically, in each situation, what You are saying and doing that I am to say and do today. (John 5:19)
18. Only to live, according to Your divine purpose for my life, by being led by Your precious Holy Spirit. (Matthew 4:1; Luke 4:1; Romans 8:14)
19. Always having and giving the Word You want me to share to impart supernatural faith in the heart of each hearer. (Romans 10:17)
20. How to open and explain the sense of the Scriptures so that the hearts of the hearers will be greatly moved and burning within. (Luke 24:32)
21. The ability to deliver the Gospel in such a way that the Gospel will bring strong conviction to each hearer. (Acts 2:36-37)
22. Wisdom to win souls for Your Kingdom. (Proverbs 11:30)

23. Everything else I need that is available to me from You, through Jesus Christ, and by Your Holy Spirit. (Matthew 7:11; Romans 8:26)

Thank You so very much, in Jesus' name! It is so! Amen! (John 14:13-14; John 15:16; John 16:23-24, 26)

Before the reading of Holy Scripture:
"Holy Spirit:"

1. Open my eyes that I may behold wondrous things out of Thy Law today. (Psalm 119:18)
2. Give me the pure and original knowledge, wisdom, understanding, and revelation of Thy most holy Word today. (Acts 8:30)
3. Impart the ministry of Jesus Christ to me and reveal Him to me more and more as I read Your holy Word today (Acts 20:24, 2 Corinthians 5:18)
4. Impart all I'm to have today of Jesus Christ's love, faith, power, compassion, authority, knowledge, wisdom, understanding, sensitivity, and everything He's providing for me. Cause me to assuredly know Your voice and the Father's will by clearly hearing, seeing, or being impressed in my spirit by You, precisely what I am to say and do to obey the Father always and to command and defeat every devil and unclean spirit at each encounter. (John 16:14; Authority-Matthew 8:5-13)

Thank You so very much, in Jesus' name!

BLESSINGS THAT BREAK CURSES

Mourning, in its natural state, is not a curse (Matthew 5:4). It is a normal human response to loss, and the Bible acknowledges that there is "A time to weep, and a time to laugh; a time to mourn, and a time to dance;" (Ecclesiastes 3:4 KJV). However, mourning can evolve into a curse when it binds people in emotional or spiritual heaviness and can prevent them from moving forward into the restoration and joy that God promises. God designed mourning to have its season, but He also intends for His people to experience restoration and joy following the course of mourning.

The power of the gospel ensures that God's comfort and freedom are available to break any natural response that appears to have trapped us in what is supposed to be a restorative process, from pain to relief. God desires to turn our mourning into joy and our sorrow into peace (Jeremiah 31:13). Recognizing this distinction enables us to understand why *mourning* and other natural responses are listed under "curses."

Isaiah 61:3 KJV provides a profound truth about God's desire to lift His people out of prolonged grief: "To appoint unto them that mourn in Zion, to give unto them beauty for ashes, the oil of joy for mourning, the garment of praise for the spirit of heaviness; that they might be called trees of righteousness, the planting of the Lord, that he might be glorified." This verse shows that God does not intend for His people to remain in mourning indefinitely. When grief becomes a "spirit of heaviness," it has shifted from a natural emotional process into a spiritual burden. God desires to replace that heaviness with the oil of joy and the garment of praise, offering freedom and healing.

Psalm 30:5 KJV reinforces this truth: "For his anger endureth but a moment; in his favour is life: weeping may endure for a night, but joy cometh in the morning." God's design is for mourning to be a temporary state. Suppose the heaviness persists as a permanent emotional state or becomes a defining aspect of a person's identity. In that case, such a result may indicate that the enemy has transformed it into a curse, stripping that person of the joy and peace God intends for them.

Fear, anxiety, sickness, and other hardships may not always stem from curses. Sometimes, they are part of life's challenges or spiritual growth. However, when they persist unnaturally, hinder progress, or cause emotional and spiritual harm, they can become curses. The blessings listed in this chart represent God's promises to replace any lingering effects of these difficulties with recovery.

God's blessings are powerful enough to reverse any curse and bring hope, healing, and restoration. His Word assures us that no curse can stand against His blessings (Numbers 23:20). As you review this chart, allow the Holy Spirit to reveal areas where you may need to receive God's blessing and release any spiritual, emotional, or physical bondage.

- When you feel **mourning**, God offers **comfort**. Find this promise in *Matthew 5:4*.
- If **fear** grips you, remember God gives **power, love, and a sound mind**. This is anchored in *2 Timothy 1:7*.
- In moments of **weakness** He provides **strength**. Look to *Isaiah 40:29*.
- Where **poverty** seems overwhelming, God promises **provision**. Reflect on *Philippians 4:19*.
- Against **sickness**, hold onto the blessing of **healing**. *Isaiah 53:5* speaks to this.
- When **loneliness** creeps in, know you have God's **presence**. *Hebrews 13:5* assures us of this.
- If you struggle with **condemnation**, embrace the truth that there is no condemnation in Christ. This is powerfully stated in *Romans 8:1*.
- For **anxiety**, seek the **peace of God**. Find guidance in *Philippians 4:6–7*.
- When facing **rejection**, remember your **acceptance** in Christ. *Ephesians 1:6* highlights this gift.
- Instead of **shame**, God offers **honor**. See this promise in *Isaiah 61:7*.

- Against **defeat**, claim your **victory**. *1 Corinthians 15:57* declares this truth.
- When **confusion** clouds your mind, God provides **clarity and direction**. *Proverbs 3:5–6* offers wisdom here.
- For feelings of **guilt**, receive the blessing of **forgiveness**. *1 John 1:9* is a cornerstone for this.
- In times of **hopelessness**, find **hope in Christ**. *Romans 15:13* shines a light.
- If **insecurity** troubles you, build your **confidence** in God. *Proverbs 3:26* encourages this.
- When battling **depression**, remember God offers **joy**. *Nehemiah 8:10* links joy and strength.
- To break free from **bondage**, embrace the **freedom** in Christ. *Galatians 5:1* is a key declaration.
- Where there is **darkness**, God brings **light**. *John 8:12* illuminates this.
- When experiencing a **lack of direction**, trust in God's **guidance**. *Psalm 32:8* promises His direction.
- For **weariness**, find **rest**. *Matthew 11:28–30* offers this invitation.
- If you worry about **provision**, trust in God's **supply**. *Matthew 6:31–33* speaks directly to this.
- In times of **isolation**, seek **fellowship**. *1 John 1:7* points toward the connection in Him.
- To overcome **bitterness**, practice **forgiveness**. *Ephesians 4:32* calls us to this.
- Against **pride**, cultivate **humility**. *James 4:10* shows the way.
- When you experience **grief**, God promises **joy**. You can find this in *Psalm 30:11*.
- Against **spiritual blindness**, He offers **spiritual sight**. *John 9:25* speaks to seeing anew.
- For **hardness of heart**, God can give a **heart of flesh**. *Ezekiel 36:26* describes this transformation.
- In **brokenness**, seek His **wholeness**. *Psalm 147:3* assures He heals the brokenhearted.

- Where there is **captivity**, He proclaims **liberty**. This freedom is found in *Isaiah 61:1*.
- Against **barrenness**, trust for **fruitfulness**. *Psalm 113:9* celebrates this blessing.
- When faced with **doubt**, choose **faith**. *Mark 11:23* encourages mountain-moving faith.
- To counter **hatred**, embrace **love**. *1 John 4:7* reminds us that love comes from God.
- In times of **ignorance**, ask for **wisdom**. *James 1:5* promises wisdom to those who ask.
- Against the **fear of death**, hold onto **eternal life**. *John 11:25* reveals Jesus as the Resurrection and the Life.
- Instead of **condemnation of the law**, receive **grace**. *Romans 6:14* declares we are under grace.
- If you feel like an **outcast**, know you are **chosen**. *1 Peter 2:9* calls you chosen.
- For **unforgiveness**, seek **reconciliation**. *2 Corinthians 5:18* speaks of the ministry of reconciliation.
- In **poverty of spirit**, find **richness in Christ**. *2 Corinthians 8:9* highlights Christ's sacrifice for our enrichment.
- When feeling **unloved**, remember God's **everlasting love**. *Jeremiah 31:3* affirms His enduring love.
- Where there's a **lack of peace**, He offers **perfect peace**. *Isaiah 26:3* promises peace to the steadfast mind.
- To overcome **anger**, cultivate **patience**. *Proverbs 14:29* praises the slow to anger.
- Instead of seeking **revenge**, practice **forgiveness**. *Romans 12:19* reminds us that vengeance belongs to the Lord.
- When faced with **injustice**, trust in God's **justice**. *Isaiah 30:18* assures that the Lord waits to be gracious and is a God of justice.
- In times of **spiritual dryness**, look for **rivers of living water**. *John 7:38* promises this flow from within believers.
- If you feel like you're **wandering**, know that you can experience being **found**. *Luke 15:24* celebrates the return of the lost.

- Against **aimlessness**, find **purpose**. *Ephesians 2:10* reveals we are God's workmanship, created for good works.
- Where there is **division**, strive for **unity in Christ**. *Ephesians 4:3* encourages us to maintain the unity of the Spirit.
- For feelings of **alienation**, embrace your **adoption** into God's family. *Ephesians 1:5* speaks of this predestined adoption.
- Instead of **spiritual death**, receive **new life in Christ**. *2 Corinthians 5:17* declares we are a new creation.
- In **hopelessness**, anchor yourself in **living hope**. *1 Peter 1:3* celebrates the living hope through Christ's resurrection.
- When dealing with **fear of the future**, trust God's promise of **hope and a future**. *Jeremiah 29:11* is a beloved assurance.
- And for **faint-heartedness**, receive **renewed strength**. *Isaiah 40:31* promises renewed strength to those who hope in the Lord.

Curse	Blessing	Reference
Mourning	Comfort	Matthew 5:4
Fear	Power, love, and a sound mind	2 Timothy 1:7
Weakness	Strength	Isaiah 40:29
Poverty	Provision	Philippians 4:19
Sickness	Healing	Isaiah 53:5
Loneliness	God's presence	Hebrews 13:5
Condemnation	No condemnation in Christ	Romans 8:1
Anxiety	Peace of God	Philippians 4:6-7
Rejection	Acceptance in Christ	Ephesians 1:6
Shame	Honor	Isaiah 61:7
Defeat	Victory	1 Corinthians 15:57
Confusion	Clarity and direction	Proverbs 3:5-6
Guilt	Forgiveness	1 John 1:9
Hopelessness	Hope in Christ	Romans 15:13
Insecurity	Confidence in God	Proverbs 3:26
Depression	Joy	Nehemiah 8:10
Bondage	Freedom in Christ	Galatians 5:1
Darkness	Light	John 8:12
Lack of direction	Guidance	Psalm 32:8
Weariness	Rest	Matthew 11:28-30
Worry about provision	God's supply	Matthew 6:31-33
Isolation	Fellowship	1 John 1:7
Bitterness	Forgiveness	Ephesians 4:32
Pride	Humility	James 4:10
Grief	Joy	Psalm 30:11
Spiritual blindness	Spiritual sight	John 9:25
Hard-heartedness	A heart of flesh	Ezekiel 36:26

Curse	Blessing	Reference
Brokenness	Wholeness	Psalm 147:3
Captivity	Liberty	Isaiah 61:1
Barrenness	Fruitfulness	Psalm 113:9
Doubt	Faith	Mark 11:23
Hatred	Love	1 John 4:7
Ignorance	Wisdom	James 1:5
Fear of death	Eternal life	John 11:25
Condemnation of the law	Grace	Romans 6:14
Being an outcast	Being chosen	1 Peter 2:9
Unforgiveness	Reconciliation	2 Corinthians 5:18
Poverty of spirit	Richness in Christ	2 Corinthians 8:9
Feeling unloved	God's everlasting love	Jeremiah 31:3
Lack of peace	Perfect peace	Isaiah 26:3
Anger	Patience	Proverbs 14:29
Revenge	Forgiveness	Romans 12:19
Injustice	God's justice	Isaiah 30:18
Spiritual dryness	Rivers of living water	John 7:38
Wandering	Being found	Luke 15:24
Aimlessness	Purpose	Ephesians 2:10
Division	Unity in Christ	Ephesians 4:3
Alienation	Adoption into God's family	Ephesians 1:5
Spiritual death	New life in Christ	2 Corinthians 5:17
Hopelessness	Living hope	1 Peter 1:3
Fear of the future	Hope and a future	Jeremiah 29:11
Faint-heartedness	Renewed strength	Isaiah 40:31

SPELL AND CURSE-BREAKING PRAYERS

As you enter this section on Prayers—and the following sections on Declarations and Affirmations—remember that these are not merely words to recite but tools to help ignite your personal journey with God. Each one is designed as a starting point, guiding you to seek out more of God's Word—the Holy Bible—and apply it to your specific circumstances. May these serve as a springboard for deeper study, prayer, and intimacy with the Lord as you grow in understanding and authority over every area of your life. Once you've found a prayer, declaration, or affirmation that speaks to your need, build on it with all else you've studied and learned. Then, add your revelation to what you'll read in these sections. God bless you on your Holy Spirit-filled journey!

When we feel overwhelmed, burdened, or in need of divine help, prayer becomes our sacred place of appeal to God. This section provides Spirit-led prayers to help us communicate with our Heavenly Father about the strongholds, struggles, and spiritual warfare in our lives. These are not just words—they are petitions anchored in faith, surrender, and the truth of God's Word.

Use this section as part of your intimate conversation with God when you need to cast your cares on Him, ask for deliverance, cry out for a breakthrough, or address other pressing deficiencies in your life.

1. Prayer for Protection from Spiritual Attacks
Father, in the name of Jesus, I ask for Your divine protection over my mind, body, and spirit. Place a hedge of protection around me and my family. Let no weapon formed against me prosper, and every tongue that rises in judgment be condemned. I cover myself with the blood of Jesus and declare that every

spiritual attack against me is broken and rendered powerless. Strengthen me to stand firm in faith, knowing that greater is He Who is in me than he who is in the world. In Jesus' name, Amen.

2. Prayer for Boldness to Walk in God's Calling
Lord, I know You have called me for a divine purpose. Today, I ask for boldness to walk confidently in my calling. Silence the voice of fear and intimidation that seeks to hold me back. Let me move forward with courage, knowing that You have already equipped me with everything I need to fulfill my assignment. Let Your strength rise within me as I follow Your leading without hesitation. In Jesus' mighty name, Amen.

3. Prayer for Healing from Emotional Wounds
Heavenly Father, I lay my emotional wounds before You. Heal the broken places in my heart that have been scarred by rejection, betrayal, and disappointment. Let Your love pour over me like healing oil, soothing every hurt and restoring my peace. I release every person and situation that has caused me pain. Fill me with Your joy, and let my heart be whole again. In Jesus' name, Amen.

4. Prayer for Wisdom and Spiritual Discernment
Lord, Your Word says that if I lack wisdom, I can ask You, and You will give it generously. Today, I ask for wisdom and discernment in every area of my life. Let me recognize truth from deception, and give me the insight to make decisions aligned with Your will. Open my spiritual eyes and ears to hear and perceive Your leading. I receive Your wisdom with gratitude. In Jesus' name, Amen.

5. Prayer for Deliverance from Generational Curses/Spells
Father, I stand before You today, forgiven for all of my sins because I have wholeheartedly repented, and You have graciously forgiven me of any sin that could bind me to a generational curse. By Your Word and power, break every generational curse operating in my bloodline and my family line. Thank You for giving me the power to renounce every sinful pattern, bondage, affliction passed down through my family, and every agreement made, knowingly or

unknowingly, with the kingdom of darkness. Father, let Your freedom reign over my family line, from this generation forward. By the blood of Jesus Christ! In Jesus' name, Amen.

6. Prayer for Strength During Spiritual Warfare
Lord, the battle feels intense, but I know that You have already secured the victory. As Your Word commands, teach me how to clothe myself with Your full armor—the belt of truth, the breastplate of righteousness, the shield of faith, the helmet of salvation, the sword of the Spirit, and my feet shod with the preparation of the gospel of peace. Strengthen my hands for battle and my heart for victory. Let me fight not in my strength, but in the power of Your might. I will not be moved, for You are with me. In Jesus' name, Amen.

7. Prayer for a Renewed Mind
Father, Your Word says that the renewing of my mind transforms me. Today, I bring my thoughts before You and ask You to align them with Your truth. Remove every negative, fearful, and doubtful thought that does not reflect Your will for my life. Let my mind be saturated with thoughts of faith, peace, victory, and all else You have for me to ponder on. I reject the lies of the enemy and choose to think on things that are true, noble, and praiseworthy. In Jesus' name, Amen.

8. Prayer for Freedom from Fear of Failure
Lord, I confess that I have allowed the fear of failure to hold me back from walking fully in my purpose. Today, I renounce that fear and declare that my success is not based on my strength, but on Your faithfulness. I will step out in faith, knowing that You will guide and empower me. Even if I stumble, You will lift me up and set me back on track. My success is secured in You. In Jesus' name, Amen.

9. Prayer for Peace in Times of Uncertainty
Father, uncertainty surrounds me, but You are the God of peace. I refuse to be anxious or overwhelmed by the unknown. Fill my heart with peace that

surpasses all understanding. Let me rest in the assurance that You are in control and working all things together for my good. Even when I don't see the way, I trust that You are leading me. I receive Your peace now, in Jesus' name, Amen.

10. Prayer for Victory Over Temptation and Sin
Father, in the name of Jesus, I come before You with a sincere heart, confessing that I have chosen sin over obedience far too many times. I ask for strength and discernment, so that when the enemy seeks to entice me, I will overcome evil with good (Romans 12:21). Deliver me from every plan designed to pull me away from Your will. Strengthen my spirit to choose righteousness over sin, and let me walk in the freedom You purchased for me on the cross.

You have given me the power to resist temptation, and today, I choose lasting freedom from the grips of enticement. Your Word says that whoever has suffered in the flesh has ceased from sin and lives to please You instead of self and the world (1 Peter 4:1). Help me to arm myself with this same mindset—to patiently endure and resist temptation rather than give in and fail to please You.

I renounce every desire I've harbored that seeks to gratify the flesh. I confess and forsake every sin I've covered, hidden, or excused. I receive Your mercy according to Proverbs 28:13. Teach me to recognize the root causes that drive me toward sin, whether loneliness, stress, rejection, or insecurity. Show me how to surrender every craving and impulse to You. I will not make provision for my flesh to fulfill its lusts (Romans 13:14). Instead, I put on the Lord Jesus Christ and choose to walk in obedience and holiness. Fill the empty places with Your presence, Lord. Be my peace, my joy, and my true satisfaction. In Jesus' name, Amen.

11. Prayer for Financial Breakthrough
Father, You are my Provider. Today, I ask for a breakthrough in my finances. Remove every barrier that stands between me and the financial blessings You have for me. Open doors of opportunity and grant me wisdom in my financial decisions. Let abundance flow into my life so that I can be a blessing to others. In Jesus' name, Amen.

12. Prayer for Protection from Evil Influences

Lord, I ask for Your protection from every evil influence that seeks to invade my life. Close every demonic portal and disconnect me from any ungodly soul ties. Surround me with angels to guard and defend me from the enemy's schemes. Let no weapon formed against me prosper, and let every trap set for me be dismantled. I walk in Your protection and safety. In Jesus' name, Amen.

13. Prayer for Emotional Stability

Father, I come to You with my emotions laid bare. Calm the storms within me and give me emotional stability. Let me not be ruled by anger, fear, or sadness. Restore my emotional balance and fill me with peace and joy. Let my heart rest securely in Your love. In Jesus' name, Amen.

14. Prayer for Relationships

Lord, I lift my relationships to You. Heal the broken places and, only if it be Your will, reunite what has been torn apart. Let forgiveness flow where offense has been. Restore trust where it has been broken. Let love, peace, and understanding be the foundation of my relationships. I receive Your blessing—that my relationships will reflect Your heart and bring glory to Your name. In Jesus' name, Amen.

15. Prayer for Freedom from Anxiety

Father, I cast all my anxieties upon You because You care for me. Let Your peace guard my heart and mind. Remove the weight of anxiety and replace it with the assurance of Your love and faithfulness. Your perfect peace rules my heart. In Jesus' name, Amen.

16. Prayer for Favor and Open Doors

Lord, I ask for Your divine favor in every area of my life. Open doors that no man can shut and align me with the right people and opportunities. Let Your favor go before me, making a way where there seems to be no way. In Jesus' name, Amen.

17. Prayer for Guidance in Decision-Making

Father, I seek Your guidance in every decision I face. Let Your Holy Spirit lead me and give me clarity and peace. Let me not rely on my own understanding, but trust fully in You. Close doors that are not from You and open the ones that align with Your will. In Jesus' name, Amen.

18. Prayer for Spiritual Growth and Fruit

Lord, I desire to deepen my relationship with You. Increase my hunger for Your Word and my sensitivity to Your Spirit. Let my faith grow strong and mature as I spend time in Your presence. Let me reflect Your character more each day. Then, when my growth is ready to produce the fruit of blessing others, use me so that You can get all the glory You desire from my life. In Jesus' name, Amen.

19. Prayer for Protection Over Family

Father, I entrust my family into Your care. Protect them from harm, sickness, and evil. Cover them under the shadow of Your wings. Let them walk in Your blessing and favor. Keep them close to You, and let them fulfill the destiny You have for them. In Jesus' name, Amen.

20. Prayer for Freedom from Bitterness

Lord, I release all bitterness and unforgiveness from my heart. Cleanse me from resentment and fill me with Your love. Let me walk in peace and freedom. I refuse to be weighed down by bitterness. In Jesus' name, Amen.

21. Prayer for Protection of the Mind

Father, I ask that You guard my mind from negative thoughts, confusion, and deception. Let my thoughts be aligned with Your truth. Silence the voice of the enemy that tries to speak lies into my mind. When I put on the helmet of salvation, I know that my mind is sound and secure in You. Let the peace of Christ rule my mind and heart. In Jesus' name, Amen.

22. Prayer for Deliverance from Fear of Rejection

Lord, I confess that I have feared rejection from others. Today, I renounce that fear and declare that I am wholly accepted and loved by You. Let me no longer seek approval from people but find my security in Your perfect love. Let me walk confidently in my identity as Your child, knowing that Your love is all I need. In Jesus' name, Amen.

23. Prayer for Restoration of Joy

Father, restore to me the joy of my salvation. Let Your joy be my strength. Remove the heaviness and sadness from my spirit and replace it with laughter and gladness. Let me walk in the freedom and lightness of heart that comes from knowing You. I receive the fullness of Your joy. In Jesus' name, Amen.

24. Prayer for Strength to Forgive

Lord, I confess that forgiveness is hard, but I choose to forgive those who have hurt me. I release every offense into Your hands and ask You to heal my heart. Give me the strength to let go of bitterness and walk in the freedom of forgiveness. Let love replace resentment, and let peace guard my heart. In Jesus' name, Amen.

25. Prayer for Divine Health and Healing

Father, thank You that by the stripes of Jesus, I am healed. Let Your healing power flow through my body and restore me to full health. I reject sickness and disease, and I stand on Your promises of health and strength. Let my body align with Your Word, and let healing be my portion. In Jesus' name, Amen.

26. Prayer for Financial Wisdom

Lord, I ask for wisdom in managing my finances. Let me be a faithful steward of everything You've entrusted to me. Open my eyes to opportunities and give me discernment in financial decisions. Let me walk in abundance, not lack. Thank You that my needs are met according to Your riches in glory. In Jesus' name, Amen.

27. Prayer for Spiritual Clarity and Direction

Father, I need to hear Your voice clearly. Remove the distractions and confusion that cloud my understanding. Let me discern Your will and walk confidently in the path You have set before me. Let my steps be ordered by You, and let me not lean on my own understanding. In Jesus' name, Amen.

28. Prayer for Family Salvation

Lord, I lift my family to You and ask that You draw them to Yourself. Let the light of Your truth shine in their hearts and remove every veil of deception. Let them know the love of Christ and receive salvation. I wholeheartedly believe that You will save my household, and we will serve the Lord together. Please send whoever they will listen to, and let the one witnessing to them have Your heart of love, compassion, and patience to help my loved ones understand You and Your never-ending love for them. If the one witnessing is the one who will plant, water, fertilize, or harvest the salvation of my loved ones, please give them the anointing, wisdom, understanding, knowledge, fruit, and gifts of the Holy Spirit needed to persuade my loved ones to come to Jesus and stay with Him. Then, have someone or others disciple them for the rest of their lives on Earth. In Jesus' name, Amen.

29. Prayer for Deliverance from Procrastination

Father, in the name of Jesus, I come to You acknowledging that procrastination has hindered me from fulfilling what You've assigned to my life. I repent for every delay that has come through fear, distraction, perfectionism, or laziness. I renounce every spiritual force that promotes delay and declare that it has no more authority in my life.

Your Word says, "The soul of the sluggard desireth, and hath nothing: but the soul of the diligent shall be made fat" (Proverbs 13:4 KJV). Lord, make me diligent in spirit. Remove from me the urge to put off what You've called me to do. Let Your fire burn in my heart with urgency, focus, and discipline to fulfill every task and assignment You've given.

I receive divine strength to act, to move, and to finish. I declare that I will no longer be ruled by hesitation or passivity. I walk in the power of the Holy Spirit, and I redeem the time, for the days are evil. In Jesus' name, Amen.

30. Prayer for Breaking Ungodly Soul Ties

Father, in the name of Jesus Christ, I come before You, fully surrendering my heart, mind, soul, spirit, and body to You. According to 1 Corinthians 6:16-17 AMPC, Your Word warns that "the two shall become one flesh," and it also promises that "he who is united to the Lord becomes one spirit with Him." Lord, I no longer desire to be one in any way with anyone or anything that You did not assign to my life. I renounce and sever every ungodly soul tie, heart tie, mind tie, spirit tie, and body tie—whether formed through sin, unhealthy emotional attachments, friendships, relationships, or experiences that were never Your will for me.

As Ezekiel 13:18 AMPC speaks of those who "hunt the souls of My people," I declare that every demonic transporter, manipulator, or spiritual hijacker that gained access through those soul ties is now cut off from me. In the mighty name of Jesus, I apply the blood of Jesus Christ over every part of me—my soul, heart, mind, spirit, and body—and I deauthorize their power and cancel their assignments now and forever.

Father, I thank You for cleansing me, restoring my purity, and aligning me with Your will. I am free, and I will remain free, from all ungodly ties and demonic connections. I receive Your peace, wholeness, and healing in every place that was once bound. In Jesus' name, Amen.

31. Prayer for the Breaking of Delay and Stagnation

Father, will You please break every spirit of delay and stagnation off of my life? Let the doors that have been closed be opened. Remove every obstacle standing in the way of my progress. Let my life move forward in alignment with Your timing and purpose. Thank You for the breakthrough and the acceleration of all You've promised in my life. In Jesus' name, Amen.

32. Prayer for Restoration of Purpose

Lord, I ask You to restore the purpose You placed on my life. Let me no longer wander or live without direction. Let my gifts and calling come alive within me. Open doors of opportunity and let me fulfill the assignment You have given me. Thank You that, through my obedience to Your plan, Your purpose for my life will be fulfilled. In Jesus' name, Amen.

33. Prayer for Release from Guilt and Shame

Father, I bring my guilt and shame to You. I confess my sins and receive Your forgiveness. Let the burden of condemnation be lifted from me. Thank You that I am cleansed by the blood of Jesus and stand righteous before You. Let me walk in the freedom of grace and mercy. In Jesus' name, Amen.

34. Prayer for Protection from Witchcraft and Sorcery

Lord, thank You that no spell, curse, or hex has any authority over my life. The blood of Jesus covers me. The gospel breaks every evil spell on my life through my belief in Jesus Christ. Your blessings crush every curse on my life to rid it from me, unto Your glory. Let every demonic assignment sent against me be canceled. Let every word spoken against me in darkness be exposed, condemned, and destroyed according to Your Word. I walk in divine protection and victory. In Jesus' name, Amen.

35. Prayer for Supernatural Favor in the Workplace

Father, I ask for Your favor to surround me in my workplace. Let my work be excellent and my reputation be honorable. Let me have favor with my superiors and colleagues. Let promotion, increase, and recognition be my portion. Thank You, Father, that I work as unto You, and my labor will be rewarded. In Jesus' name, Amen.

36. Prayer for Deliverance from Depression

Lord, I ask You to lift the heaviness of depression from my heart. Teach me how to let Your joy be my strength. Remove every cloud of darkness and let light and hope flood my soul. I reject every lie of the enemy that says I am worthless or unloved. Let me walk in peace and joy. In Jesus' name, Amen.

37. Prayer for Reconciliation in Friendships

Father, I ask You to heal the broken friendships in my life that You want restored. Let forgiveness, grace, and understanding flow where division has entered. Let there be reconciliation and restoration. Let love replace resentment, and let unity be established. In Jesus' name, Amen.

38. Prayer for Increase in Spiritual Gifts

Lord, I ask You to stir up the spiritual gifts within me. Whether it's prophecy, healing, wisdom, discernment of spirits, or another gift that the Holy Spirit has given to me, flow mightily through me for the edification of others. Let me operate in the power of the Holy Spirit. Let my gifts make room for me and glorify You. In Jesus' name, Amen.

39. Prayer for Peace During Spiritual Attacks

Father, even when the enemy comes against me, teach me how not to fear, and what I need to do in place of the anxiety that tends to cause me to shrink back when I'm attacked. Let Your peace guard my heart and mind. Let me remain calm and confident, knowing that You are my Defender. Thank You that no attack of the enemy will ever succeed against me. I rest in Your protection and strength. In Jesus' name, Amen.

40. Prayer for Increase in Faith

Lord, I ask You to teach me how to increase and deepen my faith in You. I know faith comes by hearing Your Word (Romans 10:17), so instruct me how to grow my faith by listening to and obeying Your Word. Let me trust You even when I can't see the outcome. Let my faith grow deeper and stronger as I walk with You. Let me believe the impossible and expect miracles. Let faith be my foundation and my shield. In Jesus' name, Amen.

41. Prayer for Courage to Step Into Purpose

Father, I ask You for the courage to step into the purpose You've designed for me. Let me no longer be held back by fear or uncertainty. Strengthen my heart to take bold steps of faith, even when the path ahead is unclear. Let me trust that You have prepared the way for me and that every step I take is guided by Your hand. I reject hesitation and embrace the boldness that comes from knowing that You go before me. Thank You that I will fulfill the calling You've placed on my life, and nothing will stand in the way of Your purpose. In Jesus' name, Amen.

42. Prayer for Deliverance from the Spirit of Control

Lord, I surrender every need for control into Your hands. I have tried to control outcomes, people, and situations out of fear and insecurity. I release this need to You and ask that You teach me to trust You completely. Let me walk in faith, knowing that You are in control of all things. Replace the desire to control with the peace that comes from trusting in Your sovereignty. Let me live freely under the guidance of Your Spirit. In Jesus' name, Amen.

43. Prayer for the Protection of My Home

Father, I plead the blood of Jesus over my home. Let my house be a place of peace, safety, and rest. Let no weapon formed against my home or family prosper. Thank You that no evil spirit or work of darkness shall enter my household. Let Your angels surround my house—standing guard on the perimeter of my property line and posted at every door and window as You command. Let Your presence fill my home, driving out every trace of darkness. I establish my house under the authority of Jesus Christ. In Jesus' name, Amen.

44. Prayer for Clarity in Decision-Making

Lord, I ask for divine clarity in every decision I face. Let me not be swayed by my emotions or by the opinions of others. Let me hear Your voice clearly and follow Your leading without hesitation. Give me wisdom and discernment to choose the path that aligns with Your will. Let me walk confidently, knowing that You are directing my steps. I refuse to be double-minded or uncertain. Thank You that I have the mind of Christ, and Your truth guides my decisions. In Jesus' name, Amen.

45. Prayer to Break the Spell of Laziness

Heavenly Father, in the name of Jesus, I come against every spell, curse, and demonic influence that promotes laziness, complacency, or slothfulness in my life. I repent for every time I've allowed procrastination and ease to take the place of diligence and purpose. Your Word declares, *"The soul of the sluggard desireth, and hath nothing: but the soul of the diligent shall be made fat"* (Proverbs 13:4 KJV). Thank You that excuses, distractions, or comfort no longer rule me.

I renounce every spiritual and mental heaviness that makes it hard to start, continue, or finish the assignments You've given me. Father, ignite in me a fresh fire of discipline, focus, and drive. I receive Your grace to be diligent in all things—natural and spiritual—and to do all things heartily, as unto You. I break every chain of spiritual laziness now, and I rise in strength to fulfill my purpose. In Jesus' name, Amen.

46. Prayer for Strength to Overcome Grief
Lord, I bring my grief and sorrow to You. I ask that You comfort my heart and lift the heaviness that weighs on me. Let Your peace fill the empty spaces left by loss. Help me to release the pain and entrust my heart to You. Thank You that I will not be defined by grief but will walk in the healing and restoration that comes from Your presence. Let joy replace mourning, and let hope rise again within me. In Jesus' name, Amen.

47. Prayer for Deliverance from the Spirit of Guilt and Condemnation
Father, I confess that I have allowed guilt and condemnation to weigh me down. Today, I release every mistake and failure into Your hands. Your Word declares there's no condemnation for those who are in Christ Jesus. Let me walk in the freedom of Your grace, knowing that I have repented and am therefore forgiven and cleansed by the blood of Jesus. I refuse to allow the enemy to accuse me or hold me captive to past mistakes. Thank You that I am free, whole, and righteous in Christ. In Jesus' name, Amen.

48. Prayer for Breaking the Spirit of Jealousy
Lord, I confess that jealousy has taken root in my heart. I renounce the spirit of envy and comparison. Let me be content with what You have given me and rejoice in the blessings of others. Let me celebrate the success and favor of those around me without resentment. Teach me to trust Your timing and Your plan for my life. Let my heart be pure and free from bitterness. Thank You that I will walk in love and gratitude, knowing that You have good things in store for me. In Jesus' name, Amen.

49. Prayer for Wisdom in Relationships

Father, I ask for wisdom in my relationships. Let me discern the people You have assigned to walk with me and give me courage to release those who are not aligned with my destiny. Let me walk in unity with those who are of Your Spirit and protect me from relationships that would lead me away from You. Let love, respect, and understanding govern my relationships. Let me be a source of encouragement and strength to those You have placed in my life. In Jesus' name, Amen.

50. Prayer for Supernatural Breakthrough

Lord, I ask You for a supernatural breakthrough in my life. Break down every wall and barrier standing in the way of my destiny. Let the chains of delay, hindrance, and limitation be broken off my life. Let every closed door be opened according to Your will. Let miracles, signs, and wonders follow me as I walk in faith and obedience. Thank You that I am stepping into a new season of favor and increase. Let me see the manifestation of Your promises. In Jesus' name, Amen.

SPELL AND CURSE-BREAKING DECLARATIONS

> *O you poor and silly and thoughtless and unreflecting and senseless Galatians! Who has fascinated or bewitched or cast a spell over you, unto whom—right before your very eyes—Jesus Christ (the Messiah) was openly and graphically set forth and portrayed as crucified?*
>
> Galatians 3:1 AMPC

This verse confronts the tragic reality that even believers—those who had seen Christ clearly—can come under the influence of deception. The word *"bewitched"* in the Greek implies a spiritual manipulation or spellbinding that clouds judgment, blinds the heart, hinders truth, and shifts loyalty away from the cross of Christ. Paul wasn't merely addressing immaturity—he was exposing a spiritual attack.

When believers are spiritually dulled or misled, it's not always because they've backslidden by choice. Sometimes, they've unknowingly come under a spell—fascinated by a lie, charmed by a false teaching, or entangled by emotional soul ties that override discernment. This fact is why declarations, rooted in God's Word, are not mere words of our supposing—they are spiritual weapons. A biblical declaration is *a bold proclamation of what God has already established, promised, or decreed in His Word.*

Our generation wrestles with hidden spiritual forces that seek to blind us, discourage us, and keep us bound. That's why this section isn't just a list of declarations of good intentions. They are bold, truth-rooted *weapons* for spiritual warfare—formulated from Scripture and targeted to break strongholds, cancel curses, and restore clarity.

Although a few of these declarations may sound similar in theme, each was constructed to address a specific stronghold or subject covered throughout these pages, anchored in the Word of God. They are distinct in purpose—to speak directly to the different ways spells and curses can manifest.

I did not include this section on declarations to replace your own prayer life, but to help you *jumpstart your journey* or assist as you pray more accurately, study the Bible more deeply, and become motivated to find fitting verses that perfectly align with your unique situation. These declarations are faith-fueled and will equip you with the language, direction, and Spirit-led confidence required for effective warfare strategies as you earnestly seek to follow the Holy Spirit's leading.

Only the Holy Spirit and you can create a perfectly tailor-made declaration that fits your exact need. I'm humbled and highly honored to come alongside you to help you set up and move forward from the starting line or wherever you are in your journey. From there, the Holy Spirit will guide you to obtain everything else you'll need to cross the finish line in freedom and victory.

Traveling the distance from beginning to end is not about how fast you can arrive at the destination. Our focus is on pleasing God throughout the process. Remember what you've learned in this book: spiritual warfare is about pleasing God, not ourselves.

There are times when we must rise to a higher spiritual authority and boldly proclaim what God has already promised us. These declarations are based on the unchanging truths of Scripture that have already been established in Heaven and are ready to be spoken into existence on Earth. This section serves as a part of our weaponry for spiritual warfare, helping us silence the enemy's voice and align our circumstances with God's will.

As you speak these declarations aloud, do so with confidence and authority, knowing you are partnering with the promises of Heaven. Let your faith rise because your turnaround has already begun.

1. Declaration of Authority Over the Enemy
I declare that I have been given authority to trample on serpents and scorpions, and over all the power of the enemy, and nothing shall by any means harm me

(Luke 10:19). I am seated in heavenly places with Christ Jesus (Ephesians 2:6), and I reign with Him in spiritual authority. No weapon formed against me shall prosper, and every tongue that rises against me in judgment I condemn, for this is my heritage as a servant of the Lord (Isaiah 54:17). I walk in victory, knowing that the enemy is already defeated.

2. Declaration of Empathy and Compassion
I declare that I put on compassion, kindness, humility, gentleness, and patience, as God's own chosen one (Colossians 3:12 AMPC). I reject every spirit of selfishness, coldness, and insensitivity. The love of God has been poured into my heart by the Holy Spirit (Romans 5:5 AMPC), and I am empowered to care for others deeply. I walk in love, seek to understand before judging, and extend grace as I have received it.

3. Declaration of Confidence in My Identity
I declare that I will not compare myself with others, for it is unwise and leads to deception (Galatians 6:4-5 AMPC). I examine and test my own work, and I will take pride in it alone. I am fearfully and wonderfully made (Psalm 139:14), uniquely fashioned by God for a divine purpose. I celebrate others without diminishing myself, and I walk boldly in who God created me to be.

4. Declaration of Healing and Wholeness
I declare that by the stripes of Jesus Christ, I am healed (Isaiah 53:5). I reject every sickness, disease, and infirmity in my body, for Christ Himself took my infirmities and bore my sicknesses (Matthew 8:17). I speak life and health over my body, declaring that I am whole from the crown of my head to the soles of my feet. My body is the temple of the Holy Spirit, and no disease or affliction can dwell in it (1 Corinthians 6:19).

5. Declaration of Victory Over the Enemy
I declare that I am more than a conqueror through Christ who loves me (Romans 8:37). No scheme of the enemy will prevail against me, for the weapons of my warfare are not carnal, but mighty through God to the pulling down of

strongholds (2 Corinthians 10:4). Every plot, plan, and strategy of the enemy against my life is dismantled and destroyed in the name of Jesus (Isaiah 54:17). I walk in victory, knowing that God always causes me to triumph in Christ (2 Corinthians 2:14).

6. Declaration of Supernatural Provision
I declare that my God shall supply all my needs according to His riches in glory by Christ Jesus (Philippians 4:19). The Lord is my Shepherd; I shall not want (Psalm 23:1). I am blessed in the city and blessed in the field (Deuteronomy 28:3). I have no lack because the Lord provides for me abundantly. I will not worry about tomorrow, for God is my Source and my Sustainer (Matthew 6:25-26).

7. Declaration of Renewed Strength
I declare that I can do all things through Christ who strengthens me (Philippians 4:13). When I am weak, the Lord is my strength (2 Corinthians 12:9-10). I will mount up with wings like eagles; I will run and not grow weary; I will walk and not faint (Isaiah 40:31). My strength is renewed daily because the joy of the Lord is my strength (Nehemiah 8:10).

8. Declaration of Deliverance From Anxiety and Worry
I declare that I am anxious for nothing. Still, in everything by prayer and supplication, with thanksgiving, I make my requests known to God (Philippians 4:6). The peace of God, which surpasses all understanding, guards my heart and mind in Christ Jesus (Philippians 4:7). I declare that I will not be controlled by fear or worry. I reject the spirit of worry and anxiety, knowing that God is in control of every detail of my life (Matthew 6:34).

9. Declaration of Favor and Open Doors
I declare that I am walking in God's favor and success. I declare that I am surrounded with His favor as with a shield (Psalm 5:12). The Lord goes before me and makes the crooked places straight (Isaiah 45:2). He opens doors that no man can shut and shuts doors that no man can open (Revelation 3:7). I

walk in the favor of the Lord, knowing that He delights in prospering me and giving me good success (Psalm 35:27; Joshua 1:8).

10. Declaration of Stewarding My Health
I declare that I honor my body as the temple of the Holy Spirit (1 Corinthians 6:19-20 AMPC). I do not neglect myself, for I belong to God and was bought with a price. I take time to rest, refresh, and replenish so that I may serve the Lord with strength, clarity, and joy. I choose balance and prioritize soul and body wellness, trusting God to restore and sustain me daily.

11. Declaration of Severing Soul Ties
I declare that every ungodly and evil soul tie, heart tie, mind tie, spirit tie, and body tie that I have with any person or thing is now severed in the name of Jesus Christ. I apply the blood of Jesus Christ to my soul, heart, mind, spirit, and body (Revelation 12:11). I renounce and revoke every ungodly pleasure, influence, and connection that has held me captive in any way, shape, or form. I deauthorize every demonic transporter and their assignment over my life, declaring that their access to me is now revoked by the authority of Jesus Christ (Luke 10:19). I am free, and I will remain free from every ungodly influence and connection, now and forever (John 8:36). So be it!

12. Declaration of Spiritual Clarity
I declare that I have the mind of Christ (1 Corinthians 2:16). I reject every spirit of confusion, mental fog, and double-mindedness. My mind is sharp, focused, and sound, for God has given me a spirit of a sound mind, not of fear (2 Timothy 1:7). I receive divine understanding and clarity, knowing that the Holy Spirit leads me into all truth (John 16:13). I will no longer second-guess God's direction because His Word is a lamp unto my feet and a light unto my path (Psalm 119:105).

13. Declaration of Breaking Generational Curses
I sever every generational tie God has not willed for me and my family. No curse has any legal authority over my life. Let every curse spoken over my

lineage be rendered powerless. I declare that every generational curse in my bloodline is broken by the power of the blood of Jesus Christ (Galatians 3:13). The sins of my ancestors no longer bind me; I am a new creation in Christ (2 Corinthians 5:17). I reject the inheritance of sickness, poverty, addiction, and failure that has plagued my family. Instead, I receive the inheritance of righteousness, peace, and joy through the Holy Spirit (Romans 14:17). Every curse spoken over my family line is canceled. I am free in the name of Jesus Christ (John 8:36). I declare that I am free from every generational stronghold, and I establish a new legacy of blessing and righteousness for my family.

14. Declaration of Financial Breakthrough

I declare that I am blessed and not cursed in my finances (Deuteronomy 28:12). My God shall supply all my needs according to His riches in glory by Christ Jesus (Philippians 4:19). I reject the spirit of lack and poverty; I am a lender and not a borrower (Deuteronomy 28:12). I walk under an open heaven where God's provision and favor will follow me in every area of my life (Malachi 3:10). I declare that my current circumstances do not limit me because God is more than enough. I decree supernatural increase and abundance over my finances in the name of Jesus Christ.

15. Declaration of Restoration

I declare that God is restoring everything the enemy has stolen from me (Joel 2:25). My wasted years, lost opportunities, and broken relationships are being restored by the hand of God. The Lord is making all things new in my life (Revelation 21:5). My latter days will be greater than my former days (Haggai 2:9), and I will testify of God's goodness and faithfulness.

16. Declaration of Wisdom and Discernment

I declare that the wisdom of God dwells richly within me (James 1:5). I can discern between truth and deception, light and darkness (Hebrews 5:14). False teachings, manipulative spirits, or cunning strategies of the enemy will not mislead me. The Holy Spirit leads me into all truth (John 16:13), and the mind of Christ guides my decisions.

17. Declaration of Fruitfulness and Multiplication

I declare that I am fruitful in every area of my life (Genesis 1:28). My hands are blessed, and the work of my hands prospers (Deuteronomy 28:8). I reject barrenness and stagnation; I decree increase and expansion over my life (Isaiah 54:2-3). Everything I touch will flourish because the Lord's favor rests upon me (Psalm 1:3).

18. Declaration of Divine Alignment

I declare that my life is in divine alignment with God's will and purpose (Jeremiah 29:11). My steps are ordered by the Lord (Psalm 37:23), and I am positioned in the right place at the right time. Every detour, distraction, and delay sent by the enemy is canceled, and I am walking confidently in my divine assignment.

19. Declaration of Boldness to Witness

I declare that I am not ashamed of the gospel of Christ, for it is the power of God unto salvation (Romans 1:16). The Holy Spirit has empowered me to proclaim the truth of God's Word with boldness and confidence (Acts 4:31). I am a light in the darkness. My testimony will draw others to salvation (Matthew 5:16).

20. Declaration of Strength in Spiritual Warfare

I declare that I am clothed in the whole armor of God (Ephesians 6:11). I stand firm against the schemes of the enemy, wielding the sword of the Spirit, which is the Word of God (Ephesians 6:17). No weapon formed against me shall prosper (Isaiah 54:17). I take authority over every spiritual attack and demonic influence in the name of Jesus Christ (Matthew 18:18).

21. Declaration of Divine Timing

I declare that my times and seasons are in the hands of the Lord (Psalm 31:15). I will not be anxious about the future, for the Lord makes everything beautiful in its time (Ecclesiastes 3:11). The Lord orders my steps. I walk confidently in His timing and provision (Proverbs 3:5-6).

22. Declaration of Overflow and Abundance

I declare that my cup runs over (Psalm 23:5). The Lord has blessed me abundantly so that I may be a blessing to others (2 Corinthians 9:8). I receive supernatural increase in my finances, relationships, and spiritual gifts. I will not lack, for the Lord is my source (Philippians 4:19).

23. Declaration of Joy and Peace

I declare that the joy of the Lord is my strength (Nehemiah 8:10). I reject the spirit of heaviness and depression, for God has given me a garment of praise (Isaiah 61:3). I walk in supernatural peace that surpasses all understanding (Philippians 4:7).

24. Declaration of Deliverance From Addiction

I declare that I am free from every addiction, stronghold, and bondage (John 8:36). I am no longer a slave to sin, for I have been redeemed by the blood of Jesus (Romans 6:14). Every chain of addiction is broken, and I walk in liberty (2 Corinthians 3:17).

25. Declaration of Reconciliation

I declare that God is restoring broken relationships in my life that He desires I have (2 Corinthians 5:18). Forgiveness, healing, and understanding flow freely in my relationships. The Lord is binding up the wounds of the past and, according to His will, bringing reconciliation where there was division (Psalm 147:3).

26. Declaration of Kingdom Influence

I declare that I am a kingdom ambassador (2 Corinthians 5:20). I represent the Kingdom of Heaven on Earth and carry the authority of the King. My words and actions bring glory to God and advance His kingdom (Matthew 6:10).

27. Declaration of Financial Stewardship

I declare that I am a faithful steward of the resources God has given me (Luke 16:10). I manage my finances with wisdom and integrity, honoring God with my tithes and offerings (Malachi 3:10).

28. Declaration of Deliverance From Shame
I declare that I am not condemned, for no condemnation is given to those in Christ Jesus (Romans 8:1). My past mistakes and failures no longer define me; I am a new creation in Christ (2 Corinthians 5:17).

29. Declaration of Divine Promotion
I declare that promotion comes from the Lord (Psalm 75:6-7). I am being lifted to new levels of influence and authority because I have been faithful in the little (Luke 16:10).

30. Declaration of Courage
I declare that I am strong and courageous (Joshua 1:9). I reject the spirit of fear and intimidation, knowing that the Lord is with me wherever I go (2 Timothy 1:7).

31. Declaration of Victory Over Fear
I declare that I am not a slave to fear, for I am a child of God (Romans 8:15). Fear has no place in my life because God has not given me a spirit of fear, but of power, love, and a sound mind (2 Timothy 1:7). I walk boldly and confidently, knowing that the Lord goes before me and is my rear guard (Isaiah 52:12). I reject every whisper of fear and anxiety. I declare that my mind and heart are guarded by the peace of God (Philippians 4:7).

32. Declaration of Spiritual Boldness
I declare that I am not ashamed of the gospel of Christ, for it is the power of God unto salvation (Romans 1:16). I speak with courage and conviction, knowing that the Holy Spirit empowers me to be a bold witness for Christ (Acts 1:8). I am fearless in proclaiming the truth. I will not back down in the face of opposition (2 Timothy 4:2). I walk with spiritual authority, knowing that the power of God rests upon me (Luke 10:19).

33. Declaration of God's Favor
I declare that the favor of God surrounds me like a shield (Psalm 5:12). I walk in divine favor with God and man (Luke 2:52). Doors of opportunity are

opening for me because God's favor is upon my life. I am blessed in the city and blessed in the field (Deuteronomy 28:3). I receive divine acceleration and increase because of God's favor.

34. Declaration of Sound Mind and Emotional Stability
I declare that I have the mind of Christ (1 Corinthians 2:16). I reject every lie and distortion of the enemy. My mind is stable, peaceful, and reflects on God and His goodness, for I am kept in perfect peace because my mind is stayed on the Lord (Isaiah 26:3). I take every thought captive to the obedience of Christ (2 Corinthians 10:5). I walk in mental clarity and emotional stability, free from confusion and distress.

35. Declaration of Health and Healing
I declare that I make wise choices in what I consume, for whether I eat or drink, I do it all to the glory of God (1 Corinthians 10:31 AMPC). I do not let cravings or idleness dictate my decisions. My appetite is submitted to Christ, and I choose foods that nourish and strengthen my body. I am disciplined and guided by the Holy Spirit even in my eating habits, and I reject habits that lead to destruction (Proverbs 23:2 AMPC).

36. Declaration of Overcoming Temptation
I declare that I am not tempted beyond what I can bear, for God provides a way of escape from every temptation (1 Corinthians 10:13). I have the strength and discipline to resist the schemes of the enemy (James 4:7). I am led by the Spirit, not by the flesh (Galatians 5:16). I walk in holiness and purity, rejecting every unholy desire and impulse. I declare that I am no longer a slave to sin—I am a servant of righteousness, made free by God's truth. I declare that I have victory over every temptation, and I will not be overtaken by sin.

37. Declaration of Protection
I declare that I dwell in the secret place of the Most High and abide under the shadow of the Almighty (Psalm 91:1). No evil will befall me, and no plague will

come near my dwelling (Psalm 91:10). The Lord has given His angels charge over me to keep me in all my ways (Psalm 91:11). I am covered and protected by the blood of Jesus Christ (Revelation 12:11).

38. Declaration of Deliverance From Fear of Death
I declare that I am not afraid of death, for Christ has conquered death and the grave (1 Corinthians 15:55-57). My life is hidden with Christ in God (Colossians 3:3). I will fulfill the number of my days, and I will not die before my time (Psalm 118:17). The Lord has secured my eternal future, and I walk in the confidence of His promise of everlasting life (John 3:16).

39. Declaration of Anointing and Spiritual Power
I declare that I am anointed by the Holy Spirit (1 John 2:27). The same power that raised Jesus from the dead lives in me (Romans 8:11). I walk in spiritual authority, and signs and wonders follow me because I believe in Jesus Christ (Mark 16:17-18). I am equipped to heal the sick, cast out devils, and proclaim the gospel with power.

40. Declaration of Freedom from Overspending
I declare that I walk in Holy Spirit-guided understanding concerning my finances. I do not make impulsive decisions or spend beyond my means, for the Word says:

> *"For which of you, wishing to build a [farm] building, does not first sit down and calculate the cost [to see] whether he has sufficient means to finish it?"*
>
> Luke 14:28 AMPC

I count the cost before committing to anything financially. I reject overspending and emotional purchases. The Spirit of wisdom and prudence guides my financial decisions. I am a faithful steward of what God provides, and I experience peace, not pressure, because I live by principle, not impulse.

41. Declaration of Focus and Digital Discipline

I declare that I fix my eyes on what is eternal, not on what is temporal (2 Corinthians 4:18 AMPC). Notifications, endless scrolling, or compulsive checking will not control me. I set my mind and keep it set on what is above, not on the distractions of this world (Colossians 3:2 AMPC). My time is precious, and my attention is valuable. I take control of my devices, and I live a present, focused, and purposeful life each day.

42. Declaration of Strength to Overcome Opposition

I declare that no weapon formed against me shall prosper (Isaiah 54:17). Every tongue that rises against me in judgment, I condemn (Isaiah 54:17). I am more than a conqueror through Christ who strengthens me (Romans 8:37). I stand firm and unshakable in the face of opposition, knowing that God fights for me (Exodus 14:14).

43. Declaration of Walking in Authority

I declare that I have been given authority over all the power of the enemy (Luke 10:19). I trample on serpents and scorpions, and nothing shall harm me. I walk in the power of the Holy Spirit, and the enemy flees when I resist him (James 4:7). I decree that no demonic influence will prosper in my life.

44. Declaration of Supernatural Peace

I declare that I am filled with the peace of God, which surpasses all understanding (Philippians 4:7). My heart and mind are guarded by the peace of Christ (Colossians 3:15). I reject the spirit of anxiety and turmoil. I walk in divine peace, resting in the promises of God.

45. Declaration of Deliverance From Hopelessness

I declare that I have hope because Christ is my anchor (Hebrews 6:19). I reject the spirit of despair and hopelessness. My future is secure in the Lord, and I have a good and expected end (Jeremiah 29:11). I walk in faith, knowing that God will complete what He has begun in my life (Philippians 1:6).

46. Declaration of Overcoming Self-Doubt

I declare that I am fearfully and wonderfully made (Psalm 139:14). I reject every negative thought about my identity and worth. I am complete in Christ (Colossians 2:10). I have confidence, knowing that I am God's masterpiece, created for good works (Ephesians 2:10).

47. Declaration of Patience and Endurance

I declare that I will run with endurance the race set before me (Hebrews 12:1). I will not grow weary in well-doing, for I will reap in due season (Galatians 6:9). I am strengthened with all might according to His glorious power (Colossians 1:11).

48. Declaration of Supernatural Insight

I declare that I have divine insight and revelation through the Holy Spirit (Ephesians 1:17-18). My eyes are opened to see the deep things of God. I have spiritual discernment and understanding that surpasses human wisdom.

49. Declaration of Victory Over Depression

I declare that I have the oil of joy for mourning and the garment of praise for the spirit of heaviness (Isaiah 61:3). Depression and sadness have no place in my life. The joy of the Lord is my strength (Nehemiah 8:10).

50. Declaration of Trust in God's Plan

I declare that I trust in the Lord with all my heart (Proverbs 3:5-6). I lean not on my own understanding, but submit to God's direction. He makes my path straight, and I follow Him confidently.

SPELL AND CURSE-BREAKING AFFIRMATIONS

Sometimes, the battle isn't around us—it's within us. Affirmations are *powerful, truth-based statements designed to reshape how we see ourselves and renew our minds in accordance with God's Word.* Affirmations are not casual sayings or feel-good phrases—they are truth-based articulations of agreement that align our minds (hearts), souls, spirits, and mouths with the will of God. To affirm something is to persistently, firmly, and confidently express that it is true, even when others doubt it, and even when circumstances contradict it. We see this clearly in the book of Acts:

> *14 And recognizing Peter's voice, in her joy she failed to open the gate, but ran in and told the people that Peter was standing before the porch gate.*
> *15 They said to her, You are crazy! But she persistently and strongly and confidently affirmed that it was the truth. They said, It is his angel!*
> *16 But meanwhile Peter continued knocking, and when they opened the gate and saw him, they were amazed.*
>
> Acts 12:14-16 AMPC

In this moment, the servant girl didn't just report what she believed—she affirmed it. She stood firm in her statement despite ridicule and disbelief. That's what biblical affirmations train us to do—boldly align our words and thoughts with what God says is true, even when the natural world denies it.

When our identity feels shaken or our thoughts become clouded by lies, these biblical affirmations help us internalize and materialize God's truth of who we are. Recite them slowly, repeatedly, and intentionally, allowing each affirmation to help reframe your thinking and rebuild your confidence in Christ.

1. Affirmation of Identity in Christ

I am a child of God, chosen, loved, and accepted by my Heavenly Father. My past mistakes, my weaknesses, or the opinions of others do not define me. I am fearfully and wonderfully made, created in God's image, and called to walk in His light. Nothing and no one can separate me from the love of God that is in Christ Jesus. I am His masterpiece, created to fulfill the purpose He designed for me before the foundation of the world. (Romans 8:38-39; Psalm 139:14; Ephesians 2:10)

2. Affirmation of Spiritual Authority

I have been given power and authority through Jesus Christ to trample over serpents and scorpions and all the power of the enemy. No weapon formed against me shall prosper, and every tongue that rises against me in judgment, I shall condemn. I am seated in heavenly places with Christ Jesus, and I rule and reign in spiritual authority because greater is He who is in me than he who is in the world. (Luke 10:19; Isaiah 54:17; 1 John 4:4)

3. Affirmation of Confidence in God's Protection

I dwell in the secret place of the Most High and abide under the shadow of the Almighty. The Lord is my Refuge and my Fortress; in Him, I trust. He covers me with His feathers, and under His wings, I find refuge. No evil will befall me, and no plague will come near my dwelling. God has commanded His angels to guard me in all my ways. I am safe and secure under the covering of my Almighty Father. (Psalm 91:1-11)

4. Affirmation of Freedom from Fear and Anxiety

I refuse to live in fear or anxiety because God has not given me a spirit of fear, but of power, love, and a sound mind. I cast down every anxious thought and every imagination that exalts itself against the knowledge of God. I rest in the peace of God that surpasses all understanding. The peace of Christ guards my mind, and I will not be moved by fear. (2 Timothy 1:7; Philippians 4:7; 2 Corinthians 10:5)

5. Affirmation of God's Provision

My God shall supply all of my needs according to His riches in glory by Christ Jesus. I am not anxious about what I will eat, drink, or wear because my Heavenly Father knows my needs before I even ask Him. He clothes the lilies of the field and feeds the birds of the air; how much more will He take care of me? I am free from the fear of lack, for the Lord is my Shepherd, and I lack nothing. I live under an open heaven, and the blessings of God overtake me. (Philippians 4:19; Matthew 6:25-33; Psalm 23:1; Malachi 3:10)

6. Affirmation of Breaking Spells and Curses

I affirm that the gospel of Jesus Christ breaks every spell, and God's blessings break each curse assigned against me. No enchantment or divination will prosper against me because the covenant of the cross covers me. Every generational curse is canceled and reversed in the name of Jesus. I am delivered from every dark assignment and hidden attack. I walk in the blessing of Abraham, and the favor of God surrounds me like a shield. (Numbers 23:23; Galatians 3:13-14; Psalm 5:12)

7. Affirmation of Walking in God's Favor

The favor of God surrounds me like a shield. I am blessed and not cursed, the head and not the tail, above only and not beneath. Everything I put my hand to prospers because the Lord's hand is upon me. Doors of opportunity open for me, and no one can shut them. God's favor positions me for success, and His grace causes me to stand before kings. (Psalm 5:12; Deuteronomy 28:13; Proverbs 18:16)

8. Affirmation of Healing

By the stripes of Jesus Christ, I am healed. I reject every symptom of sickness, disease, and infirmity. My body is the temple of the Holy Spirit, and I affirm that God gives me health and strength over every organ, cell, and system in my body. I am free from pain and discomfort because God has sent His Word and healed me. Healing is my covenant right, and I walk in divine health every day of my life. (Isaiah 53:5; Psalm 103:3; 1 Corinthians 6:19)

9. Affirmation of Courage
I am strong and courageous because the Lord my God is with me wherever I go. I will not be afraid or discouraged because God goes before me, and He will never leave me nor forsake me. I rise up in faith and bravery, knowing that God's strength is made perfect in my weakness. I refuse to tolerate the enemy's intimidation tactics because the Lord is my Strength and my Shield. (Joshua 1:9; Deuteronomy 31:8; Psalm 28:7)

10. Affirmation of Complete Trust
I walk by faith and not by sight. I trust in the Lord with all my heart and lean not on my own understanding. In all my ways, I wholeheartedly and faithfully acknowledge God because I need Him to direct my path. I refuse to be foolish and be moved by earthly circumstances because I am secure in my faith in God, and I believe that the Word of God is the truth. My faith is anchored in Christ, and I will not be shaken. (2 Corinthians 5:7; Proverbs 3:5-6; Psalm 125:1)

11. Affirmation of Accomplishment
God strengthens me with all might, according to His glorious power, so that I may accomplish each task, honoring Jesus Christ, who increases my ability. The Lord is the strength of my life; I will not be shaken or moved by adversity. My strength comes from the joy of the Lord, and I stand firm in obedience to His holy will by His life-giving power. (Colossians 1:11; Philippians 4:13; Nehemiah 8:10)

12. Affirmation of Refusing Captivity
The Lord is my Deliverer. He has delivered me from the snare of the fowler and from the deadly pestilence. No stronghold of the enemy will keep me bound because the Spirit of the Lord has set me free. I walk in liberty and refuse to

be held captive by fear, doubt, or oppression. (Psalm 91:3; 2 Corinthians 3:17; Psalm 34:17)

13. Affirmation of a Conqueror's Heart
I am more than a conqueror through Christ, Who loves me. God always causes me to triumph in Christ Jesus. No battle is too great for the Lord, and He fights for me. Victory is mine because the battle belongs to the Lord. (Romans 8:37; 2 Corinthians 2:14; Exodus 14:14)

14. Affirmation of Restoration
God restores the years that the locusts have eaten, and He will return everything the enemy stole from me, with increase. God makes all things new, and He brings beauty from the ashes of my life. Restoration is my portion, and I walk in the fullness of God's blessing. (Joel 2:25; Isaiah 61:3; Revelation 21:5)

15. Affirmation of Bold Witnessing
I affirm that I am a witness for Jesus Christ, empowered by the Holy Spirit to share the truth with boldness and compassion. I am not ashamed of the gospel, for it is the power of God unto salvation. I speak as one sent and called, unafraid of rejection, because I know Heaven stands behind me. The words I speak are not my own—they are given by the Spirit who lives in me. I am a light in the darkness, and I will not be silent. (Romans 1:16; Acts 1:8; Matthew 5:14)

16. Affirmation of Hope
My hope is in the Lord, and I will not be disappointed. I am anchored in the promises of God, and I know that He works all things for my good. My future is secure in Christ, and I live with expectation and confidence in His faithfulness. (Romans 15:13; Jeremiah 29:11; Hebrews 6:19)

17. Affirmation of Patience
I wait on the Lord, and He renews my strength. I will not grow weary in well-doing because I know that I will reap a harvest in due season. I will not

rush ahead of God's timing because I trust that His plans for me are good and perfect. (Isaiah 40:31; Galatians 6:9)

18. Affirmation of Pursuing God's Call

"I press on toward the goal to win the [supreme and heavenly] prize..." (Philippians 3:14 AMPC) I affirm that, when God requires me, I will run swiftly toward the distant mark, the goal or the end that God has allowed me to view, of the high invitation from God for my life's destiny in Christ Jesus. I will not be distracted by past mistakes or present challenges. My eyes are fixed on the upward call of God, and my life is committed to fulfilling His divine purpose. I let go of what's behind and stretch forward in faith. I run this race with endurance, knowing that Christ is my reward. (Philippians 3:14; Hebrews 12:1; 1 Corinthians 9:24)

19. Affirmation of God's Faithfulness

God is faithful, and He will never abandon me. His promises are true and everlasting. I can depend on His Word and trust in His character. What God has spoken will surely come to pass because He watches over His Word to fulfill it. (Lamentations 3:22-23; 2 Timothy 2:13; Numbers 23:19)

20. Affirmation of Love

God's love is shed abroad in my heart. I am rooted and grounded in His love. I love others because God first loved me. His love strengthens me, comforts me, and empowers me to love even those who are difficult to love. Nothing can separate me from the love of God. (Romans 5:5; Ephesians 3:17-19; 1 John 4:19)

21. Affirmation of Spiritual Position and Authority

I affirm by God's previous Word concerning my earthly assignment that I am positioned above and not beneath, the head and not the tail, because God has established me in His authority (Deuteronomy 28:13). I am seated with Christ in heavenly places, ruling and reigning with Him (Ephesians 2:6). Therefore, only what is allowed, legal, and loosed in Heaven is what will be allowed, legal, and loosed on Earth in my life (Matthew 18:18). I receive the peace of God, which guards my heart and mind, helping me to clearly recognize His voice and His divine guidance (Philippians 4:7). I am shielded from all satanic, spiritual monitoring. No being, physical or spiritual, is allowed to spy on my life for strategic planning purposes. I am hidden in Christ Jesus (Colossians 3:3). No weapon formed against me shall prosper, and no evil altar raised against me will stand. Every evil tongue that speaks against me is silenced and condemned (Isaiah 54:17). Because God blesses me, no curse has power over me (Numbers 23:8). I also affirm that every spiritual prison holding me captive has opened. Just as Paul and Silas experienced supernatural release, I am walking in freedom today (Acts 16:26). Thank You, Lord Jesus, for setting me free to fulfill Your purpose for my life. In the name of Yeshua Hamashiach, Jesus the Messiah, Amen (So be it).

22. Affirmation of Supernatural Peace
I affirm that the peace of God, which surpasses all understanding, guards my heart and mind through Christ Jesus. I am not troubled by the chaos of this world because I rest in the peace that God provides. His peace establishes my steps and leads me into perfect alignment with His will. Fear and anxiety have no authority over me because God's peace reigns in my life. (Philippians 4:7; Isaiah 26:3; John 14:27)

23. Affirmation of Spiritual Boldness
I affirm that I am bold and courageous because the Lord my God is with me wherever I go. I am not intimidated by the enemy's threats, nor am I discouraged by life's challenges. The Lord has filled me with a spirit of power, love, and a sound mind. I stand firm, knowing that God's strength is made perfect in my weakness. (Joshua 1:9; 2 Timothy 1:7; 2 Corinthians 12:9)

24. Affirmation of God's Timing
I trust in God's perfect timing. I am not anxious about the future because I know that God has appointed every season of my life. He makes all things beautiful in His time, and He will complete the work He began in me. I rest in the assurance that God's timing is always right, and I will not try to force

open doors that He has not prepared for me. (Ecclesiastes 3:11; Philippians 1:6; Psalm 31:15)

25. Affirmation of Family Salvation

From God's Word, in Acts 16:31 AMPC, I speak into the atmosphere: "...Believe in the Lord Jesus Christ [give yourself up to Him, take yourself out of your own keeping and entrust yourself into His keeping] and you will be saved, [and this applies both to] you and your household as well." I affirm that I and my household belong to the Lord. As I believe in Jesus Christ, salvation is flowing through my family line. Every loved one is coming to the knowledge of the truth. I declare that their hearts are softening and their eyes are opening to the light of the gospel. The same grace that saved me is pursuing them. My family will know God, love God, and serve Him faithfully. (Acts 16:31; Isaiah 54:13; 2 Peter 3:9)

26. Affirmation of God's Protection Over My Family

I affirm that the blood of Jesus covers my household. No weapon formed against my family shall prosper. God's angels are stationed around my home, guarding us day and night. The Lord builds a hedge of protection around my family, and we are hidden under His wings. (Psalm 91:10-11; Isaiah 54:17; Job 1:10)

27. Affirmation of Being Heard by God

I affirm that God hears me when I call. My prayers do not fall to the ground, for the ears of the Lord are open to the cries of the righteous. He knows my voice, and He responds with compassion and power. I am not ignored or overlooked—I am beloved and heard. My petitions rise as incense before Him, and my voice carries weight in the courts of Heaven. (Psalm 34:15; 1 John 5:14; Revelation 5:8)

28. Affirmation of Deliverance from Spiritual Bondage

I affirm that I am free from every spiritual stronghold and demonic influence. The anointing of the Lord destroys every yoke, and the chains of oppression are broken off my life. I have been delivered from the kingdom of darkness and transferred into the kingdom of God's dear Son. I walk in liberty, and the enemy no longer has authority over my life. (Isaiah 10:27; Colossians 1:13; Galatians 5:1)

29. Affirmation of Joy and Strength
The joy of the Lord is my strength. I choose to rejoice even in difficult circumstances because my hope is in God. His joy fills me with supernatural strength and empowers me to endure every trial. I am not moved by what I see; God's joy strengthens me. (Nehemiah 8:10; Habakkuk 3:18-19; Philippians 4:4)

30. Affirmation of Victory Over Temptation
I affirm that I am victorious over every temptation. God has provided a way of escape for me, and I have the strength to resist every scheme of the enemy. Sin has no hold on me because the Holy Spirit empowers me, and there is nothing on Earth that gives me more pleasure than knowing I'm pleasing God. I walk in purity and righteousness, knowing that God's strength enables me to overcome every temptation. (1 Corinthians 10:13; James 4:7; Romans 6:14)

31. Affirmation of Fruitfulness and Success
I affirm that I am fruitful and successful in all that I do. God has blessed the work of my hands, and I see an increase in every area of my life. I am like a tree planted by streams of water, bearing fruit in its season. Everything I put my hands to prospers because God's favor rests upon me. (Psalm 1:3; Deuteronomy 28:12; Joshua 1:8)

32. Affirmation of Clarity and Wisdom
I affirm that I walk in divine clarity and wisdom. God grants me understanding and insight beyond human ability. I am not confused or uncertain because the Spirit of truth leads me into all truth. I have the mind of Christ, and I think clearly and strategically. (James 1:5; 1 Corinthians 2:16; John 16:13)

33. Affirmation of Unwavering Faith
I affirm that my faith is unwavering and unshakable. I trust in the promises of God even when circumstances appear impossible. My faith is not based on what

my senses perceive but on the truth of God's Word. I believe that what God has spoken will come to pass. (Romans 4:20-21; Hebrews 11:1; 2 Corinthians 5:7)

34. Affirmation of Abundant Life

Jesus said in John 10:10 KJV, "The thief cometh not, but for to steal, and to kill, and to destroy: I am come that they might have life, and that they might have it more abundantly." I affirm that Jesus came to give me life, and I receive the fullness of life He has for me. I do not live under the weight of survival—I live in the overflow of His abundance. My life is marked by purpose, peace, joy, and grace. The enemy comes to deduct, but Jesus came to give me more than enough, and I have it; God prepares and makes it available to me in His perfect timing. I walk in the richness of Jesus' life—body, soul, and spirit. (John 10:10; Psalm 16:11; Ephesians 3:20)

35. Affirmation of Wholeness

I affirm that I am whole and complete in Christ. Nothing is missing, broken, or lacking in my life. God's restoration power is at work in me, making me whole in every area—spirit, soul, and body. I am strengthened, healed, and complete because of the finished work of Jesus Christ. (Colossians 2:10; 1 Thessalonians 5:23; Isaiah 58:12)

36. Affirmation of Light and Influence

I affirm unto God's glory that I am the light of the world. My life shines brightly before men, and they see the goodness of God through me. I am called to be a light in dark places, and God's glory radiates through me. The light of Christ within me dispels darkness, and I walk confidently as a vessel of His love and truth. (Matthew 5:14-16; Isaiah 60:1-2)

37. Affirmation of Spiritual Discernment

I affirm that even if I don't possess the gift of discernment of spirits, through the Holy Spirit, I am not and will not be easily deceived because the Spirit of truth guides me into all truth. I recognize the enemy's schemes and reject every falsehood and lie. My spiritual senses are sharp, and I will distinguish between good and evil. God grants me wisdom and insight to make righteous decisions. (1 John 4:1; Hebrews 5:14; John 16:13)

38. Affirmation of Freedom from Guilt and Shame

I am free from guilt and shame because Christ has redeemed me. I am not condemned because I am in Christ Jesus. My sins have been forgiven, and I walk in the righteousness of God. I reject every accusation from the enemy and stand boldly in the truth of my forgiveness and acceptance in Christ. I am washed, sanctified, and justified by the blood of Jesus. (Romans 8:1; 1 John 1:9; 1 Corinthians 6:11)

39. Affirmation for Governmental Leaders and the Nation

I affirm that God is sovereign over the nations, and I lift up my country, its leaders, and its influencers before Him. I proclaim that those in authority will be guided by God's wisdom, understanding, justice, and truth. God, by His Holy Spirit, has given them His Word, will, and way, presented in a manner that they won't refuse. Righteousness exalts a nation, and I declare that godly counsel will surround and be imparted to those in power. I affirm that God brings and maintains peace and welfare of my land, and I stand in the gap for my generation, knowing that the effectual, fervent prayer of God's righteous ones avails much. (1 Timothy 2:1-2; Proverbs 14:34; James 5:16)

40. Affirmation of Strategy and Dependence

I affirm that no weapon formed against me shall prosper. Every scheme of the enemy is exposed and destroyed by the power of God. The blood of Jesus covers me, and the Lord is my Defender and Protector. The enemy's plans against me are rendered powerless, and I walk in total victory and spiritual authority. (Isaiah 54:17; 2 Corinthians 10:4-5; Luke 10:19)

41. Affirmation of Protection for My Children

I affirm that the blood of Jesus covers my children. No harm will come near them, and no weapon formed against them shall prosper. God's angels surround them and guard them in all their ways. My children will walk in the truth of God's Word, and they will fulfill the purpose and destiny that God has planned for them. (Psalm 91:10-11; Isaiah 54:13; Proverbs 22:6)

42. Affirmation of Confidence in God's Leading

I trust in the Lord with all my heart and lean not on my own understanding. In all my ways, I acknowledge Him, and He directs my paths. I am not confused or uncertain because God's wisdom leads me. His voice is clear, and I follow Him with confidence, knowing that He will never lead me astray. (Proverbs 3:5-6; John 10:27; Isaiah 30:21)

43. Affirmation of Strength During Trials

I am strong in the Lord and in the power of His might. I face trials with courage and endurance, knowing that God works all things together for my good. Even in the midst of hardship, I am sustained by God's strength and encouraged by His promises. I am victorious because Christ has already overcome the world. (Ephesians 6:10; Romans 8:28; John 16:33)

44. Affirmation of Deliverance from Fear of Failure

I affirm that the fear of failure does not bind me. God's perfect love casts out all fear, and I step forward in faith and confidence. My success is determined by God's plan for my life, not by human standards. Even if I stumble, God's hand upholds me, and He strengthens me to rise again. I walk boldly in obedience to God's call. (2 Timothy 1:7; Psalm 37:23-24; 1 John 4:18)

45. Affirmation of Rest and Renewal

I can now boldly affirm that I enter into God's rest. I am not overwhelmed by life's demands because God gives me peace and restoration. He leads me beside still waters and restores my soul. I cast my burdens on the Lord, and He sustains me. I find rest for my soul in His presence. (Matthew 11:28-30; Psalm 23:2-3; Isaiah 40:31)

46. Affirmation of Deliverance from Rejection

I affirm that I am accepted and loved by God. The opinions of others do not define me, and I refuse to live under the burden of rejection. God has chosen and appointed me, and I am secure in His love. My identity is in Christ, and I am complete in Him. I am not abandoned or forgotten; my Heavenly Father cherishes me. (Ephesians 1:4-6; Psalm 27:10; Isaiah 41:9-10)

47. Affirmation of God's Overflowing Goodness

I affirm that God's goodness and mercy follow me all the days of my life. His favor surrounds me like a shield, and His blessings overflow in my life. I expect good things to happen because God is good, and His plans for me are good. His goodness leads me, and I walk in the abundance of His provision. (Psalm 23:6; Romans 8:28; James 1:17)

48. Affirmation of Steadfastness in Faith

I affirm that I stand firm in my faith. I am not shaken by trials or opposition because my foundation is in Christ. I hold fast to my confession of faith, knowing that God is faithful. My heart is steadfast, and my faith grows stronger through every test. I remain rooted and grounded in God's truth. (Hebrews 10:23; 1 Corinthians 15:58; Psalm 112:7)

49. Affirmation of Divine Assignments and Open Doors

I affirm that I am walking in my divine assignment. God has opened doors for me that no one can shut. I am equipped and anointed for every task He has given me. I walk in alignment with His purpose, and I fulfill my destiny with confidence. Every opportunity God has appointed for me is secured and released in His perfect timing. (Revelation 3:8; Philippians 2:13; Isaiah 22:22)

50. Affirmation of God's Perfect Love

I affirm that God's love is perfected in me. His perfect love casts out all fear and fills me with boldness and confidence. I am secure in His love, knowing that nothing can separate me from it. I love others with the love God has given me, and I am a vessel of His compassion and grace. (1 John 4:18; Romans 8:38-39; Colossians 3:14)

ABOUT THE AUTHOR

Shane Wall has been preaching internationally for over 40 years and is the author of two bestselling books: the #8 bestseller *Understanding: All Success is Attained by It* (hailed as the first Christian book ever written on the subject of understanding) and the #1 bestseller *The Supernatural Guide to Understanding Angels*. He also recorded a Gospel CD titled *Conversations with God*, featuring songs he personally wrote to express divine conversations between God and His children.

He is the founder and Senior Pastor of **The Feast of the Lord** in Orangeburg, South Carolina, where he resides with his two children, Joshua and Amayah. Apostle Wall regularly ministers in churches and conferences across the globe, helping people break free from spiritual bondage and walk in divine clarity. His free mobile platform, the **Shane Wall App**, offers powerful teachings, insight, and resources for those seeking to grow in their walk with God.

Contact

Shane Wall
PO Box 2005
Orangeburg, SC 29116

• • •

SHANEWALL app

www.shanewall.com

www.ingramcontent.com/pod-product-compliance
Lightning Source LLC
Chambersburg PA
CBHW042300030526
44119CB00066B/819